ALTERED EGOS

ALTERED EGOS

Authority in American Autobiography

G. Thomas Couser

New York Oxford
OXFORD UNIVERSITY PRESS
1989

Oxford University Press

Oxford New York Toronto
Delhi Bombay Calcutta Madras Karachi
Petaling Jaya Singapore Hong Kong Tokyo
Nairobi Dar es Salaam Cape Town
Melbourne Auckland

and associated companies in
Berlin Ibadan

Published by Oxford University Press, Inc.,
200 Madison Avenue, New York, New York 10016

Library of Congress Cataloging-in-Publication Data
Couser, G. Thomas.
Altered egos : authority in American autobiography / G. Thomas Couser.
p. cm.
Includes bibliographies and index.
ISBN 0-19-505833-X
1. Autobiography. 2. Authority in literature. 3. American prose literature—History and criticism. I. Title.
PS366.A88C67 1989 88-38246
810'.9'492—dc19

An earlier version of chapter 4, "Prose and Cons: The Autobiographies of P. T. Barnum," appeared in *Southwest Review* 70(4):451–69, 1985. An earlier version of chapter 5, "False 'I's': Mark Twain's Pseudonymous Autobiography," was published in *Auto/Biography Studies* 3(3):13–20, 1987. An earlier version of chapter 8, "*Black Elk Speaks* With Forked Tongue," appeared in *Studies in Autobiography* (New York: Oxford, 1988).

9 8 7 6 5 4 3 2 1

Printed in the United States of America
on acid-free paper

For Barbara

Preface

My first book, *American Autobiography: The Prophetic Mode* (Amherst: University of Massachusetts Press,1979) traced an American tradition of using autobiography as a medium for prophecy: of writing one's life in such a way as to illuminate the community's history as well as one's own. Prophetic autobiographers—from Thomas Shepard, the seventeenth-century Puritan, to Norman Mailer and Malcolm X—tend to conflate individual and communal narratives, to describe—and even to prescribe—both histories according to some exalted vision of their destinies. Prophetic autobiography, then, seeks an authority beyond the personal and the "literary" in order to exert moral and spiritual leverage on the course of actual events.

In the last ten years, my understanding of autobiography, of American literary history, and of the relation between selves, events, and texts has changed substantially in response to structuralist and post-structuralist theory. The new theory has particularly unsettling implications for autobiography, whose authority has traditionally been grounded in a verifiable relationship between a text and an extratextual referent (the writer's self, or life). The trend in recent criticism has been to undermine the apparent correspondence between the textual and the extratextual and to deny any hard distinction between fiction and nonfiction. Post-structuralism has challenged the notion of authors as autonomous beings who produce texts; instead, it argues that they are constructs produced by texts. Indeed, it suggests that the idea of a unique self may be a delusion, that "individuals" are perhaps nothing more than intersections of cultural codes and sign systems. Authors and their authority are mere language effects. From this perspective, autobiography, far from being capable of prophecy, is an inherently problematic endeavor.

The discussion that follows attempts neither to refute poststructuralism's assault on the subject and on the authority of autobiography, nor simply to apply its insights to a group of American autobiographies. While I find myself considerably more skeptical than I used to be of the authority of the genre, I remain concerned with the way in which autobiography may seek to order, even to alter, a world beyond the textual. This book is concerned, then, with the "authority" of lifewriting in America, in several related senses: first, the idea that autobiography is inherently authoritative writing because it is (presumably) verifiable; second, the idea that each individual has authority, at least in writing, over his or her own life; third, the idea that, because of the apparent congruence between the implicit ideology of the genre and that of the nation, autobiography has a special role in American literature.

Keeping the post-structuralist critique of autobiography in view—but I hope not confined to, or by, it—this book examines various ways in which the authority of lifewriting may be called into question. The body of the book is structured in two major parts. The first sequence of chapters traces increasingly antiauthoritarian gestures in the autobiographies of Benjamin Franklin, P. T. Barnum, and Mark Twain. For very different reasons, these autobiographers playfully undermined the authority of their own autobiographies, and thus of the genre as a whole. (They could afford to do so, of course, since all three were famous before they were autobiographers.)

The second sequence of chapters appraises the authority of autobiography in the rather different circumstances of the minority writer. A chapter on slave narrative discusses various impediments to authorial control and efforts to evade or surmount them, in texts by Solomon Northup, Harriet Jacobs, Frederick Douglass, and others. A chapter on Mary Chesnut examines the "ideology of form" of her Civil War "diaries." Rather than seeking a definitive label for her text, I argue that her two-stage revision of it over the course of two decades was a means of arrogating a kind of authority generally reserved to men in her culture. A chapter on Black Elk explores what happens when an autobiographical narrative is produced on a cultural frontier by collaborators with fundamentally different notions of authorship. Finally, a chapter on two contemporary bicultural autobiographers, Richard Rodriguez and Maxine Hong Kingston, illuminates the way in which recent thinking about the linguistic determination of the self has shaped lifewriting.

As a whole, the manuscript treats autobiography neither as inherently authoritative nor necessarily duplicitous, but rather as a shifty ground on which writers struggle for literary control over their lives, within and against the constraints of language and genre, race and gender—literary and extraliterary conventions.

* * *

It is conventional for scholars to acknowledge the sense in which, and the extent to which, their books are products of a collaborative process, dependent on the inspiration, assistance, and labor of others. In the case of a book, like this one, which professes skepticism about the authority of texts, such acknowledgments are evoked less by convention than by simple consistency. To put it differently, the book's argument may be taken as an expression, in another voice, of my grateful awareness of its other authors. Particular debts are duly noted in the impersonal format of scholarly documentation; let me add here that the endnotes are more suggestive than exhaustive: this book is a response to an impressive body of recent work in the field of autobiography studies. It has been a pleasure and a challenge to enter that lively dialogue.

My obligations to others' writing, while substantial, are not my only significant debts. Rick Bogel taught me the theory that has recast my sense of autobiography. Lynda Bogel offered support in the crucial early stages of this project. My departmental colleagues at Hofstra have provided a congenial environment for scholarship as well as for teaching; Robert Sargent, Chair of the Department, and Robert Vogt, Dean of the College of Liberal Arts and Sciences, have helped to make funds and released time available. David H. Hirsch has gone beyond the call of graduate school professor. James M. Cox and Albert E. Stone have not only enriched the field generally but helped me particularly to pursue my own work. And a grant from the National Endowment of the Humanities provided the necessary luxury of a year's leave, during which I brought this project to completion.

Finally, Barbara Zabel has sustained me throughout, coauthoring our life, altering my ego.

Quaker Hill, CT G.T.C.
January 1989

Contents

ALTERED EGOS

1

Prologue: The Case of the Counterfeit Autobiography

I

The Autobiography of Howard Hughes, as told to Clifford Irving, is an uncommon, if not unique, case in the annals of American life-writing: the book was withdrawn just before publication when it was exposed as a complete fraud, or hoax. In hindsight, it seems clear that the text was completely devoid of authority as autobiography because the project lacked the crucial credential it boasted of—the imprimatur and cooperation of its elusive subject. Indeed, it eventually proved to be neither autobiography nor authorized biography, but rather a rewriting of a former Hughes employee's unauthorized memoirs of his boss presented as those of Hughes himself. While it is not a representative, much less a canonical, American autobiography, it illuminates, from a singular perspective, the complex issue of the authority of autobiography.

Even at the time of its presentation to the publisher, McGraw-Hill, the manuscript should have been suspect: it was extremely unlikely that the notoriously reclusive Hughes would suddenly undertake to expose himself in autobiographical form, and that, were he to do so, he would choose to collaborate with Clifford Irving (whose most recent book, *Fake!,* had concerned the notorious art forger, his friend Elmyr de Hory). Yet, following the announcement of its impending publication, it still took more than two months for journalists, lawyers, and investigators to expose it as a hoax, despite the fact that both parties to the supposed collaboration were living and accessible, more or less, to interrogators. The remarkable thing, was not that the fraud was discovered, but that it was not discovered earlier.[1]

Both the unlikely persistence of the manuscript's credibility and the story of the fraud's eventual exposure reveal a good deal about how autobiography is regarded and how its authority is established in the "real world" —by publishers, lawyers, and judges. Though the phantom autobiography would seem to have little in common with the autobiographies that will be discussed in the following chapters, the fate of the text and the power struggle surrounding it make a good starting point for an exploration of the authority commonly ascribed to autobiography in our culture. Precisely because it seems such a clear-cut case of an autobiography without warrant in the most fundamental sense, it suggests how difficult it can be to establish the authority of any autobiography.

II

The case is admittedly unusual, and the fraud's temporary success depended on the peculiarities of both the book's subject and its composition. The first contributing circumstance was Hughes's combination of extreme wealth and his obsession with privacy. Either of these elements alone might have created substantial curiosity—and thus a market for books—about him. In combination, the two both whetted the public's appetite for and dulled the publisher's skepticism toward the inside story. These traits also made Hughes a kind of grotesque mutant of the species entrepreneur, and his life story was potentially a Gothic version of the American success story that derives from Benjamin Franklin's example because his eccentric reclusiveness and his fantastic wealth were extreme, even deviant, expressions of the fundamental capitalist notions of personal privacy and of private property—especially of intellectual property. (His fortune was founded on the careful preservation and thorough exploitation of patents on rock-drilling bits designed by his father [84].)

Hughes's sense of the property value of ideas, so rational and profitable in the mining industries, proved irrational and expensive when extended to other venues. For example, his obsession with privacy asserted itself in a lifelong attempt to monopolize and suppress information about himself. Hughes's hostility to biographers is reminiscent both of Henry Adams, who, in a letter to Henry James, characterized biography as literary homicide,[2] and of Mark Twain, who jealously repelled those who, by seeking to write about his life, infringed on what he considered his exclusive literary property. Of course, Adams finally resorted to autobiography, taking his own life as a kind of preemptive strike against future biographers, and Mark Twain's self-possessiveness was calculated to maximize his profit from his own literary capitalization of his experience. (Indeed, in order further to profit from his pseudonym, Mark Twain eventually made it a legal trademark, long after it had become a kind of unofficial signet of his brand of humor.)

Hughes singlemindedly sought to ensure his privacy, even at great financial cost. Like Mark Twain, but with different aims, he attempted virtually to patent himself. He also tried mightily to copyright his life (84). Hughes had long depended on public relations firms to control information about his business enterprises; but late in life he set up a separate concern, Rosemont Enterprises, solely to inhibit the relation of stories about him to the public. At great expense, then, Hughes endeavored to ensure his own invisibility. (In this respect, Hughes was the opposite of P. T. Barnum, who believed that publicity was good by definition; when it came to himself, Hughes felt that the only good news was no news.) Incorporated in 1965, Rosemont immediately purchased from Hughes exclusive rights to material about him—the intent of the contract, of course, being not to publish, but to squelch, such materials (82–83). Though superficially the opposite of exhibitionism, this gesture is profoundly self-centered and perversely narcissistic: in buying, through a proxy, the rights to his own life story in order to keep it *off* the market, Hughes bid for a kind of exclusive, economic form of self-possession.

Armed with its contractual monopoly, Rosemont attempted to thwart publication of information about Hughes. In one notable case, it bought up the copyright to published materials that were the main source of an impending biography and then sued for infringement of copyright. The legal status of its case—like that of its claim to exclusive rights to Hughes as a literary property—was questionable: under American law, the public's right to know about powerful and influential figures limits celebrities' right to privacy, rendering them vulnerable to all but libellous publicity (80–85). One can copyright one's life *story,* but not one's life; that is, one can secure copyright protection for a particular account of one's experience, but cannot prevent the literary use of, or reference to, one's life by others (hence the unauthorized biography). Indeed, in *Rosemont* v. *Random House* (1965), a New York State appeals court denied Hughes's right to squelch the biography: "It would be contrary to the public interest to permit any man to buy up copyright to anything written about himself and to use copyright to restrain others from publishing biographical material concerning him" (86). While Rosemont clearly acted on Hughes's strong sense that his life and self were his private property, it stretched, or violated, the law.

Despite Rosemont's opposition, several biographies of Hughes *were* published. What distinguished Clifford Irving's venture was his claim of Hughes's approval and cooperation. Exploiting Hughes's seclusion and rumored feebleness (and a sample of his handwriting reproduced in *Newsweek*), Irving and a researcher, Richard Suskind, decided to fabricate an "authorized biography" of the mysterious billionaire—to be based on published sources and some original research. In the beginning, the value of their literary property was based entirely on their claim, as evidenced in forged letters, of his authorization of the project and his participation in taped interviews. However, some time after Irving had won McGraw-Hill's confidence—and a sizable advance ($100,000)—he and Suskind somehow gained access to an unpublished manuscript of the memoirs of Noah Dietrich, Hughes's former C.E.O. and right-hand man. Dietrich's book, though rich in potential, had been sidetracked by delays in revision (63, 259–60).

Irving and Suskind took clever but illegitimate advantage of Dietrich's honest, though unauthorized, project. Dietrich's memoirs, in the form of interviews with his collaborator, Jim Phelan, were surreptitiously photocopied and then reenacted by Irving and Suskind, who took turns "interviewing" each other, paraphrasing Dietrich's comments as Hughes's (297). These performances were tape-recorded and transcribed. Thus, Dietrich's memoirs of Howard Hughes, as told to Jim Phelan, were altered in order to disguise their origin and passed off as the autobiography of Hughes, as told to Irving; the *subject* of the genuine original text was reconstructed as the "author" of the phony derivative one. (Formally, their gesture is the inverse of that of Gertrude Stein in writing *The Autobiography of Alice B. Toklas*. When Stein overtly impersonated Toklas, she wrote her own autobiography as Toklas's memoir of her; Irving and Suskind covertly passed off Dietrich's memoirs of Hughes as Hughes's autobiography.)

Greatly emboldened by access to this valuable source, Irving reconceived his project as the autobiography of Hughes and raised the price accordingly; the publisher reluctantly agreed. An autobiography was a more valuable property than an authorized biography (78–79): its value was a function of Hughes's alleged authorship and the authority it was presumed to guarantee. In any event, when the manuscript's impending publication—first in excerpts in *Life* magazine and then as a McGraw-Hill book—was announced on December 7, 1971, it had the prestige of a major publishing house and a popular mass-circulation magazine behind it. To many, however, this announcement was the first news of the book's existence, and the skepticism of certain parties made for a series of challenges that lead to its eventual exposure as a fraud. Remarkably, however, the manuscript had already convinced knowledgeable people in journalism and publishing, and it took a long time for the consensus to shift, even in the face of Howard Hughes's vehement denial that the book was genuine.

When the book was announced, Hughes's public relations firm quickly disowned it, and Rosemont tried to suppress it. But Irving's previous assurance that Hughes had kept the book a secret from his employees and advisers sustained the publisher's faith in the project; Rosemont's response was to be expected. Even when Hughes broke a long silence to disown the book—at first, off the record—his denunciation was dismissed as *re*nunciation: McGraw-Hill assumed that Hughes had simply, and understandably, changed his mind about publishing an autobiography. The publisher took comfort in the cancelled checks to Hughes as evidence of the book's legitimacy and in the apparently still-valid contract as guarantee of its publishability (151). But the publisher's confidence rested mainly on the manuscript itself. Indeed, the very man who took Hughes's first call, Time-Life's in-house Hughes expert, Frank McCulloch, was convinced by a perusal of the manuscript the very next night that whatever its subject had decided to say about it, it *was* his genuine autobiography (128–29).

In this case, Hughes's obsession with privacy proved self-defeating, for his denunciations of the book were at first taken as evidence that the book was genuine. McCulloch swore in an affidavit:

> I am convinced beyond reasonable doubt as to the authenticity of the Howard Hughes autobiography. This conviction is based upon my long-standing personal familiarity with Howard Hughes, my readings of the manuscript, and my interviews with Clifford Irving. My belief in that authenticity is not shaken by denials of that story, nor is my belief in the authenticity of the autobiography shaken by the denials which I have heard from a man I believe to be Howard Hughes. Such actions are perfectly consistent with the Hughes I know (161).

Hand-writing analysis had failed to expose the documents purporting to be written or signed by Hughes as forgeries; Irving had mastered Hughes's hand well enough to fool two sets of qualified examiners (132–33). The authority of the transcripts of the taped interviews, however, had to be tested differently. One concern was for their accuracy and verifiability—that is, their historicity: did their contents stand up to scrutiny in the light of the ample public record of Hughes's earlier life? (Despite the vigilance of Rosemont, much was known and published about Hughes.) From the point of view of the publishers, verifiability and authenticity were closely related, and the conformity of the manuscript to the known material was thought to reflect Irving's direct access to the book's subject and source. The manuscripts passed two degrees of "truth-testing": first, the haphazard informal scrutiny of any and all who read them; second, the more intense scrutiny of *Life* researchers who vetted the excerpts to be published serially early in 1972.

Of course, the manuscript's corroboration by published material reflected not its authenticity, but rather the reverse: its derivation from (indeed, its plagiarism of) secondary sources. Several impulsively invented episodes escaped detection at this time, presumably because they did not conflict with published accounts of Hughes's life. Thus, aspects of the manuscript that should have cast suspicion upon it were ignored or misconstrued. These tests proved nothing except the prevalence of the expectation, even the requirement, at least among lay readers, that autobiography should be verifiable—that its authority is in part a function of factual accuracy. In this regard, autobiography is perceived to be like biography, perhaps a subgenre of it; insofar as autobiography and biography share the same ostensible subject, they are expected to conform in certain matters of "fact" —dates, places, and so on. But "tests" of verifiability such as this reflect a naively empiricist (and legalistic) view of autobiography. The inadequacy of reality-testing in the form of fact-checking was nicely illustrated by a phone conference in which Howard Hughes again denounced the book, this time on the record, for an audience of qualified journalists. Asked a series of questions contrived to establish his identity, Hughes answered fewer than half correctly; his recall of facts and names was simply deficient. (He did, however, redeem himself by displaying a characteristic obsession with minutiae and technical detail—and by using a voice recognized as that of Howard Hughes [140].)

Though the manuscript's verifiability allayed the publisher's suspicions, it was not sufficient in itself to convince them. Their faith rested finally, and unfortunately, on other aspects of the manuscript:

its persona and tone, which were judged to be authentic by all who read it. Both of these, however, were more fraudulent simulations than the handwriting: while the handwriting was a studied imitation of Hughes's, the tone was derived from the Dietrich memoirs. One irony of this is that the Irving manuscript involved the attribution of unauthorized recollections of Hughes to the man who forbade their publication (in 1959 Hughes had forced Dietrich to sign an agreement not to publish any stories about him [80]).

In earlier years, Hughes's public image had been created largely by Noah Dietrich, trusted chief executive and spokesman. At the time of the conception and composition of the "autobiography," little was known about Hughes's current circumstances, point of view, or personality. Dietrich's memoir was the key source of Irving's book not so much because it provided exclusive material derived from intimacy with the subject as because it furnished a distinctive style that could pass for Hughes's in the absence of counter-evidence:

> Dietrich's style, the way he talks and tells his stories, is rough and ready, spattered with curses and salty phrases, uninhibited, irreverent. Brusque, rude, and impatient, he is many things that Howard Hughes is not. But he had also been, for most of his working life, Howard Hughes's public stand-in. What the outside world had seen and known of Hughes had mostly come via Noah Dietrich. . . . All Clifford Irving needed to do was to put the thoughts of Noah Dietrich into the mouth of Howard Hughes (as Noah had done for so many years), and he had the material for a rich, literary property (296).

More than anything else—the forged letters, the cancelled checks, or even the verifiability of the manuscript's facts—the authority of the submitted manuscript finally rested on its style and the persona it created, and these were purely textual effects—difficult, if not impossible, to discount. Having hidden from the public, or approached it indirectly through a single mediator, Hughes found it difficult to dispel the holographic illusion conjured up by Irving and Suskind with the unwitting assistance of his former spokesman.

The book succeeded, therefore, merely in creating a distinctive self that could be—and was—(mis)taken for that of Hughes, not in simulating Hughes's unique style. Throughout this episode, it was the manuscript's style that most convinced its readers. As Ralph Graves, the editor of *Life,* later remarked,

> It was outspoken, full of rich and outrageous anecdotes, as well as detailed accounts of Hughes's youth, his movie-making, his career in

> aviation, his business affairs, his private life, his opinions and crotchets. . . . Even the boring parts were persuasive: Howard Hughes had always been fascinated by the minutiae of aircraft design and performance, and the transcripts had lots of it (91).

The authors of *Hoax* have noted a curious or paradoxical aspect of the affair:

> Usually hoaxes convince people who do not have intimate access to the dubious material; once it is scrutinized, their veracity crumbles. But in the case of the autobiography of Howard Hughes it was the editors and publishers—the people who had read it—who believed passionately in it and who managed to communicate some of their enthusiasm to a less credulous public (157–58).

Indeed, the decisive breaks in the case came as a result of concentrated sleuthing: investigation of the cashing of the checks and of Irving's story of getting the story—the bogus autobiography of a bogus autobiography. Significantly, the financial forgeries were revealed before the literary ones, and the falsehood of Irving's miniautobiography exposed that of the larger one he tried to sell. (Intended to take the form of a story in *Life,* "Clifford Irving—My Secret Meeting with Howard Hughes," Irving's narrative eventually took the form of an affidavit when the Hughes manuscript's veracity was challenged; as such, it faced stricter scrutiny than a magazine article—and more severe penalties for deceit.) The vulnerability of the hoax lay more in peripheral acts than in the text itself, which was finally discredited only when it was compared to its true (but covert) source, Dietrich's purloined manuscript. In spite of its complete fraudulence, this "autobiography" displayed an authority that was convincing to skeptical readers knowledgeable about its subject; however, this effect was a function of clever literary impersonation of a "character" at once world-famous and obscure, not of genuine authorship. While Hughes's real voice and fingerprints finally and definitively established his identity, the falseness of his "writing"—both hand-writing and voice-writing (the recreated "interviews")—was much harder to prove.

III

Rarely do we find such an open-and-shut case of lifewriting of questionable authority; therefore, the "autobiography" of Howard

Hughes may be said to define one end of a continuum. The Howard Hughes–Clifford Irving hoax, however, not only demonstrates that the authority of autobiography may be problematic, even nonexistent, when it appears otherwise. It also shows how difficult it is to determine the authority of autobiography even in relatively favorable circumstances, for this elusive phenomenon is ultimately a function of a constellation of factors. The authorship of the subject and a verifiable relationship between the text and some extratextual referent may be desirable, and may even be deemed necessary constituents of autobiographical authority, but they are not sufficient to establish it definitively. Other, more subtle factors come into play, such as the role of the subject in the initiation and execution of the project, the relationship between the subject and institutional mediators such as collaborators, editors, and publishers, cultural assumptions about autobiography, and matters of rhetorical skill and mastery of convention.

The focus of the following chapters is on autobiographical texts from various periods whose authority is made problematic by a variety of factors. The first group concerns autobiographers who in some way, more or less deliberately, undermined the authority of their own narratives. Benjamin Franklin, even as he established the conventions for a distinctive mode of American autobiography, undermined its authority in subtle, perhaps not entirely intentional, ways. P. T. Barnum, for whom confidence tricks were a stock in trade, deliberately and playfully subverted the authority of his own text—he had the genius to see that this would enhance rather than diminish its marketability. With Mark Twain, certain expectations of autobiography—that some of its contents would be verifiable, for example—come into inevitable conflict with the ramifications of his use of a pseudonym: lacking a proper name, a pseudonymous persona has no real history to verify.

The next several chapters explore cases in which the authority of autobiography is compromised by circumstances largely beyond the control of the writers. From the start, historicity (factual authority) has been a crucial issue for the slave narrative. Recently, scholars have begun to recognize the extent to which the sponsors—including the abolitionists—may have unwittingly compromised the authority of the ex-slaves. The case has been made that the genre's conventions owe more to the authorizing institution than to the individual authors—that, in effect, the narrators were not the masters of their own Lives. In the case of the Confederate, Mary Boykin

Chesnut, the thorough, painstaking revision of a Civil War diary over a period of two decades transformed it into something subtly but distinctly different—whether a novel, a hoax, or an innovative form of lifewriting. To some extent, Chesnut's revision, however compromised as lifewriting, must be seen in terms of her aspiration to authority beyond what was generally granted women writers of her time.

Examples of bicultural collaborative autobiography, such as that of Black Elk, show that collaboration is always risky—both author and subject are inevitably composite constructions. Unlike Howard Hughes, minority collaborators may lack the clout to discredit the results. *Black Elk Speaks* illustrates, more dramatically than a slave narrative, how biracial collaboration may subvert an autobiography's authority. Finally, Richard Rodriguez and Maxine Hong Kingston reveal that the writing of bicultural autobiography remains fraught with danger: for bilingual writers like them, the initial choice of the language of the narrative predetermines not only the nature of the audience but also to a large extent, that of the self-image created.

If Howard Hughes's idea of his exclusive right to his life as a literary property is not one endorsed by American courts, it still holds much popular appeal. The history of autobiography in America suggests that for many Americans part of the promise of the new republic is the idea that anyone can write the definitive account of his or her own life. Unfortunately, the obstacles to control over one's own Life are nearly as numerous and subtle as those to dominion over one's existence. Though rarely assessed in as public (and definitive) a way as in the case of the Irving hoax, the authority of autobiography is usually more tenuous than it seems. It is also a good deal more interesting.

2

Introduction: Authority, Autobiography, America

I

In English the pronoun that signifies the self is triply singular: in number, in capitalization, and in being the sole single-letter pronoun. Typographically identical with the Roman numeral *I* and phonemically identical with the word *eye*, it puns on the notion of a single point of view. These fortuitous features of our linguistic system reinforce our sense of the privileged status of the self, and the language seems to encourage us to conceive of the first person as unique, integral, and independent—like the pronoun that represents it.

Autobiography is the literary form, and democracy the political form, most congruent with this idea of a unique and autonomous self. Significantly, both terms gained currency in English in the period following the political disturbances of the late eighteenth century,[1] and it is more than coincidence that America achieved its independence in that same era. James M. Cox has linked the "the very idea of autobiography" with that era's political revolutions: "For the American and French Revolutions, whatever else they did, were the convulsive acts which released the individual as a potent political entity and gave us what we are pleased to call modern man."[2] The dramatic inscription of the idea of individual autonomy in the texts that defined and constituted America implied the legitimacy of autobiographical discourse; the autobiography of Benjamin Franklin made a virtually explicit link between political and literary autonomy.

The values of the genre and those of American culture have long seemed to be in close congruity; and the notion of a special compatibility between American culture and autobiographical discourse has become a commonplace of criticism. For example, Robert Sayre has claimed, "Autobiography may be the preeminent kind of American expression. Commencing before the Revolution and continuing into our own time, America and autobiography have been peculiarly linked."[3] Thomas Doherty has attributed the congruence to ideology: "Autobiography is not a peculiarly American literary form, but it does seem to be a form peculiarly suited to the traditional American self-image: individualistic and optimistic."[4] Thus, autobiography has been thought to have special authority in America—prestige deriving from its apparent political warrant and its valorization of individualism.

This notion of autobiography as a form that almost literally embodies American selfhood can be seen in dramatic if somewhat crude form in the advertisements of a company called Newstrack Executive Classics, which sells audiocassettes containing abridged autobiographies of "business giants" like Henry Ford, Andrew Carnegie, J. C. Penney, David Ogilvy, and Ray Kroc. (Not surprisingly, but somewhat unfairly, Benjamin Franklin's autobiography is often cited as the prototype of these books.) In this case, autobiography is presented as a medium through which readers can make contact with, and internalize the values of, the captains of American commerce:

> Twelve of America's greatest business leaders tell you in their own words how they built vast business empires and personal fortunes with their knowledge, skill, and determination. What they have to say in their autobiographies is invaluable to today's business executive. But what executive has time to locate and read all of these amazing stories? Now, however, you can enjoy the company of these business giants and learn from their experiences . . . *without reading a page. . . . Listening to them is like enjoying a personal visit from these business leaders. They come alive on the tape as they never could on the printed page.*

Two important claims are being made for autobiography here. The first has to do with its *utility* (which in turn depends on its presumed factuality or historicity): the subgenre of the success story, at least, is presented as having a quite literal cash value. The second, which is not unrelated, is that autobiography directly delivers its author's self. (This claim is presumed here to be strengthened by the auditory medium of tape-recording, despite the fact that the books are not read by the autobiographers themselves.) In promising listeners "the company" of "business leaders," the advertisement implies that these tapes offer unmediated access to *historical* figures who had significance prior to and independent of writing their autobiography. Indeed, the value of their autobiographies is derived from their fame, rather than vice versa. These claims depend on the appropriation of the "metaphysics of presence" to autobiography.

This advertisement nicely illustrates one of the uses of autobiography in American popular culture. Its claims also illustrate a pervasive lay habit of reading autobiography as an especially, even essentially, authoritative kind of writing—if not because it is written from a privileged standpoint (the author is identical with his subject), then because it is historical and thus can offer *practical* lessons or models. Academic criticism of autobiography is never this naive, of course, but until recently much of it shared two of the advertisement's assumptions. The first of these assumptions is that autobiography is nonfictional, since it records the experience of a historical person, not an invented "character." The second assumption is that the author is present in the text, that a pre-existent unique personality can be conveyed through—or despite—literary mediation.

According to referential or transactional theories of language, autobiography has a kind of "authority" lacking in most forms of literary discourse—the authority of its grounding in a verifiable relationship between the text and an extratextual referent. For example, Elizabeth Bruss has said that the genre depends "on distinctions between fiction and nonfiction, between rhetorical and empirical first-person narration."[5] Indeed, by defining autobiography as a particular illocutionary speech act, Bruss has characterized its fundamental conventions as a series of rules:

> The author claims individual responsibility for the creation and arrangement of his text. . . . The individual who is exemplified in the organization of the text is purported to share the identity of an individual to whom reference is made via the subject matter of the text. . . . The existence of this individual, independent of the text itself, is assumed to be susceptible to appropriate public verification procedures.
>
> Under existing conventions, a claim is made for the truth-value of what the autobiography reports—no matter how difficult that truth-value might be to ascertain, whether the report treats of private experiences or publicly observable occasions. . . . The audience is expected to accept these reports as true, and is free to "check up" on them or attempt to discredit them (10–11).

Bruss views autobiography as making empirically verifiable assertions that have, or claim to have, the authority of truth. In her view, autobiographers have a natural, inevitable, and relatively secure authority over their texts because they initiate and control them as well as serve as their subjects. Not surprisingly, this view of autobiography prevails in most anthologies or writing texts built around personal narrative. The preface of one such book asserts:

> Students writing autobiographically can approach their subject with less anxiety, since knowledge of that subject is already theirs, possessed in a way that could only be approximated with an academic topic. . . . Autobiography, then, makes the writer an authority, at least about his subject, and that initial security can serve as a powerful incentive to create an authoritative style.[6]

To many, therefore, authority seems inherent in autobiography: even the style of the narrative may be held to be necessarily authoritative, at least to the extent that it is grounded in "the characteristic cadences and patterns of our own speech" (Lyons,10).

II

Recently this traditional view of the integrity of the self and of its autobiographical expression has come under heavy attack from various quarters. Indeed, recent developments in a number of fields imply that the "I" is none of the things it has conventionally been thought to be: neither first (prior) nor personal (private) nor singular (unique). For example, social psychologists known as *social constructionists* reach conclusions such as the following about the nature and development of selfhood: "The construction of the self is not . . . carried out by individuals in isolation, but requires complicity, negotiation, and collusion—terms that all refer to relationships and not to single individuals."[7] Thus the so-called individual is *not* individual. The self is not an essence, but a socially created construction—a cultural artifact fashioned collaboratively and publicly out of readymade materials, like a quilt patched together at a quilting bee.

Moreover, *identity* involves difference; because the self is contextually variable, its unity is highly problematic:

> Probably most of us present different sides of ourselves in different contexts, depending on the demands of the situation, our personal goals and intentions, and so forth. For the present it remains to be seen whether various configurations of personality characteristics are sufficiently different from each other to constitute different selves in any meaningful sense. If they do, this will not mean that there is no

> stable core to personality. . . . For most of us, our contextual selves are united by a continuously running autobiographical record: Just as we awaken in the morning knowing that we are the same person who went to sleep the night before, we are aware of the activities of our different selves. . . . In the final analysis, our personal histories provide for the continuity that is the essence of selfhood.[8]

The self may be an integrated whole, rather than a mere repertoire of roles, but its unity is to be found in continuity of consciousness, not in consistency of behavior. Personal history is not the product of prior selfhood. Rather, selfhood is the product of an internal autobiography; identity hangs by a narrative thread.

Nor is this "running autobiographical record" necessarily reliable. According to one summary of recent research on memory:

> Events we witness do not always, or even usually, remain unchanged in memory; we fill in missing details by inference, or alter them in accordance with questions we are asked or suggestions made to us, and have no way of retrieving the original—and are not even aware that anything had happened to it. . . . [A]ll of us continually revise our memories of our lives to harmonize with the events that have happened or are happening to us; we are unable to distinguish between what really happened and what we now think happened, since original memory no longer exists.[9]

Memory is not a stable, static record that could ground a reliable written narrative; rather, it is itself a text under continuous unconscious revision.

The attack on the common-sense conception of the self as an essence preceding or transcending context and language has been even more aggressive in the study of literature than in the social sciences. Thus, it is not surprising to have a prominent contemporary critic of autobiography, Paul John Eakin, assert that the search for the origins of the self, whether phylogenetic or ontogenetic, ultimately leads to the acquisition of language as the decisive generative event: "It is not a question of language endowing a hitherto mute self with the capacity for self-expression, but, quite possibly, of language constituting the self in its very make-up."[10] Terry Eagleton has economically rendered the counterintuitive thrust of the recent structuralist "critique of the subject": "The confident bourgeois belief that the isolated individual was the fount and origin of all meaning took a sharp knock: language predated the individual, and was much less his or her product than he or she was the product of it."[11] (Thus, in one currently fashionable formulation, it is not we who speak the language, but the language that speaks us.)

From a Marxist point of view, the idea of a unique self is a bourgeois delusion; from a semiotic point of view, "individuals" are, like texts, merely fields where different cultural codes intersect. Indeed, they *are* texts. From a poststructuralist viewpoint (in Eagleton's account),

> it is an illusion for me to believe that I can ever be fully present to you in what I say or write, because to use signs at all entails that my meaning is always somehow dispersed, divided and never quite at one with itself. Not only my meaning, indeed, but *me:* since language is something I am made out of, rather than a convenient tool I use, the whole idea that I am a stable, unified entity must also be a fiction. Not only can I never be present to you, but I can never be fully present to myself either. I still need to use signs when I look into my mind or search my soul, and this means that I will never experience any "full communion" with myself. It is not that I can have a pure, unblemished meaning, intention, or experience which then gets distorted and refracted by the flawed medium of language: because language is the very air I breathe, I can never have a pure, unblemished meaning or experience at all (129–30).

The critique of the autonomy of the self and the "metaphysics of presence" has taken different forms, and has advanced at different rates, in various disciplines. For better or for worse, the overall trend has been steady retreat from the idea of the self as an embodiment of the attributes of the first-person singular pronoun. We seem to have entered the age of the dot-matrix "I": that crucial personal pronoun, once impressed on the page by an integral piece of type, is now merely a particular configuration of the otherwise indistinguishable dots that serve to make up all the other characters. (Indeed, as "I" write this, "I" am even less substantial than a constellation of dots mechanically imprinted on a page of paper: "I" consist of pixels dancing on a video screen. The steadiness of my image is an illusion produced by the speed of the scanning beam.) The tenuous dot-matrix "I" may stand as an emblem of the contemporary conception of the subject.

Inevitably, the critique of the subject has extended to autobiography. If the self is inherently a function—even a fiction—of language, then autobiography is doubly so; after all, it is a *literary* capitalization of the "I." Thus, the trend in recent autobiography studies has been to erode the distinction between fiction and nonfiction and to deconstruct the apparent relation between the self and its textual embodiment. Structuralism and post-structuralism as we have seen, suggest that autonomy is found not in individuals but in the working of linguistic codes. Autobiography, then, is seen not as *produced by* a preexistent self but as *producing* a provisional and contingent one. Indeed, that self is seen as bound and (pre)determined by the constraints of the linguistic resources and narrative tropes available to the "author."

III

Of course, the authority of autobiography had been challenged before structuralism and poststructuralism emphasized the linguistic dimension of the self. It is sharply circumscribed even in Georges Gusdorf's classic essay, "Conditions and Limits of Autobiography"[12]—an example, according to Avrom Fleishman's survey of genre theory, of "the literalist or purist position, which maintains that an autobiography is a self-written biography designed and required to impart verifiable information about the historical subject."[13] Gusdorf notes the temporal and spatial limits of the genre (the cultural circumstances under which autobiography is, or can be, written):

> The concern, which seems so natural to us, to turn back on one's own past, to recollect one's life in order to narrate it, is not at all universal. It asserts itself only in recent centuries and only on a small part of the map of the world. . . . This conscious awareness of the singularity of each individual life is the late product of a specific civilization (28–29).

To point out that autobiography occurs only when "humanity [has] . . . emerged from the mythic framework of traditional teachings and . . . entered the perilous domain of history" (30) is to characterize the genre (correctly) as a cultural construct whose "authority" is not universal or natural but conditioned, and limited, by certain unspoken assumptions.

Moreover, in practice, it is not always clear when and where the necessary conditions of autobiography have been established. Gusdorf recognizes that this turning point is not passed once and for all by "humanity" or even by Western Europeans. Some critics of American literature, however, have been too eager to see the genre as open to all Americans—as universal, at least during the national era.

That is, they have prematurely identified autobiography with a monolithic "American culture," ignoring its remoteness from, or inaccessibility to, minority groups within the larger population. In different ways, Maxine Hong Kingston and Richard Rodriguez testify to the difficulty of constructing a bicultural self. Indeed, both suggest that the writing of their autobiographies required defiance of ethnic proscriptions since autobiography had little or no warrant in Chicano or Chinese-American culture. The emergence of "minority autobiography" may signal the contact of particular individuals with mainstream culture, or even a subtle form of cultural imperialism, rather than the development of generic preconditions in minority cultures. Texts involving bicultural collaboration, such as some slave narratives and native American autobiographies, are particularly problematic because they are produced on, or across, a cultural frontier by means of "collusion" or "negotiation" (to use Gergen's words for the construction of the self). Even noncollaborative minority autobiographies involve complex transactions among conflicting or even incompatible cultural codes. Sidonie Smith has recently reminded us of how deeply androcentric the prevailing conventions of autobiography may be because the kinds of life stories that count as autobiography tend to reinforce or assume "hegemonic paradigms of psychosexual development."[14]

Just as problematic as the limited extension or currency of autobiography is the question of its truth value. Gusdorf succinctly states the purist position, which assigns autobiography a unique authority:

> The witness of each person about himself is . . . a privileged one: since he writes of someone who is at a distance or dead, the biographer remains uncertain of his hero's intentions; he must be content to decipher signs, and his work is in certain ways always related to the detective story. On the other hand, no one can know better than I what I have thought, what I have wished; I alone have the privilege of discovering myself from the other side of the mirror—nor can I be cut off by the wall of privacy (35).

As we have seen, social psychology is skeptical of the reliability and uniqueness of self-knowledge. Kihlstrom and Kantor report that people

> readily perceive themselves as responsible for positive outcomes [but] tend to deny responsibility for negative outcomes . . . [and] tend to seek information that confirms their theories about themselves and to revise their autobiographical memory so that it accords with their current self-concept (31).

While admitting that individuals may have "some degree of direct introspective access to their own mental states," which can be known to outsiders only through "verbal reports," they caution:

> This is not to say that our introspections are always accurate. . . . [U]nder some circumstances we can be entirely wrong about the reasons for what we think and do. . . . Nor can it be denied that subjective states themselves are often the product of inference and other constructive activity, based on what individuals observe themselves doing (35–36).

To his credit, Gusdorf is also skeptical. He concedes that autobiography will tend inevitably toward apologetics: the identity of author and subject that distinguishes it from biography also compromises it. (In effect, this view makes autobiography the extreme case of authorized biography; the self-biographer has unique access to, and knowledge of, the book's subject, but is also loyal to, and constrained by, that subject.) Gusdorf also acknowledges that

> the narrative of a life cannot be simply the image-double of that life. . . . [T]he original sin of autobiography is the first one of logical coherence and rationalization. . . . The act of reflecting that is essential to conscious awareness is transferred, by a kind of unavoidable optical illusion, back to the stage of the event itself (40–41).

He asserts that, in the end, autobiography's literary "function" is more important than its historical one (43).

Thus, he adopts a variant of the referential theory. For him, the authority of autobiography depends less on the relation between narrative and life-history than on the more immediate link between text and self: "The creative and illuminating nature thus discerned in autobiography suggests a new and more profound sense of truth as an expression of inmost being, a likeness no longer of things but of the person" (44). Gusdorf, then, moves away from the strict purist position, with its simple equation between life and text, toward an expressive view of the genre. He concedes that autobiography is more artifactual than factual, that in some ways it is inevitably fictive. He insists, however, on generic truth value and authority; autobiography inevitably and truthfully corresponds to the self that generates it.

John Sturrock takes a step further in this direction when he argues that " 'authoritative' is synonymous with 'autobiographical' since whatever an autobiographer writes, however wild or deceitful, cannot but count as testimony." According to Sturrock, "It is impossible for an autobiographer not to be autobiographical. . . . The peculiarity of the genre is that the untruth it tells may be as rich, or richer in significance, than the truth."[15] Sturrock ingeniously solves the problem by defining it out of existence—it is the *nature* of autobiography to be authoritative. What Sturrock seems to mean is that insofar as it is an emanation of the writer, autobiography is inevitably self-revelatory: although an autobiography's statements may not be empirically true of the historical figure portrayed, they will nonetheless truthfully characterize their *utterer.* (In Peirce's terms, Sturrock suggests that autobiography furnishes a reliable *index* of its author even when it provides a deceptive *icon* of its subject.)

This view may be unassailable, but only because it gives up so much. In any case, Sturrock's position will be of small consolation to the purist because the quality he calls "authoritativeness" or "autobiographicality" inheres no more necessarily in what we like to call "autobiography" than it does in any other kind of writing, including that which we like to call "fiction." Still, Sturrock's assertion helpfully reminds us of a distinguishing feature of autobiographical discourse: it functions *simultaneously* as an index and icon of the same person. One way of reading it is to determine what is "wild or deceitful" in it (and hence the significance of its untruth) by scrutinizing its iconic function and comparing it with its indexical one—a strategy not demanded, or permitted, by most other genres.

Of course, it is not always easy—nor is it enough—to do so. As we have seen in the prologue, it is quite possible for a counterfeit autobiography to pass itself off not only as an accurate icon but as an authentic index of its subject; neither its (Dietrich-derived) style nor errors in reference gave Irving's hoax away. Yet the Irving–Hughes manuscript reminds us that the value of autobiographical texts is linked to their authorship in a unique way. A "Hemingway" story might retain some aesthetic value in its own right even after it was exposed as forged, or misattributed; it would remain a story with a potential claim to the status of "literature." In contrast, while Irving's "autobiography" of Howard Hughes might retain value as a curiosity (or even as literature) after its exposure, it can not be valued *as* autobiography. (At least, not as that of Howard Hughes; perhaps, for Sturrock, it would be a covert but nonetheless "authoritative" autobiography of Irving.) This distinction suggests that the very nature and idea of autobiography are bound up with the values of validity, authority, and authenticity—and with the identity of its author, narrator, and subject.

IV

As we have seen, this last is the feature on which Elizabeth Bruss staked the authority of the genre. In doing so, she was adapting a view of the genre first developed in Philippe Lejeune's *Le Pacte Autobiographique.*[16] This position also has been assailed recently—by Michael Ryan, for example, who deploys both deconstructive and Marxist strategies.[17] A consideration of his vigorous Marxist critique of Lejeune will illuminate the predicament of the critic of American autobiography today, for the assumptions that Ryan challenges are precisely those on which the supposed congruence of autobiography and American culture is based.

For Lejeune, the existence of an autonomous, self-identical individual is a self-evident truth, and the institution of autobiography is founded on the oneness of author, narrator, and subject. For Ryan, however, "nothing can be self-evident which has been worked out through time and the conflict of interested opinion. To possess a prehistory in this sense is to lose authority" (4). Thus, Ryan takes issue with Lejeune's projection of "the decision of the bourgeois class—that the abstract individual subject shall be the norm—as a universal norm" (10). We may be reminded here of Gusdorf's observation that autobiography, like modern Western culture, assumes the autonomy of the self. (Gusdorf did not project the individual subject as a universal norm, but neither did he quarrel with it as a Western one.) From a Marxist point of view, the assumption of the autonomy of the individual is intellectually spurious and politically invalid, if not reactionary: "The isolation of an identity of personhood, a self-repetitive sameness, from the movement of differentiality or history is ultimately impossible" (11).

Ryan points out that Lejeune's textual pact, which is modeled on a contract between two free and equal agents, "presupposes the possibility of a whole truth which would be the property of the subject and which he would convey at will." That this is a popular notion, in both senses, is evidenced by the Newstrack Executive Classic cassette autobiographies, which presume to deliver, for a price, the autobiographer's truth and self. The literary careers of P. T. Barnum and Mark Twain also involved shrewd exploitation of the same notion, and the essence of the Irving–Hughes case was a strategic, legal, and moral conflict over this notion of autobiographical truth as private property.

As Ryan points out, autobiographical truth is "produced by a rhetorical . . . and a metaphysical system which promotes a notion of privately possessed, ideal truth detached from history and language." But Ryan is at pains to deconstruct that process: "The concept of a private, autobiographical truth which can be exchanged through contract is, like the bourgeois notion of private property, historically produced, socially constructed, and coequal with, not anterior to, contractual rhetoric" (13). Indeed, while Barnum, Twain, and the producers of the Newstrack autobiographies may revel in, and capitalize on, this conception of a contractually conveyable autobiographical truth, the history of collaborative bicultural autobiography demonstrates the inadequacies, and hidden costs, of projects based on such premises.

The Marxist views the subject as inextricably bound up with a socioeconomic system, so that his or her very sense of "self-identity" is produced by class relations rooted in the historical development of the economy. In this sense, "[t]he subject is a repository of effects, the causes of which . . . are absent" (14). A strict Marxist critique, then, would view autobiography as a reflection of a delusive sense of autonomy in its producer that encourages a similar belief in its consumers. Especially in America, where the ideology of the genre and of the mainstream culture seem so well matched, autobiography would seem to function as an opiate of the masses precisely because it *denies* their massiveness, their collectivity. In a sense, then, autobiography is always "done with mirrors" ; it tends merely to reflect prevailing cultural assumptions rather than adequately to enact or express the relation between the individual, on the one hand, and social and historical forces on the other. Thus, the deepest assumptions of the form seem to bar—or to cancel out—radical insights. Insofar as it *singles out* its subject, autobiography is a form of self-mutilation—a voluntary amputation of the "individual" member from a larger sustaining body.

Working in a seemingly remote field, textual editing, Jerome McGann has also recently criticized the notion of authorial authority. His critique is rooted in the sociology of literary production, and his aims are more modestly historicist than Ryan's. But he argues for the restoration of the social dimension of authorship in terms that sound at times faintly Marxist:

> As the very term *authority* suggests, the author is taken to be—for editorial and critical purposes—the ultimate locus of a text's authority, and literary works are consequently viewed in the most personal and

> individual way. . . . The result is that the dynamic social relations which always exist in literary production—the dialectic between the historically located individual author and the historically developing institutions of literary production—tends [sic] to become obscured in criticism (81).

McGann points out that the notion of the "author's final intentions" is often an inappropriate standard for editing because it arbitrarily invokes a Romantic conception of the author as an isolated genius, when a work may owe its form to a voluntary collaboration among author, publisher, and editor (sometimes in response to an audience's reaction).[18] As he puts it,

> those relations of production do not sanction a theory of textual criticism based upon the concept of the autonomy of the author. . . . "Final authority" for literary works rests neither with the author nor with his affiliated institution; it resides in the actual structure of the agreements which these two cooperating authorities reach in specific cases (54).

Indeed, he seems to argue that "authorial" intention may be a function of editorial work:

> [T]he concept of authorial intention only comes into force for criticism when (paradoxically) the artist's work begins to engage with social structures and functions. The fully authoritative text is therefore always one which has been socially produced; as a result, the critical standard for what constitutes authoritativeness cannot rest with the author and his intentions alone (75).

As McGann recognizes, his approach has important implications for autobiography, especially collaborative, or ghostwritten, narratives. Indeed, he cites *The Autobiography of Malcolm X* as a problematic text:

> An editor who came to deal with this work might be tempted to say, simply, that Alex Haley is the principal authority for the "words" while Malcolm X is the authority for the material and "ideas." Needless to say, it does not require much imagination to realize the problems which would await an approach based upon such distinction (85–86).

The problems are even greater when we consider earlier, more obscure bicultural collaborations, such as those involved in the production of most slave narrative and native American autobiography. In many of these cases, the texts were initiated, and later heavily edited, by ghostwriters, rather than by the subjects; moreover, the relationship between collaborators was rarely one of true equality or reciprocity.

The questions of authorship and authority here are difficult but fundamental: to challenge the texts' authorship is to ask whether—or how—they can be read as autobiography. Recent criticism reflects the concerns of both Ryan and McGann in looking more closely at the means by which autobiographical texts are produced. In particular, it has reexamined the "sites" in which collaborative texts were produced, paying careful attention to the method of their presentation and authentication, and to their "dialogic" potential, in an attempt to acknowledge more fully their corporate production and to determine the nature and extent of their authority.

V

With the undermining of the referential theory of language and the consequent emphasis on the self-reflexive nature of all texts, the writing of autobiography has been declared to be, on the one hand, problematic—if not impossible—and, on the other, a paradigm for all writing. Some critics see autobiography as nonexistent or exhausted, while others see it as inescapable and universal. If anything is clear in contemporary autobiography studies, it is that recent developments in theory have challenged the most fundamental assumptions of the genre. Indeed, because the term *autobiography,* the idea of the author as the sole originator and proprietor of a text, and America itself were all produced at about the same time by related forces, contemporary theory poses an especially stimulating challenge to the student of American autobiography. Recent critiques of the autobiographical subject threaten not only the idea that autobiography is a uniquely authoritative kind of writing, but also the significance of its place in American literature because they question the whole "episteme" that underlies the relation of the culture to the genre.

This brief overview of the current complexity—and perplexity—in the field was not meant to answer the questions it raises. Most are not susceptible to final resolution. As Paul John Eakin has recently observed, it is difficult to see how the conflicting views of the relation between language and the self can be definitively adjudicated (191). Nevertheless, the recent debate forces us to rethink our relation to language and culture, and it illuminates autobiography from an important, and often troubling, new perspective. This study endeavors to reread a number of American autobiographies in the wake of recent developments in theory. Although the questions may be ultimately unresolvable, the positions taken have vital implications for our reading of Lives, and thus for our lives.

In light of the attention given earlier to the recent assault on the common-sense notion of the referentiality of autobiography, it is only fair to note that the tenuousness of the authority of autobiography did not require structuralists and post-structuralists to expose it. In a less formal and academic way, the more self-conscious practitioners of autobiography have always understood it to be an inherently tricky enterprise. Certainly Benjamin Franklin, arguably its first practitioner in America, intuited and exploited its provisional nature. Beginning with his unfinished narrative, I will proceed to examine, in more or less chronological order, texts whose authority has been interestingly placed in doubt—either by their authors or by the circumstances of their production or reception. What I will attempt in the following pages, then, is to investigate the degree and kind of the authority manifested by various American autobiographies: how those texts create, erode, or negotiate it; and where, in textual or extratextual considerations, it lies.

3

The Autobiography of Benjamin Franklin: *Self-Constitutional Conventions*

I

According to James Boyd White,

> [i]n separating from Great Britain and setting up their own government, Americans claimed the freedom and the power to remake their world. That claim was of course not absolute. . . . Nevertheless, what was proposed, and perhaps achieved, in America was nothing less than the self-conscious reconstitution of language and community to achieve new possibilities for life.[1]

What White has in mind here is the way in which the Constitution and, to a lesser extent, the Declaration of Independence established the conditions of, and defined the parties to, a distinctively American political discourse. His statement is especially provocative, however, if we consider its relevance to other forms of discourse. In particular, I want to examine the idea of American autobiography in the context of this reconstitution of language and community, and to suggest that Franklin's autobiography represents both the theory and the practice of an "authorized" form of American discourse in which autonomous individuals constitute themselves in writing.

The redefinition of political authority required by the founding of a new nation was accomplished in America primarily by means of constitutive texts that were simultaneously antiauthoritarian and authoritative documents. On the one hand, according to Charles W.

Hendel, "[a]uthority in its American phase . . . abolished not only divinely authorized royal lineage and perpetual rule but also any absolutely fixed rights and powers of the government. . . . The nation is always in the making. So is liberty, so is authority."[2] On the other hand, according to Catherine L. Albanese, although the Constitution and the Declaration pointed " . . . to a human past grounded on human acts rather than either divine events in the lives of the gods or divine events occasioned by a God who acted in history," they quickly became virtually sacrosanct documents, the Scripture of a new anthropocentric civil religion.[3] In the new republic, secular texts assumed the authority that might elsewhere be vested in sacred texts or dynasties; indeed, (by definition) the Constitution inaugurated a world in which it was itself the ultimate textual authority.

It is interesting that both texts have autobiographical dimensions. The Declaration was drafted by three autobiographers—Jefferson, Franklin, and Adams. More important, the Declaration is itself a form of communal autobiography. As Edwin Gittleman has seen, it is a variant of the slave narrative, in which the American people as a whole assume the role of the enslaved.[4] Because Congress suppressed what John Adams referred to as Jefferson's "vehement philippic against negro slavery," the official document commits a serious hypocrisy that later (black) slave narratives would endeavor to expose and correct. This collective American autobiography called forth a subgenre that would amend the original document by, in effect, restoring the missing philippic. Slave narrative was in this sense evoked—or provoked—by a master text whose comprehensiveness and moral authority it questioned.

Unlike the Declaration, a unique speech act addressed to a particular historical moment, the Constitution was intended, according to White,

> to establish the conditions on which, and many of the materials with which, life will actually be led by a people no longer claiming to be united in a splendid moment of common sentiment but now engaged in, and divided by, their ordinary activities and moved by their ordinary motives (240)

One of its conscious and explicit purposes is to create some of the rhetorical rules, conventions, and precedents of American political discourse:

> At its most successful, [the Constitution] can be said to establish the fundamental terms of new kinds of conversation; for it creates a set

> of speakers, defines the occasions for and topics of their speech, and is itself a text that may be referred to as authoritative. . . . The Constitution—like other such instruments—is thus in a literal sense a rhetorical constitution: it constitutes a rhetorical community, working by rhetorical processes that it has established but can no longer control. It establishes a new conversation on a permanent basis (245–46).

Explicitly, it defines rules for "conversation" within and among the several branches of national government, but it establishes the conditions of other forms of expression as well—even of "literary" discourse. The most obvious way in which it pertains to literature, of course, is, in its provision for copyright protection. Under section 8 of Article I, Congress is expressly empowered "To promote the Progress of Science and useful Arts, by securing for limited Times to Authors and Inventors the exclusive Right to their respective Writings and Discoveries." Here, the Constitution followed the lead of British law (specifically, the Statute of Anne of 1709) in recognizing the right of authors to control the disposition of their intellectual property. With the inclusion of a copyright clause in the Constitution (followed by the enactment of the first American copyright statute in 1790), the new nation officially endorsed the ideology of authorship: the idea of an author as originator (and sole proprietor) of a text. The most significant features of the copyright provision, for my purposes, are the assertion of the authority of authors as opposed to the monopoly held earlier by stationers, and the reliance on the marketplace rather than on patronage as a stimulus to invention. (As Franklin's career already showed, literacy was becoming a valuable form of capital, and the writer was becoming an entrepreneur.) This redefinition of the economic relations that governed the production and distribution of literature was an important aspect of what White calls the reconstitution of the rhetorical community. Authorship was thus a privileged phenomenon from the very conception of the new Republic.[5]

If the Constitution is not itself a form of autobiography, the Preamble's prominent deployment of the first-person plural—"We the People" —puts it, like the Declaration of Independence, in a proximate relation to autobiography broadly conceived. Moreover, with the requirement that each house "keep a Journal of its Proceedings, and from time to time publish the same," the collective author of the Constitution ensures that the people's future acts (including "speech acts") will be literally represented in print; it mandates a kind of perpetual national autobiography in microcosmic cipher. This provision for published congressional records not only authorizes a special form of official discourse, it may also by implication inspire or favor autobiography of a more idiosyncratic sort.[6]

The Constitution encourages autobiography generally by institutionalizing a state in which individuals will be free, equal, and self-governing (at least in theory—it excluded whole categories of people from the full benefits of citizenship). As Robert F. Sayre has put it,

> Where everyone's life was as good as the next man's, where no one needed to feel constrained by tradition or by traditional forms, in that state every man's life was of potential interest. Any man could become President, the saying went, and any man could be an autobiographer.[7]

If autobiography is, as William Dean Howells put it, the most democratic province of letters, then democracy should be the most autobiographical of political systems. Indeed, autobiography would seem to be the inevitable literary expression of democracy, for like democracy, autobiography depends on belief in one's significance, and in one's ability to chart one's destiny. Insofar as the Constitution is the literal instrument creating this democratic climate, it establishes a rhetorical community of individuals, each of whom is a potential autobiographer entitled to write and then to copyright his or her own Life. Franklin's narrative of his life, which he began shortly before the Revolution and worked on intermittently until just after the public announcement of the Constitution's adoption, is, in this context, an especially authoritative American text because in it this eldest Founding Father established the conventions of American self-(re)constitution.

II

Of course, both the Constitution and the *Autobiography* are verbal constructs, and thus their authority is open to question from various perspectives. Under examination, neither political nor literary autonomy is as simple or as substantial as it may at first seem. For one thing, there is the curious ontological status of the speakers of the Constitution. As White points out, " 'we the people' . . . existed only in their act of constitution, in a kind of momentary incarnation. . . . The people thus left behind them a testamentary trust that has something of the character of a sacred text" (255). With a very different implication—the demystification of authorship—recent theory has suggested that *all* writing momentarily incarnates its author: an "author" is brought into existence by an utterance, and is thus its effect, rather than its cause. While this may not be disturbing when said of lyric poetry or the novel—utterances long construed as issuing from personae not necessarily identical with their creators—it may be unsettling when said of the Constitution or of an autobiography—texts we imagine to have greater authority than that of fiction or poetry, and a more stable relation to historical events.

White has suggested that the Constitution's classic use of the first-person plural creates "a single imaginary author, consisting of all the people of the United States, including the reader, merged into a single identity in this act of self-constitution" (240). But this notion is highly problematic—linguistically, rhetorically, and politically. According to Emil Benveniste, the first-person plural pronoun can never properly be considered a *pluralization* of the singular, for a multiple of identical subjects is a meaningless concept. (As Ambrose Bierce put it: "In grammar [I] is a pronoun of the first person and singular number. Its plural is said to be *We,* but how there can be more than one myself is doubtless clearer to the grammarians than it is to the author of this imcomparable dictionary."[8]) Rather, it should be seen as the first person *amplified*—"a *junction* between 'I' and the 'non-I.' "[9] This reading of the pronoun reveals the artifice of its construction.

Similarly, Kenneth Burke has observed that

> in actual point of fact, a Constitution is addressed by the first person to the second person. In propounding a Constitution, "I" or "we" say what "you" may or should and may not or should not do. . . . In adopting Constitutions, men may impose commands not only upon others . . . but they may also impose commands upon themselves [in the form of their future selves]. . . . This vagueness of address helps greatly to make us forget that commands are addressed.[10]

Gordon S. Wood has pointed out that the Constitution redefined "the people"—which in European tradition meant an organically unified "estate"—as an "agglomeration of hostile individuals coming together for their mutual benefit to construct a society" (607). Moreover, the substitution of the phrase "We the People" for "We the States," not only signaled but also effected the annihilation of the authority of the more popular state governments.[11] In effect, then, the Constitution produced the illusion rather than the reality of popular government: "The representation of the people, as American politics in the Revolutionary era had made glaringly evident, could never be virtual, never inclusive; it was acutely actual, and always tentative and partial" (600).

Viewing the crucial first-person plural pronoun from a different perspective, Edmund S. Morgan has suggested that its use endows the Constitution, that supremely authoritative document, with a fictional dimension: "Those who rescued American representative government . . . by means of the Constitution of 1787 . . . did it by an additional fiction. They invented the American people, a fictional body comprising all the people of the whole nation."[12] Morgan argues that all government depends on fictions, the willing suspension of disbelief in ruling ideas or myths—whether the idea of popular sovereignty or that of the divine right of kings. In America, the idea of representation is the crucial conceit that sustains the larger fiction of popular sovereignty. In any case, this critical pronomial gesture erases potentially problematic differences between speaker and audience, or between past, present, and future Americans—between "the people" and their government. (It also implies an inclusiveness that it did not enact.) Of course, a similar illusion is crucial to autobiography, in which the integral first-person pronoun gives the impression of "representing" a whole, coherent, pre-existent self and minimizes differences between the author and subject—or within either. (The motto of the genre might also be *e pluribus unum.*) In both cases, the first-person shifters are, at best, makeshift—at worst, they are shifty.

Insofar as the Constitution creates the American people and endows them with sovereignty, it is the original (the "great") American novel—the founding (and sometimes *con*founding) fiction. To the extent that the Constitution legitimizes and privileges the form of discourse that came to be known as autobiography, the revelation of its fictive dimension has unsettling implications for autobiography as well. These issues are directly pertinent to Franklin's autobiography because it was undertaken in the period when, according to Morgan, the taxation of the colonies finally exposed the fiction that the colonists could be represented by men elected in England (337), and it was terminated at the time when "the Constitution of 1787 restored the fictional purpose of representation, namely to persuade the many to accept the government of the few" (338). The tenuousness of the Founding Fathers' self-constituted authority is also inscribed in Franklin's autobiography.

III

Catherine Albanese has characterized the experience of the founding fathers as follows:

> The sons of the fathers became fathers themselves in the course of the Revolution because of a series of events which made them new centers of authority and power. . . . As traditional people, they had seen themselves as the heirs of a long and indefinite series of heroes and deeds. . . . Their actions possessed warrant and metaphysical validity because they were patterned on the model which had existed from time immemorial: they in the present were secure because they were repeating an exemplary action from out of the past. Yet while still invoking their fathers, the patriots were finding in their actions a creative power without reference to the models from the past. They began to function as self-constituting and self-commanding figures (46).

Franklin's involvement in this crisis of authority as a historical figure is obvious; it is part of what we mean when we identify him as a Founding Father (a term that itself plays a powerful role in the transference and securing of authority). Since he began his *Memoirs* (as he called his narrative) several years before the War of Independence began, however, and since the narrative line never reaches the 1770s, the degree of his participation in the crisis as an autobiographer is not so obvious. Nevertheless, it is significant. The letters that introduce the second part (1784) clearly indicate that the narrative was *continued* with the Revolution in mind, and Franklin's concern with constitutional issues is certainly evident in the brief last section, which is dominated by an account of an earlier political crisis. (At that time, Lord Granville, President of the Privy Council, lectured Franklin: "You Americans have wrong ideas of the Nature of your Constitution. . . . THE KING IS THE LEGISLATOR OF THE COLONIES.")[13] It can even be argued that Franklin anticipated the Revolution as he wrote the first part in 1771: in a letter written two weeks before he began the autobiography, Franklin accurately forecast the probable course of events leading to America's overthrowing the authority of the king.[14] That Franklin wrote much, if not all, of the manuscript with the Revolution in mind—prospectively or retrospectively—seems clear.

Still, the relation between the narrative and the Revolutionary politics remains surprisingly difficult to assess. Most critics of the narrative have argued that the first part flows smoothly enough into the second; indeed, the editors of the recent "genetic text" claim that Franklin "faithfully (with some significant omissions, additions, and rearrangements of the topics) followed his [initial] outline throughout the entire course of composing the autobiography."[15] Even allowing for prescience, this unperturbed continuity is troublesome insofar as it suggests that the intervening Revolution merely interrupted, rather than deflected, the course of the narrative. James Cox has argued, however, that the narrative does significantly register, or mimic, the Revolution. According to Cox, the decisive conflict is inscribed in the autobiography—not explicitly, as plot, but implicitly, as *form.* The narrative's innovative conception expresses the crucial event that remained always beyond its chronological reach:

> [T]he history of the revolution, in which Franklin played such a conspicuous part, is displaced by the narrative of Franklin's early life, so that personal history *stands in place of the revolution.* . . . But this represented history was not the actual revolution. There still remained the form which would realize the revolution and thus stand for it. That form was the autobiography—the life of a self-made, self-governing man written by the man himself (259).

This an appealing view of Franklin, as one who clearly foresaw the political revolution and who enacted its literary equivalent by inventing a new form of autobiography distinguished by its self-governed and autonomous "I."[16] But while Franklin vividly renders the transition from traditional to self-constituting agent, the transition is not without uncertainty and unforeseen consequences. At critical junctures, the narrative betrays concern about authority in many forms.

Charles Hendel has observed that "[a]uthority . . . can hardly be dissociated from the notion of the Author of all being. The metaphor in the term 'authority' is of the word spoken by the Supreme Being declaring the law, the requirement, or the responsibility enjoined upon his creatures here below" (8). One of Franklin's most fundamental, and audacious, gestures in writing his life, however, was to effect just such a dissociation, and to negate the metaphor Hendel refers to. The most compact expression of Franklin's seizure of authority in and over his narrative is a trope in the very first paragraph, which radically revised one informing an epitaph he had composed for himself in 1728. The original epitaph attributes authority over his life—and afterlife—explicitly to the supreme being:

The Body of
B. Franklin,
Printer;
Like the Cover of an old Book,
Its Contents torn out,
And stript of its Lettering and Gilding,
Lies here, Food for Worms,
But the Work shall not be wholly lost:
For it will, as he believ'd, appear once more,
In a new & more perfect Edition,
Corrected and amended
By the Author. (43–44n)

Apart, perhaps, from his apparent confidence in his own resurrection, the implications of Franklin's trope here are more or less consistent with orthodox Christian theology: while the flesh decays, the spirit will endure by the grace of God. Insofar as it identifies the self with a book, the trope inevitably evokes the idea of autobiography; here again, its implications are quite orthodox and thus consistent with contemporary theory of spiritual autobiography, according to which personal narrative is a tentative tracing by a mortal hand of God's design in the writer's experience. The authority for the narrative, as for the life, rests ultimately with the divine Author, from whose work and Word all human creations derive.

What is striking and significant about the opening of the autobiography is that in it Franklin assumes the role he had earlier assigned to God (and thus commits figurative deicide):

> [W]ere it offer'd to my Choice, I should have no Objection to a Repetition of the same Life from its Beginning, only asking the Advantage Authors have in a second edition to correct some Faults of the first. So would I if I might, besides corr[ectin]g the Faults, change some sinister Accidents and Events of it for others more favourable, but tho' this were deny'd, I should still accept the Offer. However, since such a Repetition is not be expected, the next Thing most like living one's Life over again, seems to be a *Recollection* of that Life; and to make that Recollection as durable as possible, the putting it down in Writing (43–44).

Franklin's gesture here abruptly and decisively breaks with the tradition of the conversion narrative, the most—in a sense, the only—authoritative form of life-writing he knew. In a gesture befitting Turgot's epitaph, which praised him for snatching the lightning from the sky and the scepter from tyrants, he transfers authority over personal narrative from Heaven to earth, or from God to self.

As Lewis Simpson has noted, "in Franklin's epitaph salvation by faith in the regenerating grace of God becomes faith in the grammatical and verbal skills and in the printing shop know-how of a Deity who is both Man of Letters and Master Printer."[17] In the epitaph, then, Franklin took the liberty of playfully creating a God in his own image. But in the opening of the autobiography, he went further, and usurped divine authority: by the logic of his trope, the self-written life becomes the "new and more perfect Edition, Corrected and amended by the Author" that his soul was to be in the epitaph, and Franklin becomes the Author of his own (unconditional) immortality. With a seemingly casual and apologetic introductory comment, then, he assumes authority over his Life, if not his life, and thus commits, as Cox suggests, a proleptic revolution in personal narrative.

Speaking of confession in a sense that includes, but is not limited to, formal penance, Michel Foucault has called it

> a ritual that unfolds within a power relationship, for one does not confess without the presence (or virtual presence) of a partner who is not simply the interlocutor but the authority who requires the confession, prescribes and appreciates it, and intervenes in order to judge, punish, forgive, console, and reconcile; [and] . . . a ritual in which the expression alone, independently of its external consequences, produces intrinsic modifications in the person who articulates it: it exonerates, redeems, and purifies him; it unburdens him of his wrongs, liberates him, and promises him salvation.[18]

What is remarkable about Franklin's narrative is the extent to which he seems able to alter this paradigm; indeed, Franklin's narrative might be said to initiate, or at least advance, the secularization and dissemination of confession that Foucault traces, from its medieval origins as religious duty to its adaptation in modern Western educational, penal, and medical institutions.

Like the Declaration of Independence and the Constitution, Franklin's autobiography appropriates authority to itself, but here, too, the democratic gesture of self-constitution is problematic. For one thing, Franklin seems to have lacked the courage of his self-conception: in the very next paragraph, he attributes his happiness to Providence, and to God alone knowledge of "the Complexion of my future Fortune" (45). Furthermore, other implications of his trope tend to diminish the authority it seems to consolidate in his pen. On the one hand, his open admission and correction of his errata bolster confidence in him: he seems to have internalized the role of the God who audits and judges the confession. On the other hand, the gesture hints at the possibility—indeed, the inevitability—of other, *silent* corrections of errata. His printer's analogy entails some uncertainty about authorial candor and integrity; Franklin undermines his own authority in the very act of creating it.

Thus, as one kind of authority (responsibility for initiating and producing the text) is appropriated for individual autobiographers, another (credibility) is sacrificed or lost by the genre as a whole. Like collaborative autobiography, spiritual autobiography is always "as told to" a specific second party; the fact that the second party is divine tends to enhance its authority. When the ultimate Author of autobiography is no longer God but the self, and its audience is not divinity but posterity, its credibility will be more questionable—more a matter of rhetorical skill and negotiation among interested parties. Franklin's secularizing impulse necessarily compromises autobiography's authority in the act of seizing it. In any case, by flaunting his total editorial control over his manuscript, Franklin reminds us of the artifactual nature of autobiography. As with a constitution, the acknowledgment that an autobiography is amendable, rather than definitive, in some ways diminishes its authority. Franklin creates a New World in which authority will be an unstable textual effect.

IV

Some of the text's other strategies for securing authority are also problematic—in particular, the epistolary gestures that open the first two parts. These passages were written from very different spatial and temporal vantage points—England and France, before and after the Revolution, respectively—and Franklin's role shifts decisively from the first part to the second. In the first, he addresses his son, whereas two friends address him in the second. In both cases, however, the letter writer has specific designs on his reader: the first person seeks to exert authority over the second. Also, in both cases, the bases of that authority are more tenuous than they first appear.

In view of the maturity and station of Franklin's son at the time of composition (1771), the initial salutation—"Dear Son"—has often been dismissed as a pretext, a way of exorcising the specter of vanity or egocentricity that haunted personal narrative.[19] However, two recent students of the father–son relationship—William Sterne Randall and Hugh Dawson—take it as sincere.[20] Whether a public or a private audience was foremost in Franklin's mind, the salutation deserves close attention, for, as Jay Fliegelman has shown, eighteenth-century political conflicts between authority and liberty were typically encoded in familial metaphors.[21] Indeed, the first several pages of the narrative display concern, latent as well as manifest, with legitimacy and authority of various kinds.

Fliegelman has called the autobiography an "antipatriarchal classic" because it demonstrates the advantages of Lockean contractualism between parent and child (42); however, this is truer of the career of the autobiographical *character*—as he chafes under, and eventually liberates himself from, patriarchal restraints—than it is of the performance of the *narrator.* Whatever the intention of the salutation, its effect is to cast the autobiographer in the role of a *father*—one, as it happens, who is concerned with defining and exerting authority in terms of a tradition. As I read it, then, the opening is not entirely antipatriarchal. On the one hand, the trope of autobiography as a self-authored and self-edited text liberates the narrator from a kind of ultimate patriarchal authority. On the other hand, as if in compensation for his audacity, the narrator locates himself in a tradition that reaches back through his English heritage and forward through his son's life and career. This sense of historical continuity receives its extreme expression in his joking reference to the striking resemblance between him and his uncle Thomas, who died exactly four years before Franklin was born:

> The account we receiv'd of his Life and Character from some old People at Ecton, I remember struck you, as something extraordinary from its Similarity to what you knew of mine. Had he died on the same Day [as Franklin's birth], you said one might have suppos'd a Transmigration (47–48).

Here Franklin imagines himself not as an autonomous, let alone unique and original, individual, but rather as the reincarnation of an English ancestor.

In locating himself and his son in the family tradition, Franklin may be attempting to legitimize both of them. Although his son's illegitimacy was used against both father and son at various times by political opponents (Randall 180–82), it hardly seems to have hindered either's career. Ultimately, the irregularity of his son's birth proved less embarrassing to Franklin than that of his politics: Franklin took his son's Loyalism as disloyal to *him,* and it occasioned a bitter estrangement. His patriarchal stance toward his son is clear in his written response to William's request for a conciliatory meeting in 1784,

> I ought not to blame you for differing in Sentiment with me in Public Affairs. . . . Our Opinions are not in our Power. . . . Your Situation was such that few would have censored your remaining Neuter, *tho' there are Natural Duties which precede political ones, and cannot be extinguish'd by them.*[22]

The final dependent clause here effectively retracts the forgiveness implied in the preceding lines; Franklin's lasting resentment of his son's self-assertion, his not "remaining Neuter," is obvious.

The opening pages of the autobiography, in which Franklin writes himself and William into a continuous family tradition, may have been an attempt to cement an alliance in the face of their already diverging interests and conflicting loyalties, to imply that his natural son should be loyal to his biological rather than to his political father, to consolidate his waning paternal authority over his son, and even to work out his own relation to his political fathers. Caught up in complex political and family conflicts, Franklin's attitude on authority was inconsistent. With regard to his own father, the King, and even God himself, Franklin might at times hazard an antipatriarchal stance; but with regard to his son, he reverted at times to a subtle authoritarianism.

In view of the suggestion that Franklin may have anticipated the impending separation of the colonies from England—an act of political patricide—his tracing of his ancestry in the opening pages would seem odd. But Franklin's gambit may be read as an attempt to justify himself as well as his son—that is, to constitute himself as loyal to English tradition, if not to particular institutional expressions of it such as the Church, the King, or the Parliament. Indeed, the Founding Fathers' rationalization of their self-authorization involved exactly this kind of search for precedents and principles in the (unwritten) English Constitution. According to Norman Jacobsen,

> in the Philadelphia Convention and afterwards, many of [the patriots] accepted the view that the new Constitution was much more a summary of the best in Anglo-American tradition than a noble experiment in free government. Like Columbus they attempted to convince themselves that the new world they had brought into being was actually an old one.[23]

Franklin's gesture, therefore, may not be inconsistent with revolutionary autobiography or politics, both of which require the elision of gaps in a tradition in order to secure their own authority. What Franklin finds in his past is exactly the oxymoron he requires: a tradition of nonconformity (50–52). To put it differently, in the Nonconformity of his forebears, he discovers authority for his future participation in a Revolution: he portrays himself as predestined, in effect, to be free. Of course, the retrospective search for antecedents is not a neutral process; an autobiographer as much invents as discovers a past consistent with what "follows" in his narrative. What an autobiographer isolates as "causes" of his later behavior may be instead the literary effects of it. What is interesting here is the way in which—after the Revolution could be foreseen, though before it occurred—Franklin prospectively characterized himself as a proto-Revolutionary, albeit a reluctant one. Positioned thus ambiguously, he remained flexible before the opportunities and requirements of the future.

The paradox of these opening pages is also legible in Franklin's name, which he reminds us is "the Name of an Order of People" who were freeholders. While Franklin seems to value the name as a sign of his freedom, it denotes freedom only within a social system in which rank and land-ownership are inherited. It is thus the nominal equivalent of his stance toward tradition. It also illuminates his relationship with the illegitimate son to whom he passed on the name because he seems to require from him a *filial* loyalty, loyalty to family rather than to principle—to the "name" rather than to what it signifies. (His deployment of the first-person plural pronoun to minimize differences between parties in conflict anticipates that of the Constitution; in effect, in the early pages, he and his son are at times, "We the Franklins.") Whether out of personal and familial or public and political motives, these pages reflect substantial ambivalence about autonomy and authority. Moreover, in significant ways, they tend to *minimize* Franklin's originality and uniqueness.

V

If one purpose of the epistolary strategy in part one was the avoidance of vanity, the transcription of letters from Abel James and Benjamin Vaughan at the beginning of the second part better serves the same end. By locating Franklin's narrative firmly in a public and historic context, the letters obviate the need for a private pretext for continuing the autobiography. The nature of the letters, however, further complicates the matter of the text's authority. Both urge Franklin, in very flattering terms, to resume and complete his narrative, but Vaughan's effusive letter is essentially an extensive gloss on James's short one, which Franklin had sent to Vaughan for his response (134). Since Vaughan had already brought out the first extensive edition of Franklin's nonscientific writings, he could hardly have been expected to contravene James and discourage Franklin from resuming his autobiography. Nor did he disappoint him; indeed, Franklin could hardly have written a better letter himself.

In soliciting Vaughan's letter in this manner, however, he very nearly did write it himself, and the circumstances of the letter's genesis detract somewhat from its message. In any case, what occurs here is not just the well-meaning intervention of two friends on opposite shores of the Atlantic, but a collaborative explication of the manuscript as outlined and partially drafted, and a projection of its future trajectory. Though Franklin was presumably aware of the way in which the Revolution changed the context of his narrative, he portrays himself here as receiving direction rather than shaping his own account of the events that led up to the Revolution of which he is purportedly the "author." He seems to relinquish a measure of the initiative he seized, at least metaphorically, in the opening of part one; Vaughan is allowed both to describe and to prescribe the amended and expanded document. The result is a text whose authority is less clearly defined and less autonomously exercised by the author. In the epistolary transition that bridges the gap occasioned by "The Affairs of the Revolution," Vaughan bids to become the "Author" of a "new and more perfect Edition" of Franklin's Life.

It is worth dwelling on Vaughan's letter because it so clearly expresses the conception of autobiography that governed the second part. One of its interesting features is its assertion that if Franklin does not write his own "history," someone else will do so—very likely in a such a manner "as nearly to do as much harm, as your own management of the thing might do good" (135).[24] This goes beyond the idea that one has a *right* to write one's life to the idea that some people, such as Franklin, have a *duty* to do so. Vaughan implies that Franklin's self-biography will be his only *authorized* biography; moreover, he suggests that it will be *authoritative* (i.e., definitive): "Considering your great age, the caution of your character, and your peculiar style of thinking, it is not likely that any one besides yourself can be sufficiently master of the facts of your life or the intentions of your mind" (139).

One of the key passages of the entire epistolary transition is this:

> Besides all this, the immense revolution of the present period, will necessarily turn our attention towards the author of it; and when virtuous principles have been pretended in it, it will be highly important to shew that such have really influenced; and as your own character will be the principal one to receive a scrutiny, it is proper . . . that it should stand respectable and eternal (139).

Here, Vaughan's letter does (quite explicitly) for Franklin's autobiography what, according to James Boyd White, the Constitution does for American political and legal discourse:

> [it] provides a way of testing the claims of individuals to speak in the roles it creates and on the occasions it establishes. In many instances it also defines the topics of argument appropriate to various rhetorical circumstances, telling the speaker, and others, what kinds of speech are authorized or appropriate for him (245–46).

Ironically, while Franklin initiated his autobiography before the War with an audacious trope of self-authorization, he continued it after the Revolution as a document elicited and authorized by third parties.

In a larger context, the effect of the letter is to establish a rhetorical community and to define some of the conventions of self-constitution within it. According to Vaughan, Franklin is not just the author of the Revolution to which the nation owes its existence, he is also to be the author of a definitive Life of himself that will become a kind of model text encouraging "more writings of the same kind . . . " (138). What the letter gives us, then, is an Englishman's theory of American autobiography. In Vaughan's view, just as the new nation needs a special form of autobiography to preserve its virtuous character (and thus its democratic government), the genre needs Americans like Franklin to rescue it from domination by "various public cutthroats and intriguers, and . . . absurd monastic self-tormentors, or vain literary triflers" (138). Moreover, raising the stakes, Vaughan specifically urges the production of a text that will withstand politically motivated "scrutiny."

But the implications of Vaughan's elaborate letter, are sometimes self-contradictory: Vaughan, an Englishman, *appoints* Franklin the Founding Father of American autobiography. Similarly, he conceives of the genre's relation to the nation's revolutionary origins and to its democratic ideology as requiring constraints on the autobiographer's initiative and autonomy— the writer's authority over the text. (Indeed, Vaughan's letter virtually deconstructs itself, for his editorial advice compromises the very authority he explicitly assigns to Franklin.)

There are several problems in this transitional passage. For one thing, while Franklin is asked to write what amounts to the autobiography of the Revolution, he is asked not to celebrate it, but to defend it. In a sense, the function of the text, like that of the Declaration of Independence, is to justify a fait accompli. In the parts of the narrative written after the War, however, Franklin at times seems more resigned to, than resolved on, independence. For example, in recounting his proposal for a Plan of Union of all the Colonies at the Albany Congress in 1754, he makes the conciliatory (and self-serving) assertion that, had it been adopted,

> The Colonies so united would have been sufficiently strong to have defended themselves; there would then have been no need of Troops from England; of course the subsequent Pretence for Taxing America, and the bloody Contest it occasioned, would have been avoided (211).

Here, Franklin reconstitutes himself as an early constitutionalist— one whose plan, if adopted, would have obviated the need for the Revolution. Wittingly or not, he characterizes himself here as an unheeded visionary or failed negotiator, not as a successful and virtuous revolutionary. Another problem is that in encouraging the writing of a sanitized life (an auto-hagiography), Vaughan is in effect urging the creation of a founding fiction like those that Morgan discusses; indeed, he suggests that American autobiography should be governed by the fiction of Franklin's self-representation. Similarly, in urging Franklin to write a consciously exemplary life, he contradicts his assertion of Franklin's uniqueness. Both Roger J. Porter and William C. Spengemann have noted the conflict between the exemplary impulse and the assumption that autobiography expresses unique individuality. According to Spengemann, "[h]ad the *Autobiography* been true to Franklin's remarkable career, we feel, it would have failed in its attempt to set an example for posterity."[25] Porter reads Franklin's *style* in terms of this tension:

> The writing, in its unadorned chronicling style, testifies to the desire to suppress individualism or at least not to assert an identity so particularized and distinct that it will run counter to the democratic ideal in which the common man with the proper will may achieve what Franklin has.[26]

This is especially, if not exclusively, a dilemma of democratic autobiography because democracy is conceived both as a social organization in which one is permitted—even encouraged— to develop one's unique potential, and as one in which authority must be exercised in such subtly constraining forms as exemplary autobiography.

In any case, the genre Vaughan envisions is not entirely democratic, or at least egalitarian, in its implications. Both James and Vaughan hope for a master text that will serve to discipline present and future Americans, as well as to give the new nation a respectable international image. Thus, what Franklin is being asked to produce is only nominally a revolutionary book; in a sense, it is a counterrevolutionary text that would account for the past revolution in such a way as to forestall future ones.[27] Vaughan's advice contains a degree of noblesse oblige: autobiography is characterized not as an opportunity for all, but as the duty of a ruling elite—those who have matched Franklin in eminence and achievement or otherwise assimilated his model. Autobiography in America is thus both a "privileged" form of discourse and the discourse of the privileged. The very form of the epistolary solicitation characterizes autobiography as something to be undertaken by invitation rather than by self-initiation, an endeavor dependent on the authorization of someone other than the author.

Franklin's "compliance with the Advice contain'd in these Letters" (133) is evident in his emphasis in the next part on his "bold and arduous Project of arriving at moral Perfection" (148). This section is not without humor, of course. For example, one cannot be sure that Franklin's statement of his thirteenth virtue does not contain a joke: "HUMILITY. Imitate Jesus and Socrates." Nor are his rules as restrictive as they may at first appear. Under scrutiny, the one advocating "CHASTITY" seems full of convenient loopholes: "Rarely use Venery but for Health or Offspring; Never to Dulness, Weakness, or the Injury of your own or another's Peace or Reputation" (150). Nevertheless, this illustration of self-discipline compensates for, or revises, the drama of self-liberation that was the essence of the first part.

Indeed, what Franklin invents here, in his bookkeeping method of self-examination, is, to use Michel Foucault's phrase, a "disciplinary technology." While it essentially consists of making check marks on a grid, the keeping of the book is a rudimentary form of self-life-writing, a reductio ad absurdum of autobiography. Conversely, the autobiography is the conduct book writ large. Both are forms of secular confession and self-surveillence—personal panopticons. Both are also characteristic of the progressive individualization of modern Western culture—the shift from regimes in which individuality was marked at the top in the high visibility of royalty and nobility, to ones in which the masses are individualized. If the epic is typical of the first sort of society, the dossier and the autobiography are typical of the second.[28] Foucault has shrewdly noted that both "meanings of the word *subject:* subject to someone else by control and dependence, and tied to his own identity by a conscience or self-knowledge . . . suggest a form of power which subjugates and makes subject to."[29] While Franklin is no longer a subject of the king, the message of the second part is that he is still subject to others and to himself. Even as the "subject" of his own autobiography, he exemplifies the kind of self-discipline upon which his society depends.

This passage suggests the full significance of Cox's description of Franklin as a "self-governing man," for he does not seek or undergo conversion—the sudden discovery of a master plot in his life—nor is his narrative the passive tracing of such a plot. Rather, as autobiographical character and/or narrator, Franklin assumes all three functions of constitutional government: he drafts reasonable laws of conduct, tries to execute them faithfully, and judges himself accordingly. Moreover, his narrative is increasingly concerned with government in what Foucault refers to as the

> very broad meaning which it had in the sixteenth century. "Government" did not refer only to political structures or to the management of states; rather it designated the way in which the conduct of individuals or of groups might be directed: the government of children, of souls, of communities, of families, of the sick. It did not only cover the legitimately constituted forms of political or economic subjection, but also modes of action, more or less considered and calculated, which were destined to act upon the possibilities of action of other people. To govern, in this sense, is to structure the possible field of action of others (220).

Franklin personifies government in this sense: even before the new republic is established, he devises a kind of universal disciplinary methodology and several informal structures—voluntary organizations, public institutions—that will order American life. While he promises liberation from tyrannical authority to self-government, he establishes numerous networks that subject individuals to authority in new and subtle forms.

The utopian element of the book consists in his ambition to free himself, and others, from vicious influences, external and internal—

"to conquer all that either Natural Inclination, Custom, or Company might lead me into" (148). He concludes his account of his "Project of arriving at moral Perfection" —which, predictably, falls short— with a telling image:

> yet I was by the Endeavour a better and a happier Man than I otherwise should have been, if I had not attempted it; As those who aim at perfect Writing by imitating the engraved Copies, tho' they never reach the wish'd for excellence of those Copies, their Hand is mended by the Endeavour, and is tolerable while it continues fair and legible (156).

This passage exposes a deeply conservative strain in the narrative. While his conception of himself as author of his own Life sets him outside the tradition of autobiography that is ultimately derived from Biblical sources, this passage reveals that Franklin still conceives of individual conduct in terms of written models. Here he portrays individual perfection as conformity to prevalidated, anonymous (and mechanically reproduced) copies. Conduct is envisioned as a recognizable "hand" at once individual and imitative of an accessible model. While D.H. Lawrence's complaint that Franklin "set up the first dummy American" fails to take his irony into account, it also isolates a disturbing tendency of the text.[30]

VI

Probably the most prominent model of lifewriting familiar to Franklin was the narrative of spiritual growth—especially as allegorized, or novelized, by John Bunyan in *Pilgrim's Progress,* and Franklin's autobiography *can* be seen as a secularization of the spiritual narrative. Still, it does not correspond very closely to any single model. Rather, it incorporates features of several genres. Indeed, scholars have proposed a range of different sources for the text, from Cotton Mather to Defoe.[31] Perhaps it seems so original, therefore, not because it lacks a single source, but because it has so many. The story that stands as a parable of this aspect of the narrative is the one in which Franklin singlehandedly rectifies the lack of a "Letter Founder in America": "I now contriv'd a Mould, made use of the Letters we had, as Puncheons, struck the Matrices in Lead, and thus supply'd in a pretty tolerable way all Deficiencies" (110). As a novice writer, Franklin apprenticed himself informally to acknowledged prose masters—painstakingly forging a distinctive style by slavishly imitating, then improving on, the styles of others. Later, as a life-writer, he melted his various models down until they were indistinguishable in the final form of the American letters produced.

This is especially significant with respect to the long line of autobiographies of "self-made men" that derive from Franklin's example. Their general failure to retain our interest lies not in their lack of originality alone; no one was more self-consciously imitative than Franklin. Rather, the pallor of their writing—even when it is not ghostwriting—may stem from their reliance on a single accredited source, whose visibility inevitably veils or diminishes what might be distinctive or original in them. These texts betray the extent to which their authors are *not* self-made. They may fall short of Franklin as well, precisely in the extent to which they offer an integral self and a conclusive story. The illusion of originality may depend on obscuring one's end as well as one's beginnings.

In any case, Franklin's autobiography is not merely the Life of a "self-made" man—the retrospective writing down of his "making" of himself. His opening trope, which portrays autobiography as the second, corrected edition of one's life, implies that existence is already textual. If reliving one's life—whether or not in the durable form of a written narrative—is equivalent to editing a book of which one is the author, then living is already a form of writing. This implication should not be surprising coming from one who displayed a tendency to write his life even before it happened—to *pre*scribe it—as when, returning from his first trip to England, he wrote in his Journal a Plan "for regulating my future Conduct in Life. It is the more remarkable, as being form'd when I was so young, and yet being pretty faithfully adhered to quite thro' old Age" (106). On the face of it, this tendency is consistent with Franklin's impulse to extend his authority into forbidden territory—he assumes control of his own life (as its author) as well as his autobiography (as its author/editor). This conceit implies, however, that instead of being the empirically verifiable account of an extraliterary reality, a Life is a compounding of an already textual phenomenon. (This notion of life as textual was implicit even in Franklin's seemingly pious epitaph, which compared him, body *and* soul, to a book, or *literary* work.) The relation, therefore, between narrative and life, or history, is not between "language" and the "reality" to which it refers, but between one text and another that it revises.

This intimation of the textuality of experience is clearly bound up with Franklin's conception of himself as a printer and man of letters. Whether or not subjectivity is essentially a function of the acquisition of language, as Emil Benveniste and Jacques Lacan have argued, it seems to have been largely so for Franklin. His claim that he did not remember when he could not read (53) is more than a prodigy's boast: it is an acknowledgment that for him memory was coextensive with literacy. In the first part of the narrative, the story of his imitation of the *Spectator* is the most obvious example of his emulation of literary models and of his progressive inscription of himself into the English tradition—and vice versa. Indeed, he wrote and rewrote himself throughout his life, using the whole range of secular eighteenth-century models: prosaic and poetic, aphoristic and narrative, analytical and polemical, pseudonymous and signed.

Significantly, Franklin achieved the status of published author when he submitted manuscripts anonymously to his master printer, his brother James. Only by veiling his authorship (behind the pseudonym Silence Dogood) from the arbitrary power of a jealous brother could he accede to authority of his own. The story of his pretending to have written a poem of James Ralph's in order to evade the prejudice of the hypercritical Charles Osborne reinforces the idea that the authority of a text is not, or ought not to be, entirely a function of the identity of its author.

For various reasons, then, it is finally not possible to look through the autobiography to the life and self behind it. To seek the historical Franklin in his autobiography is to peer into a hall of mirrors. For example, consider the meaning of the term *character*. Usually, Franklin uses it to mean "reputation," as when he says: "I had therefore a tolerable Character to begin the World with, I valued it properly, and determin'd to preserve it" (115). Elsewhere, he associates character in this sense with credit, and treats both as business assets: "In order to secure my Credit and Character as a Tradesman, I took care not only to be in *Reality* Industrious and frugal, but to avoid all *Appearances* of the Contrary" (126). He also uses it to refer to a form of writing, his uncle's system of shorthand: "My Uncle Benjamin . . . propos'd to give me all his Shorthand Volumes of Sermons I suppose as a Stock to set up with, if I would learn his Character" (53). The association of reputation and system of writing is significant: both render an individual public, visible, and legible, and both may be self-consciously crafted or manipulated.[32] His self-authorized and, according to Vaughan, authoritative text warns us that its author is only to be located in the form of the letters he founded.

Hovering behind both senses of "character" is perhaps another—

that of a personage in a literary work. As writer, printer, and man of letters, Franklin tended to view characters of this sort as artifactual, provisional, and variable. We can only take Franklin's word for it that he had a "tolerable character to begin the world with"; all we have is the "character" with which he begins the autobiography. That character, as he occasionally hints, is irreducibly a textual effect—a man of literal letters on the page. In the end, his statements about securing and preserving his character must be read as statements of the omnipotent autobiographer about the character he is in the process of inventing. Having learned from his disappointment in Governor Keith not to rely on others to write letters of credit, Franklin eventually wrote his own.

VII

Far from appearing, as he boasted his immortal soul would, in a new and more perfect edition, Franklin's unfinished autobiography first saw print in versions that were incomplete and flawed. Within the decade following his death, a number of corrupt versions of his Life appeared: a paraphrase of the first part ("History of the Life and Character of Benjamin Franklin," in the *Universal Asylum and Columbian Magazine*); a continuation based on Franklin's outline (published as a sequel in the same magazine); a condensation of all four parts (published by Matthew Carey in his magazine, *American Museum*); a French translation of the first part (the first publication in book form); and two *re*translations of this French version into English. (In part, this reflects the narrowness of turn-of-the-century copyright protection, which prohibited only the printing of exact copies, not abridgment, translation, or other forms of transformation [Lardner 65].)

When his grandson, Temple Franklin, finally brought forth the first full edition, *Memoirs of the Life and Writings of Benjamin Franklin,* in 1818, it proved to be nearly as illegitimate as its predecessors (and its editor). Instead of correcting the errors of the earlier versions, this edition compounded them. According to the editors of the new genetic text, when Temple Franklin was not relying on earlier versions, including the retranslations, he took it upon himself to replace colloquialisms and Americanisms with expressions in standard English. The result is a corrupt conglomerate text, rather than an accurate version of the holograph manuscript (which he had traded for a press copy). The general effect, even though subtle, was to sanitize and formalize the text; in effect, the editor reconstructed his grandfather as more loyal to English idiom and culture than he had been.[33]

Though the editors of the genetic text may have made an authoritative text possible, what they have given us is in some way an author's as well as a reader's nightmare. While it comes as close as editorial skill and state-of-the-art technology can bring a *printed* text to the original holograph manuscript that it painstakingly attempts to reproduce, their text includes virtually every blot of the pen. Every cancellation, addition, and emendation is recorded, and each editorial violation is exposed. In the manner of a modernist text, the genetic text shifts the burden of constructing a coherent text to the reader—or it defies such an intention. We are left with the chastening irony that Franklin's narrative, remarkable for its audacious self-authorizing gestures, first appeared in various unauthorized editions and continues to resist publication in a truly authoritative text. In more ways than one, therefore, the autobiography of the Founding Father defers delivery of his definitive self.

4

Prose and Cons: The Autobiographies of P. T. Barnum

I

There is some truth to the view that Franklin's autobiography is the original American success story—the prototypical story of the self-made (business)man (a model that, as we have seen, is widely imitated and marketed even today).[1] Features of P. T. Barnum's autobiography place it in this persistent tradition of self-improvement and self-advertisement. Like his precursor, he tells a story of humble New England origins and migration to an urban center more congenial to his talents, of initiative and resourcefulness that bested the competition, of the eventual channeling of his aggressive impulses into politics and reform projects, and of fame that carried him abroad and into the presence of royalty. The similarity goes beyond these structural parallels—verbal echoes occasionally reveal Barnum's appropriation of Franklin's model. For example, his advice, "Put on the *appearance* of business,and generally the *reality* will follow,"[2] revises one of Franklin's comments about the building of character: "In order to secure my Credit and Character as a Tradesman, I took care not only to be in *Reality* Industrious and frugal, but to avoid all *Appearances* of the Contrary."[3]

In Barnum's use of the terms, the relationship between appearance and reality is subtly but significantly altered: appearance literally precedes reality. More important than this shift in emphasis, however, is the belief shared by Barnum and Franklin that character is malleable, and that the self can be reconstituted from the outside in.

Among the nineteenth-century businessmen-philanthropists who emulated Franklin's model, Barnum alone seems to have probed his implication of the artifactuality of the self. The ludic quality of Barnum's *Life* also has its precedent in Franklin, but its development far exceeds its source. Partly because of his sense of responsibility as a Founding Father, Franklin balanced self-liberation with self-discipline, and self-authorizing gestures with appeals to authority. Barnum was less circumspect, both in life and in autobiography. Franklin's early writings may have made him persona non grata in Puritan Boston, but the contentious editorials of Barnum's *Herald of Freedom,* which attacked sectarian influence in politics, eventually landed him in jail for libel. His first autobiography gives us the self-portrait of a self-styled Connecticut Yankee—shrewd, avaricious, hostile to constraints of many kinds. Full of delighted "confession" of his humbugs, Barnum's *Life* was not at all what Benjamin Vaughan had in mind as the proper offspring of Franklin's seminal American autobiography. Indeed, it exposes a link between Founding Father and the nineteenth-century confidence man that we are not eager to acknowledge.

One of the con man's early manifestations in American culture was the stereotype of the Yankee peddler. While Barnum was never simply a traveling peddler, he acquired his business acumen in a Connecticut general store, and later took to the road to exhibit suspect "goods." Perhaps not coincidentally, his first autobiography was published shortly after the exploits that first gave currency to the term *confidence man* (in 1849, one William Thompson, alias Samuel Willis, was arrested for "borrowing" the watches of trusting strangers)[4] and only two years before Herman Melville's novel gave the figure perhaps its fullest and most perplexing literary treatment. (This American variant of the Trickster, known in Poe's fiction as the "diddler," went on to figure importantly in the fiction of Mark Twain.)

While Barnum preferred to think of himself as a showman—even an impresario—he functioned, in many of his activities, as a kind of con man who played, for profit, with others' faith. In private, he displayed a talent for mimicry, a taste for parlor tricks, and an interest in ventriloquism. In public, his exhibits generally created or exploited doubts about their authenticity. For example, the obvious question about the exslave Joice Heth was whether she had been, as she claimed, George Washington's childhood nurse. When interest in her waned, Barnum revived it by writing anonymous letters that denounced her not merely as a fraud but as an automaton—a simulation of a person. Barnum made a habit, and a career, of exploiting the elusiveness of identity—impersonation was part of his stock-in-trade as a showman.

It is not surprising, then, that the autobiography is full of incidents involving impersonation or mistaken identity. To distract crowds, Barnum passed off his daughter as Jenny Lind, and when the public got wise to this, he passed off Lind as his daughter trying to pass for the popular singer. In his own case, he took equal pleasure in anonymity and in celebrity. When mistaken for someone else, he would often solicit unflattering comments about "Barnum," then reveal his identity, to the embarrassment of his victim and the amusement of onlookers. On the other hand, he savored the fact that he received mail addressed simply to "Mr. Barnum, America." Since no first name or local address was necessary to identify him, the arrival of such mail was gratifying testimony of his distinctiveness and fame.

Though his autobiography owes much to Franklin's precedent, his life-long manipulation of that model explores the freedom of play rather than that of self-government. Much of his first version, *The Life of P. T. Barnum, Written by Himself* (1855),[5] deliberately and dramatically subverts authority of many kinds. It very nearly makes an autobiography out of practical jokes, and a joke of autobiography. After the Civil War, he suppressed this early uninhibited self-portrait, and replaced it with a sanitized account of his life, *Struggles and Triumphs* (1869). By revising and reissuing his autobiography continually until his death in 1891, however, he flamboyantly exercised the American freedom (or compulsion) to constitute and reconstitute one's self in words. The ultimate effect of his prolific production and circulation of different accounts of his life during the second half of the nineteenth century was to undermine the authority of his own autobiography and, by implication, that of the genre as a whole. In Barnum's hands, autobiography inevitably became—or was revealed to be—a form of prose that cons.

II

At its inception, the autobiographical project was closely linked to Barnum's American Museum. Intended to serve as a history of and advertisement for the Museum, Barnum's *Life* in effect became its literary extension, or annex: America's Barnum Museum; however, the link between text and Museum is more than opportunistic—it is conceptual. For one thing, the *Life* is structured less as a linear narrative than as an arrangement of exhibits; it is less the *story* of Barnum than a *storehouse* of Barnumana. It purported to display directly what the institution on Broadway manifested obliquely—its creator.[6] Moreover, both are variants of Barnum's fundamental form of self-expression—the practical joke. Unlike verbal jokes, which are intended to be told, and then retold in new circumstances, practical ones are contrived to be 'played' (acted out) only once in unique circumstances. Barnum's genius was to invent two lasting, institutional versions of this supposedly ephemeral form of humor—a museum and an autobiography.

As Freud pointed out, the joker requires the presence of an audience as well as of victims: the audience confirms the reality of the joke (and thus of the joker). Barnum's paying customers provided him with both an audience and victims. Part of the museum's attraction for visitors was presumably that it made a joke of business: it converted the fear of being *taken* (always a threat in a commercial transaction) into the pleasure of being taken *in.* After all, Barnum displayed "goods" of admittedly questionable value and authenticity—one paid for the experience of determining their value, risk-free, for oneself. By putting an aesthetic frame around a potentially anxious transaction, Barnum rendered it amusing. His impulses may have been exhibitionistic, aggressive, and even hostile, but his ingenious institutionalization of the practical joke enabled him to discharge them impersonally, playfully—and profitably.[7]

The practical joke serves Barnum's autobiography both as subject and model, content and form. Nature and nurture seem to have combined to make him a practical joker at an early age, for his legacy from his maternal grandfather took the form of an elaborate and astonishing joke. From him, Barnum inherited not only his given names (Phineas Taylor), but also the deed to a tract of land called Ivy Island, which was to be his at maturity. During his boyhood, relatives, friends, and townspeople—all, apparently, in on the joke—impressed on him a powerful sense of the property's value and of the status that owning it would convey. When he was about twelve, however, he discovered it to be a worthless bit of swampy ground covered with stunted ivy. Furthermore, for a period of years his family frequently reminded him of his cruel disillusionment.

But "cruel disillusionment" is my phrase, not his. Curiously, he suppressed any anger he may have felt and declined to salvage the experience with a moral about the value of self-reliance, for example—or of rural real estate. Rather, he recorded his sense of present amusement. His pleasure in recollecting the incident is confirmed, if not created, by his later use of the barren land as collateral in the acquisition of the American Museum. While his inheritance of the land, his discovery of its worthlessness, and his use of it are widely separated in the *Life,* the connection among them is clear enough. Almost the first thing mentioned in the book is his grandfather's gift-deed of the land—the deed through which Barnum was to discover his true gift, a knack for practical joking. So it is appropriate that he should later acquire the Museum, which was the first permanent institutional outlet for his compulsion—and hence his *true* ancestral estate—by reenacting the joke, and passing off the same worthless property as a valuable commodity. The gesture is psychologically as well as financially economical: as he converted a liability into an asset, he transformed humiliation into triumph: he changed a joke *on* him into a joke *by* him.

This primal joke assumes all the more importance in view of the fact that Barnum's father died insolvent, owing money even to his sixteen-year-old son. The trauma of the grandfather's patrimony was thus compounded by the father's, which it ironically foreshadowed. Whereas Franklin, the prototypical self-made man, had reveled in the opportunity to determine his own fate, and to author his own life, Barnum implied that he was less free than *compelled* to seek his own fortune and forge his own identity. He treated autonomy as a kind of confidence game forced on American sons by their confounding fathers. Barnum's way out of his predicament was typically ingenious. He assumed as his true legacy his grandfather's character, rather than his land. That is, in taking the joke of his patrimony, he took on the ready-made identity of Phineas Taylor—a Yankee prankster liberated from inhibiting self-examination and tedious self-development to playful self-expression, self-enjoyment, and self-dramatization.

Thus, the first autobiography is dominated by the pleasure principle. (Barnum is reported to have responded to a woman who expressed her gratification in reading his *Life:* "My dear madam, that is nothing to the way I enjoy living it.") This is particularly evident in his playful treatment of the controversial issues of the antebellum period. Barnum explicitly identified himself as a Yankee in the dedication:"To the universal Yankee nation, of which I am one." Given its date, the dedication may seem provocative, for in 1855 the nation was deeply divided along political and regional lines. But the autobiography betrays little evidence of partisan ideals or ideas. (In this way, the 1855 self-portrait differs significantly from the composite portrait drawn by his many biographers.) For example, there is no hint of his conversion from Democratic to Republican politics, which took place during the 1850s, nor of the motives that would lead him, during the Civil War, to pay four substitutes to fight in the Union Army. Instead, his *Life* jokingly suggests he was devoid of patriotism as well as courage: "[W]ere I forced to go to war, the first arms that I should examine would be my legs" (12). Elsewhere, he casually sidesteps the issue of racial violence. Faced with the defection of a Negro-singer while traveling with his troupe in the South, Barnum blacked his own skin and replaced him. When—still in makeup, but no longer in character—he spoke impudently to a white man after the show, he narrowly escaped a beating. He saved his skin only by hastily exposing its true color. Instead of moralizing on race at this opportune narrative moment, he treats it as a contingent phenomenon, allowing the incident to stand as a practical joke that nearly backfired.

The extent of his self-license in the 1855 autobiography is evident in his account of exhibiting Joice Heth—an aged, toothless, blind, and crippled black woman—as George Washington's boyhood nurse. He sharply curtailed this incident in postwar revisions, perhaps because of its irreverent association of the nation's sacrosanct father figure with its most volatile issue, slavery. Nevertheless, his *Life* shows Barnum beginning to carve out his own niche in history by unscrupulously linking the first President with the stereotype of the devoted slave. To entice the public to pay to hear this apparently pious old woman reminisce about the legendarily honest Washington, Barnum published documents, including a bill of sale, that purported to prove her authenticity. The autobiography cites an autopsy, however, indicating that she could not possibly have been as old as she—and he—had claimed; thus, it exposes her oral narratives, and his promotion of her, as fraudulent. Indeed, his reproduction in the text of the exslave's (false) documents of identification is a kind of grotesque and tasteless travesty of the authenticating rituals of abolitionist slave narration, both in person and in print. His first autobiography thus mocks the seriousness and authority of slave narrative.

Barnum's preoccupation with practical jokes was such that he included anecdotes in his *Life* that would not seem to be truly autobiographical: stories of jokes played neither by him or on him. In fact, whole chapters contain nothing but retold pranks that he had observed or heard of. While they are often omitted from abridgements as extraneous, these miscellaneous chapters are important manifestations of Barnum's conception of himself and of autobiography. In content and form, they express an important truth about Barnum: he apparently saw himself as a man whose essential character was that of a practical joker. In his later autobiographies, Barnum stressed his reform and philanthropic activities, but the provision of mass entertainment is his only benefaction in the first.

Indeed, implicit in his *Life* is a vision of America as an anarchic society in which there is free play for all. The episode that most clearly suggests this is one of those that Barnum neither participates in nor witnesses first hand. Its hero is his grandfather. En route by boat from Connecticut to New York with an assortment of other Yankees, mostly businessmen, his grandfather contrived to embarrass them all by delivering them to the city with one side of their faces completely shaved. The particulars of the ruse, which is as implausible as it is ingenious, are not important. Rather, it is the situation that matters: the vessel is becalmed, and the passengers become a self-contained community. They agree deliberately, even formally, to channel their energy into play: they sign a "solemn compact" that licenses joking by stipulating that any expression of anger will be fined.

Thus, these pilgrims rediscover—or invent—a primal America by means of a revisionist compact that subverts the Protestant work ethic. They become citizens of a kind of miniature utopia, a radical democracy, in which conventional status and authority are neutralized. Advantage is gained solely through the exercise of Yankee ingenuity. Power thus accrues to the humorous, for the laughter that greets a successful joke amounts to an involuntary vote of confidence in the jester. This is essentially an anarchic and amoral world—with a joke, one *gets* the better of others without *being* better they are. In this hermetic world, no harm nor good, nor work, is done. The citizens devote all of their time to making, and having, fun.

The episode's tone is nostalgic. It is set well in the past in the time of his grandfather. Indeed, the ship is the island of the grandfather that Barnum really covets—his ideal America is not a fixed property conveying status but a kind of floating con game. Its temporal equivalent in his life is his youth, when he was relatively free of responsibility and ethical restraints. What was inaccessible in time was not only available through retrospective narration, but also through psychological regression, which Barnum achieved by conflating work and play. Indeed, the essential thrust of his career was to reconstitute the lost world of his youth in space. The Museum and, to a lesser extent, the circus were places where risks were controlled, responsibility was shed, and play was licensed. Indeed, his *Life* suggests that Barnum's vision of an American Renaissance was the rebirth of the New World's workplace as an antiauthoritarian playground.

III

Of course, Barnum had to admit the constraints on his freedom. Just as his grandfather and his fellow travelers had to reenter the world of work, Barnum was doomed to age and, alas, to mature. The narrative most clearly acknowledges this in its final episode, the promotion of Jenny Lind, whose appeal as an artist depended on the purity of her morals—she spurned opera as too risqué—as well as on the clarity of her voice. The narrative assumes an uncharacteristically serious tone as it recounts this episode, which represents Barnum's first bid for respectability. Indeed, one of its few jokes hints at the significance of their relationship and thus of this climatic episode of his *Life.* When Lind reports hearing rumors that they are to be married, he attributes them to the fact that they are already "engaged." His pun not only deflects suspicion of an affair between them, but also reflects his sense that their contract wedded him to a personification of the Victorian ideal of a chaste, genteel, and cultured woman.

If Barnum's *Life* veered from the ludicrous toward the grave with the Jenny Lind episode, he buried his playful self even deeper in *Struggles and Triumphs.* The thrust of the postwar revision is suggested by its renaming, by which *Life* becomes *Struggles and Triumphs:* a loose anthology of anecdotes, incidents, and jokes is reconceived as a linear narrative of victory over adversity. The earlier title points simply to Barnum's abundant and diffuse energy, while the later one promises themes and morals—not life as energetic play, but experience as significant conflict. (Moreover, as Barnum was born in 1810, the new subtitle, *Forty Years' Recollections of P. T. Barnum* indicates a shift in emphasis from his childhood and adolescence to his career.) The tendency of this narrative is to trace a progress along the "Road to Riches" (the title of chapter 9) or up the "ladder . . . to fortune" (a phrase from the same chapter) rather than to offer a series of jokes as metaphors for his experience. The simultaneous introduction of moral, aesthetic, and political seriousness transforms the autobiography. The antiauthoritarian impulse of the first version is held firmly in check.

That Barnum's second edition of his life is not to be a sequel to the first, but a reconception of it, is indicated in the preface. There, he introduces the new version as a "complete and continuous narrative . . . new and independent of the former" (vi). Carl Bode has handily summarized Barnum's 1869 revisions of his life to 1855:

> He condensed the story of his boyhood in Connecticut, where he had learned sharpness. . . . Barnum recognized that cunning had played too much of a part in both his career and his book. He allotted Tom Thumb and Jenny Lind more space, giving his deceptions less. He philosophized more about life, he dwelt on the importance of Christianity. He expounded further on success and how to win it. He had grown a little pontificial.[8]

A number of pressures may account for the book's sobriety and propriety. The reviews of his *Life* probably played a role. British reviewers were especially severe; they were eager to condemn the self-celebration of this uncouth Connecticut Yankee who had invaded Queen Victoria's court behind the midget "general," Tom Thumb. The reviewer for *Blackwood's Edinburgh Magazine,* for example, expressed "amazement at [the book's] audacity, loathing for its hypocrisy, abhorrence of the moral obliquity it betrays, and sincere pity for the wretched man who compiled it. He has left nothing for his worst enemy to do."[9] If Barnum had unwittingly assassinated his own character in his first autobiography, then the subsequent version represents his attempt to revive and redeem himself. (Insofar as the revision responds to reviewers' criticism, its authorship acquires, in Jerome McGann's sense, a corporate dimension.)

Personal and national concerns between 1855 and 1869 also help to explain the tone of the later autobiography. For example, in 1855, "the Jerome Clock entanglement" left Barnum bankrupt. He was unable to see this as a joke like Ivy Island. In this case, serious, possibly permanent, financial harm had been done to him as an adult. This was no mere humbug (in his definition, a *harmless* confidence trick); it was a swindle. Indeed, the fact that he felt compelled to make this distinction both in *Struggles and Triumphs* and in *Humbugs of the World* (1865) suggests how defensive he had become about his reputation. He apparently resented the low status accorded a showman in a society that privileged high culture over popular culture.

The fate of an entertainer in such a society—not to be taken seriously—rankles the ambitious. Thus, in his quest for respect, Barnum increasingly emphasized the moral value of his entertainments and his involvement in politics and reform.

The intervening national crisis of the Civil War no doubt also contributed to the gravity of the second autobiography. In it, he portrays himself as an ardent Unionist; indeed, he treats his home-front activities as equivalent to military campaigns and characterizes the Jerome clock disaster as a kind of private "Bull Run." One sign of the book's seriousness, and of Barnum's pursuit of prestige, is this tendency to conflate personal and national history. *Struggles and Triumphs* is thus very much a Reconstruction autobiography. Just as the North attempted to discipline the South in restoring it to the Union after the War, so Barnum reconstituted his earlier self in conformity to the higher principles that emerged triumphant from his inner Civil War. In both cases, the more righteous cause prevailed. In Barnum's case, moralistic politics and high culture defeated low humor and anarchic play. The second autobiography, then, rehabilitates rather than simply resuscitates his earlier self. Moreover, it attempts to restore the authority of the genre treated so cavalierly the first time around.

IV

One of the notable features of Barnum's autobiographical enterprise is its sheer scope. Indeed, no scholar seems prepared to state exactly how many different editions of his autobiography Barnum published—let alone how many copies were sold—because Barnum so frequently updated the 1869 edition with supplementary chapters. In addition, two years before his death in 1891, Barnum published a third major version—*Struggles and Triumphs, or Sixty Years' Recollections of P. T. Barnum.* (This edition radically condenses his life, so although it is the most inclusive, chronologically, it is neither the most comprehensive nor the most engaging account.)

Barnum promoted the book in all its forms with great energy and ingenuity. At first, it was sold by subscription; later, it was hawked at the circus. Anyone who bought a copy *or* a circus ticket got a discount on the other. In the end, he maximized distribution by offering the copyright free to interested publishers. Barnum boasted of a million sales, and Carl Bode has estimated that after the Bible his autobiography was the most widely read book in America in the second half of the nineteenth century.[10] One thing is clear: quantitatively, at least, Barnum out*lived* the competition; he mass-produced and circulated his literary self-embodiment on an unprecedented scale.

Jean Starobinski's theory that a radical change in the author's life is the necessary precondition for autobiography fails to account for Barnum's lifelong tinkering with his autobiography—especially his periodic refurbishing of the 1869 edition. For Starobinski, all autobiography is a species of conversion narrative (i.e., it is all about self-transformation).[11] But Barnum could not have undergone metamorphosis as frequently as he amended his Life. More plausible, but less profound, motives for his undertaking are profit and publicity, which Barnum continued to pursue avidly even after his attainment of respectability. He saw that an autobiography—unlike, for example, a novel, which aspires to a timeless wholeness—can be periodically supplemented as long as one lives. Indeed, an autobiography virtually *demands* to be serially composed because its authority—whether as an icon of its subject or an index of its author—begins to diminish the moment it is "finished." Barnum made a virtue of the necessary obsolescence of the form: again and again he turned out a new, more complete (and, by implication, more definitive) version of his Life. Again and again he marketed a new, improved version of his most vital product.

There is, however, another powerful motive at work here. Autobiography always constitutes a bid for immortality, and all the evidence suggests that Barnum was especially fearful of death and obsessed with his posthumous fame and fate. For example, in his last illness, he never spoke of his own death, and his wife arranged to have news of his illness suppressed so that he would not read of its gravity in the papers. His adoption of Universalism in place of the Presbyterianism in which he was raised is perhaps also pertinent here because the gentler religion would guarantee a place in heaven even to a showman. There is harder evidence as well. Lacking male heirs, he endowed a museum at Tufts University that would perpetuate his name. In further pursuit of nominal immortality, he bound the circus legally to carry his name for fifty years and paid a nephew to change his name from C. Hallett Seeley to C. *Barnum* Seeley.[12]

One of the notable features of autobiography, considered as a species of biography, is its exclusion of the subject's death. As John Sturrock has pointed out, the teleology of autobiography differs crucially from that of biography: while biography moves toward and concludes with its subject's demise, autobiography leads toward its own conception, the moment when the author decides to compose a narrative of his life.[13] Thus, that moment is to autobiography what the subject's death is to biography. Henry Adams was acutely aware of this; he spoke of writing autobiography as taking his own life, and he enacted the conceit formally by adopting a third-person point of view. Barnum seems to have intuited what Adams so clearly saw, and his compulsive reissuing of his Life can be seen as a repeated warding off of death; but he was caught in a vicious circle. Each appendix was both a rebirth and a new death, a self-resurrection and a suicide (i.e., each new edition simultaneously extended, and ended, his Life).

In any case, his prolonged engagement with the genre suggests that the implicit equation between his existence and his autobiography was both gratifying and threatening to him. (From one angle, Franklin's arrogation of responsibility for his own immortality—as author of his own Life—is an inspiring Promethean gesture; from another, the conception of immortality as an effect of one's writing may render it alarmingly contingent.) In any case, at the end of his life, Barnum played with the limits of the genre: the final chapter of his autobiography seems to pull off the impossible when it includes an account of his demise. The solution to the generic problem was simple: his wife wrote the "Last Chapter" for him. This final installment in his life story portrays him as piously resigned to God's will in his last days. The very medium through which we witness this piety, however, ingeniously sidesteps the limitations of mortality—and of the genre. Unable to elude death by prolonging his life, he extended his Life to take in his death.

The joke is a literary analogue of one for which he is well known: on a day when his museum was overcrowded he enticed innocent visitors to leave it by means of a sign, "*To The Egress.*" Of course, instead of a final exhibit ahead of them, his customers found the exit behind them. (The joke not only enacts but exposes the essential dynamics of the confidence game. What is revealed is a diminished version of what is hinted at; what the victim is shown to deserve is an ironic distortion of what the victim desires.) Similarly, Barnum's autobiography promises his audience a unique last display—misleadingly, for a reader beginning the last chapter finishes the autobiography proper. This autobiographical gesture purports or appears to correct precisely that deficiency of the genre—its necessary incompleteness—that Barnum had capitalized on so many times. When he was about to expire, Barnum drafted his wife as his authorized biographer, or (insofar as she displayed him in his final state) as his literary undertaker. Thus, his autobiography achieved the definitiveness of complete closure only by compromising its authorship. Barnum closed out a career of mass-producing textual surrogates by resorting to a surrogate author—though not a ghostwriter in the usual sense.

V

Questions about the authorship of Barnum's autobiography did not originate with the "Last Chapter." Rather, they commenced with his *Life.* One of the editors of Barnum's *Illustrated News,* Charles Godfrey Leland, claimed that Barnum had asked him to ghostwrite it, and, when he declined, had turned to Rufus Griswold.[14] Indeed, doubts about the authorship still linger—some twentieth-century writers, such as Constance Rourke and Irving Wallace, have expressed skepticism about the author of the autobiography. But the trend (like most of the evidence) seems to be in Barnum's favor: George Bryan, who edited a composite version of the autobiographies, Neil Harris, author of the most scholarly book on Barnum, and A. H. Saxon, who has recently edited Barnum's letters, believe that Barnum did write it himself. It certainly seems unlikely that Barnum would have entrusted such an important undertaking to another. In fact, the scope of the project suggests that it was central rather than peripheral to his life and career—as much obsessive as opportunistic. In any case, no one has turned up convincing counterevidence, and the style of the texts seems consistent with his surviving correspondence. His autobiographies probably involve ghostwriting only in the sense that all autobiography does—insofar as it constitutes the deliberate verbal inscription of an immaterial essence that will survive the subject on earth.

A separate but related issue—that of the text's authority (in the sense of reliability)—was also raised by the earliest readers. For example, even as he denounced the *Life,* a British reviewer admitted that it might be a hoax that Barnum himself would expose (Wallace,178). Neil Harris has resolved the question of Barnum's sincerity this way: "In admitting his own cunning motives, Barnum appeared an honest author, however much he had been a deceitful entrepreneur" (213). This distinction is a valid and helpful one: the book may be *about* hoaxes without being one itself. Also, most of the cunning in the book *is* attributable to the protagonist rather than to the narrator. It is clear in the second autobiography, and even late in the first, that Barnum was not content to be seen simply as a professional joker. Barnum may have seen that the best way to rehabilitate himself was to expose his own tricks. Perhaps he sought to bolster public confidence in him by writing a book whose substance was true confession.

At any rate, Barnum's explicit intentions in revising and reissuing his autobiography were quite serious. The preface to his *Life* had frankly admitted the playfulness of the text. Anticipating the charge that it contained too much of the "ludicrous," Barnum attributed this feature to his "constitutional bias" and the merry "associations of his youth." In contrast, the preface to *Struggles and Triumphs* emphasizes its utility. Barnum echoes Franklin in offering his experience as "a help and incentive to the young man" and in portraying himself as "constrained" by the solicitation of publishers, friends, and relatives "to put in a permanent form what . . . may be instructive, entertaining, and profitable." More important, in dismissing its out-of-print predecessor (whose plates he had had destroyed) as "very hastily, and, therefore, imperfectly, prepared," he presented his new edition as the definitive version of his life.

Still, one must always be wary of a man who sent out form letters headed "Strictly Confidential." There are also moments when—deliberately or not—the new narrative puts its own credibility into question. Some anecdotes are simply too good to be true, such as when they involve repartee whose wit and polish seem written rather than spontaneous. The "true story" of Tom Thumb's courtship of Lavinia Warren is a good example. Barnum offers it as evidence that their engagement was a result of true love rather than of his instigation, but he did not witness the crucial scene, which continues for pages full of detail and verbatim dialogue. His source is the testimony of two "mischievous young ladies" who were visiting him at the time and who eavesdropped from an adjacent hallway—or so he says. To validate his account, he notes that he read it to the concerned parties, who approved it—"except that Lavinia remarked, 'Well Mr. B., your story don't lose any in the telling'" (607).

This passage cleverly tips the reader back and forth between skepticism and credulity. Barnum did not witness the scene, but he admits that; by his own description, his sources sound unreliable ("mischievous young ladies"), but he checks their account with the principles; they accuse him of exaggeration but vouch for its essential truth. Even as it acknowledges its distortion of the truth, Barnum's account demands belief in itself. Indeed, the autobiographer's conduct here is very much that of the confidence man, whom Gary Lindberg defines as "a manipulator or contriver who creates an . . . effect, an impression . . . of confidence that surpasses the grounds for it."[15]

An incident in his *Life* (which he omitted from *Struggles and Triumphs*) acknowledges, even flaunts, the untrustworthiness of autobiography. In response to Barnum's request for material for his autobiography, an uncle quickly offers to supply incidents Barnum would *not* want to include; naturally, the incipient autobiographer declines his offer. The anecdote makes the point that autobiography is necessarily a *partial* account of one's life: to write an autobiography is to "fix" one's life in more ways than one. Here, Barnum echoes a point made by Franklin: that while an autobiographer surely knows things about himself that no biographer could, he will not necessarily divulge them. Franklin alerts his readers to this by the way in which he corrects the errata of his life. His witty use of printers' terms reminds us how completely he controls his medium, in which silent corrections are both inevitable and undetectable. The identity of author and subject that distinguishes autobiography from biography is revealed to be a source of authority only in theory. In practice, both Franklin and Barnum show that autobiography is inevitably and hopelessly subjective.

In any event, in his very attempt to establish the authority of *Struggles and Triumphs,* Barnum undermined it, whether wittingly or not. Playful elements lurk even in his sober introduction to this more "matured and leisurely review" of his career. For example, he cannot resist a punning defence of the book's inevitable vanity:

> All autobiographies are necessarily egotistical. If my pages are as plentifully sprinkled with "I's" as was the chief ornament of Hood's peacock, "who thought he had the eyes of Europe on his tail," I can only say, that the "I's" are essential to the story I have told. It has been my purpose to narrate, not the life of another, but that career in which I was the principal actor.

Here, Barnum admits to being a literary peacock—an exhibitionist in print. His reference to the plurality of the book's "I's" may also hint at the multiplicity of the autobiography's supposedly singular first person.

Ultimately, his introduction of *Struggles and Triumphs* as a more reliable text than his *Life* is self-defeating. To begin with, under the circumstances it is obligatory: even Barnum was not likely to present a new autobiography as *less* reliable than its predecessor. Moreover, his claim that this version is "matured" and more trustworthy, which *might* be true, is coupled with a conception of autobiography that undermines it: "[A]n autobiography has attractions and merits superior to those of a 'Life' written by another, who, however intimate with the subject, cannot know all that helps to give interest and accuracy to the narrative, or completeness to the character" (vii). According to this view, the identity between the author and the subject of autobiography guarantees its superiority to conventional biography: autobiography *is* definitive biography. But if autobiography were by nature authoritative ("accurate" and "complete"), there would be no reason, or justification, for supplanting the first version. In any case, the incident in his *Life* in which the autobiographer declines his uncle's offer of material reveals this view of the genre to be naive—as does the omission of the episode from the revised text.

Finally, the act of issuing a "new and independent" life, rather than a sequel, may be counterproductive because the very proliferation of autobiographical texts exposes the correspondence between life and Life as provisional. Each new text, required to keep up with the development of the subject, inevitably supplants its predecessor; each narrative exposes the previous one as a flawed account demanding revision and correction from a newly distanced, and presumably more objective, viewpoint. Such a process erodes the credibility of the genre by suggesting the unattainability of a definitive Life.

In destroying the plates of his first autobiography and replacing it with a new "matured" one, Barnum ironically fulfilled the expectation of the hostile critic who feared the *Life* was a hoax that Barnum would later revoke. His insistent revision of his Life, which culminates in the fraudulent last chapter, reminds us that all autobiography, as Irving Horowitz put it, "provides strong intimations of a confidence racket, of seeking credibility for a highly selective presentation of evidence."[16] The con man as autobiographer thus exposes the autobiographer as con man.

Perhaps the anecdote from Barnum's autobiography that best

exemplifies its own credibility concerns a notorious teller of stretchers. When his audience finally challenged a particularly implausible assertion, he offered this splendidly equivocal self-defense: "It is as true as anything I have told you" (198). That might serve as the proper epigraph to any of his autobiographies, which remind us in a number of ways of the essential duplicity of the genre. Like Barnum's life-writing, although not to the same extent, all autobiography demands a degree of belief that it cannot command. Autobiography may be a historical genre, but in the best of circumstances it cannot render unmediated history. Indeed, the commonplace assertion that autobiography lies somewhere between fiction and history can be rescued from banality simply by emphasizing the verb: autobiography *lies* between fiction and history. Beginning with the practical joke that defines his character, and ending with a joke on the genre itself, Barnum's long-running narrative reminds us that autobiography is a kind of elaborate confidence game that is best played willingly and wittingly.

VI

After Barnum's death, a securely fastened strongbox marked *"Not to be opened until the death of P. T. Barnum"* was found at the circus's winter headquarters. This curiously inscribed box inspired visions in his workers of a valuable bequest from their employer; however, when it was opened, it contained only copies of the autobiography (Werner, 372). As with Barnum's own inheritance, it is hard to tell whether his legacy to his employees was intended as a lesson or as a practical joke. This ambiguous gesture nicely completes the symmetry of his life: Barnum left the world as he entered it, with that form of humor fundamental both to his self-conception and to his self-expression.

The number of narratives Barnum left to his modern editors is also an ambiguous heritage—possibly the final posthumous joke he played with his autobiography—for no single text seems adequately to represent him. The first version is appealing because of its lack of inhibition, but Barnum disowned it. Moreover, its chronological reach is insufficient; for example, it does not touch on the circus, with which most modern readers associate Barnum. The 1889 version gives the most chronologically complete record of Barnum's life, but its compression robs it of vitality. The 1869 version is the most detailed, but it slights his formative years on the one hand, and omits the last twenty years of his life on the other.

As a result, editors have resorted to various ploys, each of which further compromises whatever authority might be claimed for any one of the narratives. For example, the routine omission of many jokes from modern editions, while understandable, is misguided. This practice does have some claim to authorial sanction: it continues the self-rehabilitation Barnum initiated in his own revisions. But in excising "extraneous" jokes from his *Life,* these editors sanitize a text Barnum chose to suppress. On the one hand, then, they disinter the narrative he tried to bury; on the other, they censor one of Barnum's distinctive voices, a voice he seems to have lost during the Civil War. The result is true neither to the Barnum of 1855 nor to that of 1869. This emendation of his Life by twentieth-century editors jeopardizes the autobiography's historicity.

By compiling excerpts from various versions into a composite full-life narrative, George Bryan also constructed a synthetic, ahistorical Barnum. Bryan assembled a single master text out of materials whose inconsistencies demonstrate the problematic nature, as well as the richness, of autobiography. Such a practice not only blurs significant differences among the texts, but also impresses a uniform identity on a project that explicitly and implicitly demonstrates the contingency and elusiveness—the diversity and perversity—of the self. No one of Barnum's texts adequately represented him, or he would not have issued as many as he did. Taken in its self-contradictory entirety, rather than as an integrated whole, however, the autobiography continues to function as a permanent version of Barnum's museum: a rambling funhouse in which he can be forever found, and lost.

5

False "I's": Mark Twain's Pseudonymous Autobiography

I

There are suggestive similarities between P. T. Barnum and Mark Twain. Both enjoyed hoaxes, practical jokes, and low humor, yet both aspired to be more than mere entertainers or funny men; both consciously and cleverly advertised themselves, even in the architecture of their lavish and quirky homes. Both also carried on lifelong experiments with autobiography in which humor played an important role. As we have seen, Barnum's autobiographies started and ended with practical jokes. Mark Twain was even more intent on, and consistent in, parodying or undermining the conventions of autobiography, particularly its referentiality. Like Barnum, he disowned an early autobiography and, late in his career, attempted to create a definitive record of his own life. Of the two, however, Mark Twain far more playfully and self-consciously exposed the tenuous links between what is narrated and what happened, between the textual and the pretextual.[1]

Marilyn Davis DeEulis has rightly called "the forty-year enterprise Mark Twain called his 'Autobiography' . . . one of the most perplexing compilations in American letters."[2] This collection, however, is only a fraction of his autobiographical writing. Indeed, the autobiographical impulse seems to have been coextensive with Mark Twain's writing career. For this reason alone it would be difficult, if not impossible, to distinguish definitively between his autobiographical and his non-autobiographical works.

Another dimension of the problem is manifest in his well-known joke about his memory: "When I was younger I could remember anything, whether it had happened or not; but my faculties are decaying now, and soon I shall be so I cannot remember any but the things that never happened."[3] At first glance, this appears to be a self-deprecating joke about the loss of memory (and thus of mental potency) that accompanies aging. It may also be a kind of boast construing that loss as its own compensation: if, as he gets older, Mark Twain remembers *less* of what has happened to him, then in a way he reverses the normal process of aging, which involves the accumulation of experience in the compressed form of memory. To put it another way—in terms reflecting Mark Twain's dual occupation as autobiographer and novelist—as his memory (as record) of his origins fades, his memory (as faculty) becomes more original. Thus, the joke, which makes a virtue of senility, is also a warning: *caveat lector.*

If, as Neil Schmitz has suggested, "Humor . . . is skeptical of any discourse based on authority—misspeaks it, miswrites it, misrepresents it,"[4] then this joke both demonstrates and illuminates Mark Twain's virtually compulsive subversion of autobiography. Autobiography depends fundamentally on memory; indeed, one view locates the genre's authority in its exclusive access to this unique source. As the joke points out, however, recall is not only selective and often unverifiable, it is also subject to continual unconscious revision. Because memory is such an impeachable source, the credibility of autobiography is always problematic. One distinguishing feature of Mark Twain's autobiography is the degree to which it invites skepticism as to whether what it "remembers" happened *at all.*

There is always a degree of uncertainty, too, about to whom the narrated events happened: the authority of Mark Twain's autobiography is greatly complicated by the fact of its pseudonymity. Since his pen name is in effect his trademark as a humorist, the pseudonymity of his autobiography is intimately related to its humor, and therefore reinforces its subversive effect. While pseudonymity is not particularly problematic for novelists, for example, it *is* for autobiographers because for many readers, especially "pact" theorists like Lejeune and Bruss, the genre's authority rests precisely in the nominal identity of the author, narrator, and subject of the narrative. Pseudonymous autobiography is thus something of a contradiction in terms—a "true" (historical) account of a "false" (literary) identity. It might seem, therefore, that in redefining himself as Mark Twain, Samuel Clemens annulled his personal history and disqualified himself as an autobiographer. Instead, this act seems paradoxically to have made his past accessible as autobiographical material. Of course, as James M. Cox has noted, "Mark Twain," unlike many nineteenth-century pen names, did not obliterate the identity of its inventor; rather, it defined a constantly fluctuating relationship between two linked identities and stories.[5] Still, insofar as it subtly displaces his historical self and associates authorship with self-invention, it puts the authority of his autobiographical writing inevitably in question.

The chapter briefly considers an early parodic autobiography, reviews the origins of the pseudonym, and then discusses the humor and pseudonymity of the Mississippi autobiographies, "Old Times on the Mississippi" and *Life on the Mississippi.* These early texts generally violate the conventional expectations that (1) autobiography will constitute a verifiable narrative of a historical individual, and (2) its author, narrator, and subject will be identical, at least in name. Mark Twain's humor defines itself in terms of deviation from facts, and he inevitably subverts the principle of self-identity because of the fact and the fiction of his pseudonym. Pseudonymity and humor are far less prominent in *Mark Twain's Autobiography.* His playfulness in the autobiography apparently serves to revitalize the genre by expanding its repertoire, rather than to parody or undermine it. Toward the end of his life, he boldly sought new ways of giving verbal form to preverbal phenomena—of springing himself from the prisonhouse of narrative. But, as a result of the inconsistent and intermittent process of its production and the conflicting motives behind it, the *Autobiography* remains an unfinished and inconclusive experiment. Like Barnum's 1891 autobiography, Mark Twain's late attempt at a definitive self-biography ultimately tends to illustrate the limits and limitation of the genre.

II

Mark Twain's first published work to be *called* an autobiography—*Mark Twain's Burlesque Autobiography and First Romance*—vividly demonstrates the ludic impulse that characterized his lifelong approach to the genre. Indeed, this early caper seems more burlesque than autobiography: its apparent purpose is not to recount the life of the writer in any recognizable form, but rather to mock certain conventions of genteel autobiographical discourse, especially the apologetic opening and the respectful account of one's ancestry. Both of these conventions are present in Part One of Franklin's narrative, an antecedent of which Twain was painfully aware. He had good reason to be impatient with the inspirational uses to which Franklin's narrative was put in the nineteenth century—his elder brother Orion consciously emulated Franklin, and even named his printing shop (in which young Samuel Clemens worked) after him. In fact, one year before publishing his *Burlesque Autobiography,* Twain satirized Franklin as a model for young boys in a magazine piece entitled "The Late Benjamin Franklin."[6] In any case, the text opens with a lame excuse that aptly parodies Franklin's attempts to disguise his egotism: "Two or three persons having at different times intimated that if I would write an autobiography they would read it when they got leisure, I yield at last to this frenzied public demand, and herewith tender my history."[7] The transformation, within the course of a single sentence, of the lukewarm interest of a few friends into "frenzied public demand" economically exposes the vacuity of this opening gambit and the vanity of all autobiography.

The bulk of the narrative consists of a tracing of the author's ancestry through a rogue's gallery of highwaymen, cutthroats, forgers, and pirates. One evident motive here is parody of the "story-book" history of England and America. For every hero of conventional histories—Renaissance scholar, explorer, soldier, missionary—the Twain family provides a negative counterpart. By representing autobiography as "history" writ small, Twain impugns both genres as self-serving rationalizations of the past. The basic (and somewhat tiresome) joke is the transparently evasive or euphemistic nature of the account: one ancestor is said to have died "suddenly" at "one of those fine old English places of resort called Newgate" (4). Thus, while seeming to defend his ancestors, the narrator manages to indict them, whether purposely or not; moreover, his clumsy attempts to sanitize his past expose him as a charlatan in the family tradition. When the narrative breaks off without recounting the author's life, the motive appears to be avoidance of self-incrimination rather than modesty.

In any case, the correlation between the writer's family history and the narrative he produces is minimal. As we have seen, however, according to one theory, "It is impossible for an autobiographer not to be autobiographical. . . . The peculiarity of the genre is that the untruth it tells may be as rich, or richer in significance, than the truth."[8] Beneath the burlesque surface of this truncated narrative,

Justin Kaplan has detected a genuinely autobiographical impulse. In doing so, he has located an important source of both Twain's humor and his autobiography. In effect, Kaplan has read this "pseudo-confession" as a true one, full of "hostility and self-hatred." He views it as Twain's crude attempt to "joke away" his Presbyterian sense of inherited guilt: "by taking the initiative in accusing and, symbolically, punishing himself, the humorist achieves a kind of immunity from the disapproval of society."[9]

Interestingly, its account of one ancestor, Beau Twain, associates writing itself with illicit impersonation in that what is euphemistically described as playful and aesthetically pleasing is in fact criminal forgery: "He wrote a beautiful, beautiful hand. And he could imitate anybody's hand so closely that it was enough to make a person laugh his head off to see it. He had infinite sport with his talent" (6–7). The tracing of the author's ancestry to a "friend of the family by the name of Higgins" and not to a patriarch named Twain implies that the line *originates* in illegitimacy. The effect is simultaneously to insist on and to excuse its author's illegitimacy; the extensiveness of the family's corruption at once implicates the author and mitigates his guilt. On the one hand, his family and his occupation are condemned, while on the other, the sources of his own corruption are located beyond his control or choice.

Though Mark Twain later repudiated this prankish autobiography (Kaplan 124), in some ways it foreshadows the more fully developed versions. For one thing, it obviously undermines its own authority; indeed, it is so clearly unreliable a narrative that it is virtually self-correcting. In addition, in stopping just short of the narrator's life, it anticipates the more subtle ways in which later installments in the autobiographical project also evade direct treatment of it. Moreover, it draws attention to its pseudonymity both by making the use of an alias a family tradition, and by exposing the author's name as kind of misnomer, or improper name. (In doing so, the author hints at one of the pseudonym's powerful functions—to distance him from male precursors and their unwelcome legacies.) Behind the manifest parody of particular conventions of genteel autobiography is the intimation of its inevitable unreliability. By taking advantage of the lack of real Twain ancestors to invent highly improbable ones, Mark Twain exposes the pseudonym as a license to lie and pseudonymous autobiography as autonomous pseudobiography. Thus, at the heart of this most false of his autobiographies lies a true confession about the genre.

III

To attend to the matter of the pseudonym is to entertain the possibility that Mark Twain's accounts of its origins are the *true* autobiography of "Mark Twain." The choice of a pseudonym and the characterization of its genesis are profoundly autobiographical acts: self-concealment is a form of self-revelation. In this case, the circumstances of these acts, though not their motives, are quite well known. According to Henry Nash Smith, the pseudonym was first used when Samuel Clemens was a reporter covering the first Nevada Constitutional Convention (November 2–December 11,1863) for the Virginia City *Enterprise.* Though the assumption of the pseudonym was, in retrospect, decisive, it did not effect a complete rupture with the past, nor did it reflect a neat division between the "writer" and the "man," for writing continued to appear under the name of Samuel Clemens. According to Smith,

> the *Enterprise* recognized two aspects of Clemens' work: routine political reporting, a technical process without a personal flavor, ascribed to Clemens; and personal journalism mostly humorous, ascribed to Mark Twain. . . . Although Mark Twain was privileged to say anything—or almost anything—he pleased, Sam Clemens was expected to practice serious journalism, and most of the time he accepted this professional responsibility.[10]

Evidently, the self-division (or self-doubling) enacted by the pseudonym provided Clemens with a neutral territory for which he could light out whenever he wanted to flee the constraints of serious journalism. The assumption of the name was thus an expansive gesture: as the budding writer explored new geographical and political territory, he annexed new literary territory by reconstituting himself under a new name.

This impulse later took a cruder and more external form. In the early 1870s, he devised a plan whereby a stand-in or literary stunt man, James H. Riley, would explore remote territories and have adventures that would furnish material for autobiographical treatment. In a letter of November 28, 1870, he informed his publisher, Elisha Bliss,

> I have put my greedy hand on the best man in America for my purpose and shall *start him to the diamond fields of South Africa within a fortnight, at my expense.* I shall write a book of his experiences for next spring, . . . and write it just as if I had been through it all myself, but

> will explain in the preface that this is done merely to give it life and reality.[11]

Twain whimsically likened this project to Defoe's "collaboration" with Crusoe (as Gertrude Stein did her *Autobiography of Alice B. Toklas*). But this plan to have an alter ego keep careful diaries, and then return to live with him and tell him his story in daily installments curiously anticipates, in reverse form, his later collaboration with his official biographer, Albert Bigelow Paine. (Here, however, what was in effect *Riley's* authorized biography was to be passed off as Mark Twain's autobiography.) Though the scheme fell through when his double died in 1872, this bizarre literary scheme reveals an important impulse at work in his choice of a pseudonym, and in much of his writing.

To be sure, the assumption of his pseudonym at a crucial point in his career involved self-alienation as well as self-aggrandizement. Even as the Nevada territory was incorporated into the Union in a period of division nearly fatal to the nation, Samuel Clemens divided himself into two parties and began the process of suppressing his Confederate past and reconstituting himself as a Union sympathizer. Ultimately, the writer made his literary name with humorous narratives of the river that literally and vitally connected the two warring sections. Thus, he internalized and transmuted the painful politics of his day, making his pseudonym the marker both of self-division and of the humor that might make pleasure out of self-partition.

The conflicting impulses behind this act of self-begetting can be discerned in his various accounts of it. The accounts differ considerably, and none quite corresponds to the facts as scholars have reconstructed them, yet they have significant elements in common. One of these is the attribution of the name "Mark Twain" to Captain Isaiah Sellers, who may never have used it. The first published explanation appeared as a letter in the *Alta* of June 9,1877:

> "Mark Twain" was the *nom de plume* of one Captain Isaiah Sellers, who used to write river news over it for the *New Orleans Picayune*. He died in 1863 and as he could no longer need that signature, I laid violent hands upon it without asking permission of the proprietor's remains. That is the history of the *nom de plume* I bear.[12]

It is curious that Samuel Clemens chose not to claim the name as his own invention—if it was his—because the attribution of the pseudonym to Sellers gratuitously makes its appropriation a violation of his literary remains (a name- rather than a body-snatching). By this account (as well as that in his burlesque autobiography), "Mark Twain" is an illegitimate conception—an identity purloined from a dead man. (In fact Sellers died in 1864, *after* the "theft" of the pseudonym.) This act, which has patricidal implications (in its displacement of Clemens' patronymic as well as its hostility toward this patriarch of the river), is also a form of self-elevation, a way of linking himself with an acknowledged authority on the river, as Edgar Burde has shrewdly suggested: "[I]n playing him false, his memory here created something that was true to his imaginative (and wished for) conception of things: 'Mark Twain' was the patriarch of piloting."[13]

What is really accomplished here, apparently, is not the *theft* of the name from Sellers but the *gift* of it to him—and with it, the gift of a son and heir. Thus, in becoming Mark Twain, Samuel Clemens indulged in the simultaneously regressive and aggressive fantasy of choosing a father other than his biological one. To put it differently, Clemens invented a surrogate literary father whom he could easily surpass, at least as a writer, because Sellers, while he was a pilot of considerable stature, was only semiliterate; his river reports required careful editing before publication (Cardwell 183).

The assumption of a pen name probably always carries a significant emotional burden, in part because it entails the renunciation of familial for literary immortality. Mark Twain's accounts of his origins quite clearly expose the psychic violence involved in the transplantation of the self into an alternative genealogy. Instead of just assuming his chosen pseudonym, Mark Twain seems to have created an illustrious predecessor for the sole purpose of killing him off and stealing his name. As the diction and tropes of this very brief letter show—"I laid violent hands upon it without asking permission of the proprietor's remains"—this self-begetting gesture did not relieve him of anxiety about the past. Indeed, the variety of his accounts of it and their particulars indicate that the gesture may have both arisen from and aroused guilt.

An expanded version of this account of his self-conception in *Life on the Mississippi* displays conflicting impulses. In an extended portrait, the Captain is described as a "fine man, a high-minded man, and greatly respected both ashore and on the river, . . . very tall, well built, handsome," a "patriarch of the craft." But he is also self-important: "He knew how he was regarded, and perhaps this fact added some trifle of stiffening to his natural dignity, which had been sufficiently stiff in its original state."[14] Moreover, his authority stifles the other pilots:

> Whenever Captain Sellers approached a body of gossiping pilots, a chill fell there, and talking ceased. For this reason: whenever six pilots were gathered together, there would always be one or two newly fledged ones in the lot, and the older ones would be always "showing off" before these poor fellows; making them sorrowfully feel how callow they were, how recent their nobility, and how humble their degree, by talking largely and vaporously of old-time experiences on the river; always making it a point to date everything back as far as they could, so as to make the new men feel their newness to the sharpest degree possible, and envy the old stagers in the like degree. And how these complacent bald-heads *would* swell, and brag, and lie, and date back—ten, fifteen, twenty years,—and how they did enjoy the effect produced upon the marvelling and envying youngsters!
>
> And perhaps just at this happy stage of the proceedings, the stately figure of Captain Isaiah Sellers, that real and only genuine Son of Antiquity, would drift solemnly into the midst. Imagine the size of the silence that would result on the instant (517–18).

The son of Antiquity itself, Sellers has no mortal father or sons; he is an oppressive father figure, a disabler and emasculator of younger men. (His characterization incorporates some not very subtle phallic imagery.) Mindful that Sellers was noted for originating river signals that became the "universal custom of this day" (517) and for monopolizing the spoken discourse of the pilot-house, we can recognize this as a classic scenario of the anxiety of influence. The obvious and salutary response to any such forerunner would be parody—that literary mingling of resentment and respect, disdain and affection. Not surprisingly, Mark Twain goes on to say that his first newspaper article, while he was still a cub, took the form of a burlesque of Sellers' "Mark Twain" paragraphs. In his account of this episode, the fledgling writer completely supplants his predecessor:

> He never printed another paragraph while he lived, and he never again signed "Mark Twain" to anything. At the time that the telegraph brought the news of his death, I was on the Pacific coast. I was a fresh new journalist, and needed a *nom de guerre;* so I confiscated the ancient mariner's discarded one (519–20).

This account adds the injury of silencing Sellers to the posthumous insult of stealing his pen name. Here the patricidal implications of the act are obvious: the cub's parody seems to bring about the death of the father figure on which his own accession to full authorship depends.

Yet Mark Twain's attitude is ambivalent. On the one hand, he takes evident pleasure in muzzling Sellers and seizing his literary license. On the other hand, having became virtually a patriarch of the river himself, he expresses compassion and a degree of remorse for the old man's pain: "I did not know then, though I do now, that there is no suffering comparable with that which a private person feels when he is for the first time pilloried in print" (519). The appropriation of the name is here somewhat less violent. The name was "discarded" before Clemens "confiscated" it; aggression is displaced from the name-snatching to the name itself, which has become a *nom de guerre*. Finally, his declaration of a patently false intention to make the name "remain what it was in his hands—a sign and symbol and warrant that whatever is found in its company may be gambled on as being the petrified truth" (502) suggests the paradoxical traits—the appearance of authority (petrified truth) and the freedom to play (gambling)—that Clemens sought to incorporate as Mark Twain.

It appears then that the initiation of Mark Twain's career as humorist, if not as autobiographer, required the *invention* of a precursorial identity to be parodied, squelched, and finally appropriated: literary self-emancipation necessitated the fictive assassination of an oppressive master. The motives of this complex act remain obscure, but their very obscurity may paradoxically illuminate Mark Twain's peculiar, lifelong flirtation with autobiography. Perhaps unable to "know" himself according to the prescriptions of secular autobiography, or unwilling to submit to the discipline of confession, Samuel Clemens sought to subvert or elude the constraints of those conventions, including the obligation to fact. That is, he sought to have the pleasure without the responsibility of autobiography.

The ambiguity of the act may be understood another way, by reference to what Derrida calls the dissemination of one's name—the drawing out, in puns, of the common nouns it contains or suggests. To do this is to relinquish the mystique of the "proper name," but the blurring of the distinction between proper and common nouns involves gain as well as loss:

> By disseminating or losing my own name, I make it more and more intrusive; I occupy the whole site, and as a result my name gains more ground. The more I lose, the more I gain by conceiving my proper name as the common name. . . . The dissemination of a proper name is, in fact, a way of seizing the language, putting it to one's own use, instating its law.[15]

Since writing and publishing one's Life is also a way of putting one's name in circulation, it should come as no surprise to find autobiographers playing self-consciously with their names. As we have seen, Franklin drew on the meaning of his name as a common noun to appropriate certain political and economic values: when defined as a common noun, *Franklin* occupies and consolidates valuable cultural territory. Similarly, a clergyman's pun on P. T. Barnum's name links him and his wife to certain cherished Victorian values: "My friend the Rev. Dr. Chapin . . . says that my wife and I are the most sympathetic couple he ever saw, since she is 'Charity' and I am 'Pity' (P. T.)."[16] At the same time, the use of his last name as a verb encodes a conflicting popular perception of him: " 'We never thought Charlie [Tom Thumb] much of a phenomenon when he lived among us,' said one of the first citizens of [Bridgeport], 'but now that he has become "Barnumized," he is a rare curiosity' " (256). Apparently, to *Barnumize* is to transmute the unremarked, though not necessarily unremarkable, into the curious by means of clever packaging and promotion. One might say, therefore, that all autobiography, and not just Barnum's, involves Barnumizing.

Of particular significance here is that part of Barnum's success in promoting his exhibits lay in his genius for choosing clever aliases, such as General Tom Thumb and Commodore Nutt—aliases that played with common nouns. The creation of a pseudonym like "Mark Twain," made up of two common words, is also an economical and powerful way of "seizing the language, putting it to one's own use." Like the "dissemination" of one's name, this gesture combines loss and gain. The adoption of any pseudonym means relinquishing the precious historicity and particularity that attend one's proper name. But "Samuel Clemens" is an adjunct to the language, while "Mark Twain" is already inscribed within it. Thus, "Mark Twain" automatically achieves a visibility and memorability inaccessible to "Samuel Clemens." (If one measure of fame is making one's name a household word, then the adoption of a common phrase as a pseudonym is a kind of shortcut to celebrity.) Of course, lasting fame would depend on subscribing the pen name to work of distinction. But the name makes its own contribution by appropriating the Mississippi River as the writer's "natural" habitat and his distinctive literary subject; the false name "authorizes" and empowers the writer.

In the end, as James M. Cox has reminded us, "Mark Twain" is a transparent and transparently humorous pseudonym (18–20); as such, it communicates its own autobiographical message. It is distinguished from some pseudonyms—"George Eliot," for example—in being quite literally a false name, a phrase that mimics a name. (It is rather like "Strike Two," in both its syntax and its intimation of danger; in its original context, it signified perilously shallow water.) As a phrase, rather than a combination of a given name and a surname, it is an indivisible *unit.* (This is why purists object to calling him "Twain," although doing so carries no risk of being misunderstood, and even though the writer himself sometimes clove his pseudonym, signing correspondence "Mark.") Paradoxically, this indivisible unit means "sign of two" or, as Neil Schmitz would have it, "discern duplicity" (60). It is, then, not only an obvious pseudonym; it is also a self-reflexive one because it comments on the self-doubling that a pen name not only licenses but enacts.

IV

Having discussed an abortive early autobiography and the origins of the pseudonym, I want to turn to "Old Times on the Mississippi" to explore the relationships among its humorous, pseudonymous, and autobiographical elements. Because its humor at times depends on a reader's sense that the text is autobiographical, and at other times confounds it, "Old Times on the Mississippi" employs humor in a distinctively autobiographical way. And because it recounts the period of Samuel Clemens' life from which (though not during which) he fashioned his pseudonym and his identity as a humorist, the narrative unfolds a kind of primal scenario in which Mark Twain is conceived and named, but not quite born. Thus, "Old Times on the Mississippi" provides both the humor of autobiography and the autobiography of a humorist.

It is often noted that the autobiographical character in "Old Times on the Mississippi" is never shown in possession of the authority to which he aspires—the seemingly absolute power enjoyed by the pilot. It is only as *autobiographer* that Mark Twain displays any mastery of the pilot's skills—memory, intuition, and instinct. Thus, the text is sometimes read as autobiography once removed: as a narrative of the apprenticeship of a writer (Mark Twain) rather than of a pilot (Samuel Clemens). (Clemens made explicit the link between writing and piloting in a letter of December 8, 1874, which suggested that his "authorizing" was a substitute for piloting, which his wife prevented him from resuming.[17]) By this account, Mark Twain accedes only to the authority of the writer: at its best, this is the literary analogue of the "boundless authority" of the pilot, but at its worst, it is a pathetic come-down from it— "writers of all kinds are manacled servants of the public" (313).

Like the truncation of the narrative, its pseudonymity invites us—or compels us—to read it as the story of Mark Twain, not as the history of Samuel Clemens. Of course, to do this is to relinquish, to some degree, the historicity ordinarily associated with autobiography: the idea that the text arises from and refers to some verifiable extra-textual reality (i.e., the writer's life and identity). It is to agree to tarry in the labyrinth of the text, mindful that its author's pseudonym is virtually a synonym for duplicity. The phrase first shows up in the chapter that recounts Bixby's triumphal crossing of Hat Island, "A Daring Deed."[18] (Here, as elsewhere, the phrase appears as a leadsman's cry: the text never admits it as a *name.*) The cub is listening to experienced pilots trading river stories. Since he is able to contribute neither to the piloting nor to the yarning, he feels like "a cipher in this august company." After one pilot has told how he ran Plum Point, a second offers: " 'I had better water than that, and ran it lower down; started out from from the false point—mark twain—raised the second reef abreast the big snag in the bend, and had quarter less twain' " (269). The phrase "Mark Twain" appears here innocently and unemphatically, rather than hyphenated or italicized, as it is in two later uses. Despite its innocent appearance, however, it is not allowed to pass unchallenged. The next speaker by questioning the amount of water claimed, successfully "settles" his predecessor.

This, the very first instance of the phrase, occurs in a framed narrative, and the episode may be read as a comment on the uses of autobiographical narrative. The hazard signaled by the phrase lies not in the pilot's running of a stretch of the river, but in his "stretching" of a run of the river. His transparent attempt to put down his predecessor predictably backfires. Though a "fact" *is* called into question here, the implication is that the narrative's authority depends not so much on the veracity of its facts as on the manner of its delivery. It is not exaggeration that undoes this narrator—that is inevitable, even desirable— but lack of finesse. Authority is a textual, and contextual, matter. This passage questions the reliability of autobiography not only by having a self-serving narrative challenged but also—on another level—by associating "mark twain" with a "false point" and an exaggerated sounding—that is, with both a false *land*mark and a false *water*mark.

Like the pseudonym lying camouflaged on the surface of the text, the humor of the narrative undermines its authority as autobiography. Consider that much of the humor is generated by the cub's inability to learn the lessons of the river, and that this incompetence is attributed specifically to the inadequacy of his *memory*. Though the narrative demonstrates different models of memory, the cub's failure to emulate Bixby's selectively retentive memory would seem to disqualify him from autobiography as well as from piloting. As we know, it does not, but it certainly compromises, if it does not entirely undercut, his opening remark about the power of his memory to summon up a scene: "After all these years, I can picture that old time to myself now, just as it was then" (253)—a claim repeated in the much-praised Quarles Farm passage of the *Autobiography*.

In addition to impugning autobiography's source, the narrative, like the earlier burlesque, parodies various generic models. For example, the story of this apprentice inverts, if it does not subvert, the classic American account of apprenticeship by Benjamin Franklin, a printer-journalist who quickly and effortlessly surpassed his master: "Old Times on the Mississippi" is no success story. As a story of failed education (an aspect emphasized by the chapter titles—"Perplexing Lessons," "Completing My Education," "I Take a Few More Lessons,"), the narrative also sends up that prominent nineteenth-century autobiographical trope: life as education, or the evolution of mind (a conceit travestied in a very different way by Mark Twain's contemporary, Henry Adams).

A related source of humor is the mocking of that most earnest of autobiographical genres, the conversion narrative. From the beginning, the narrative of the apprenticeship is cast as a quest for a kind of salvation. The cub's sense of his goal is expressed in terms appropriate to redemption: his ardent desire is to become a pilot and "come home in glory." Moreover, the rhythm of the cub's experience—periods of false confidence followed by mortification before a superior being (in this case, the river-god, Bixby)—is closely analogous to the traditional morphology of conversion, in which humiliation is a prerequisite to salvation. The style also periodically mimics the language of spiritual autobiography. Just setting out on his travels precipitates a false sense of assurance in the cub: "I became a new being, the subject of my own admiration. . . . I was in such a glorified condition that all ignoble failings departed me" (256–57). The genius of the style is at once to simulate and to satirize the cub's expectations, to convey—by means of pious cliches—the narrator's sense that those expectations were not only naive but grandiose.

Still another source of humor in "Old Times on the Mississippi" is the narrator's awareness of the conventionality of all narrative, even that which claims, like autobiography, to recount actual events and to embody unique selfhood. Thus, the humor at times has to do with the failure of language to render experience directly. An extreme and fairly obvious instance of this is the "autobiography" of the drunken nightwatchman, "who had absorbed wildcat literature and appropriated its marvels, until in time he had woven odds and ends of the mess into [his] yarn, and then gone on telling it to fledglings like me, until he had come to believe it himself" (260). The flaw in the nightwatchman's autobiography is not its insincerity (*he* believes what he says) nor its excursion into fictional territory (after all, Mark Twain, like the nightwatchman, remembers things that never happened). Rather, it is the *triteness* of its literary sources, and their obviousness—to anyone but the awestruck cub.

One of the challenging features of the narrative as a whole, therefore, is its suggestion that linguistic and literary conventions precede and shape experience—and thus threaten to supplant it. Consider the basic "initiation" plot. One way to explain the relationship between its materials and its humorous perspective would be to say that the former *demanded* the latter—this is, that the experiences of the cub, which must have been *to him* painful rather than funny, could be narrated only if they were reworked (or replayed) as humor. By this account, his humiliating failures made humor necessary to their recovery and narration (i.e., the trauma of these events determined that the character would become a humorous narrator—or none at all). In that sense the narrative is the autobiography of humor; it is an account of the creation of a humorist. Of course, this view of the narrative assumes both that the narrator and the protagonist are one person and that what is narrated really happened. This is the traditional way of seeing autobiography, as writing produced by the prior experience of a pre-existent, unique, and self-identical individual.

From another, competing perspective, the fact of the humor dictates the plot, which is thus a kind of fiction. Whatever the origins of the pseudonymous "Mark Twain"—and they remain ultimately inaccessible to us—once conceived, he can *only* produce his past as humor: he can formulate his experience only within the genre that defines him (and *con*fines him). After all, should the cub learn his lessons and become a licensed pilot, the humor would cease and

"Mark Twain"—the licensed humorist—would expire. Because it is pseudonymous and because it obstructs the conversion of cub into pilot, the narrative frustrates the usual way of reading autobiography: reading it as the story of how the character (the I-then) became the narrator (the I-now). In "Old Times on the Mississippi," the character is a cub and the narrator an ex-pilot, and the two selves never converge. (Even *Life on the Mississippi,* which fills in the temporal gap between the cub's apprenticeship and the writer's return to the river in the 1880s, absurdly compresses the transition.)

To "explain" the relationship between plot and narrator this way is to complement the previous explanation; it is to look through the other end of the telescope. From this perspective, autobiography does not recall or recapture experience, nor can the past be reliably recuperated from it. By its failure, or refusal, to close the gaps—nominal as well as narrative—between character and narrator and author, "Old Times on the Mississippi" reminds us that autobiography inevitably papers over cracks in the ego and that narrative in some sense always produces one's "life" and identity (rather than vice versa)—that experience is always already constructed by linguistic and generic patterns. Instead of telling a story of autonomy, "Old Times on the Mississippi" demonstrates the autonomy of storytelling.

This is evident in the classic passage comparing the river to a book. The narrator's claim that his acquisition of the language of the river had cost him "all the grace, the beauty, the poetry . . . of the majestic river" (284) is itself problematic in that insofar as his "before" picture illustrates his former perception of the river, it reproduces what he claims is irrecoverable. (He is rather like the plaintiff in the accident suit who undermines his claim of bodily injury by demonstrating how easily he *used* to be able to move.) In any case, becoming a pilot is not a matter of replacing an idiosyncratic and unmediated view of the river with a shared and conventional one, nor even of replacing a superficial "romantic" one with a penetrating "realistic" one; rather, it involves supplementing one cultural code with another. In learning to read the river as a pilot, the narrator learns that he has *always* been reading it, through one set of conventions or another. One of the disturbing implications of this passage, then, is its suggestion that the river is already written, since this suggests the impossibility of ever expressing or perceiving anything directly, spontaneously, or originally.

At the heart of the passage referred to earlier is "a long, slanting mark . . . sparkling upon the water" that the narrator had learned to read as "a bluff reef which is going to kill somebody's steamboat one of these nights" (284–85). Despite its benign appearance, it is a sign of danger. As the preceding episode reveals, it is also an ambiguous mark, for the cub's embarrassment there had resulted precisely from his inability to distinguish a bluff reef from a wind reef. (The difference is crucial—literally a matter of life or death—but Bixby can only say that telling the difference is a matter of instinct rather than perception.) This may stand as a synechdoche of the text, whose central dilemma is how to read *its* enigmatic Mark, whose reflection glimmers tantalizingly on the page.

As the autobiography of humor, "Old Times on the Mississippi" traces the learning of the discourses (of the river and of autobiography) through which Mark Twain comes into existence both as humorous character and as humorist. To put it differently, one of its subjects is the acquisition of the stylistic traits that identify its author. By learning to write the river, Mark Twain succeeded spectacularly in putting his name in place, and in play, on the Mississippi. (Returning to it in 1882, to research his big book, he discovered a steamboat already named after him.) And it is tempting to say that "Old Times on the Mississippi" inscribes his signature, permanently and indelibly, on water.

But as a pseudonym, that signature constantly threatens to dissolve before our eyes. As we have already seen, it will not do to think of Samuel Clemens as the "man" and Mark Twain as the "writer"—the former as the man of flesh and blood, the latter as the man of letters. And "Old Times on the Mississippi" reminds us that one meaning of the latter phrase is "man *made* of letters"—that is, of marks on the page. In many ways, the narrative thwarts the tracing of "Mark Twain" back to a historical figure named Samuel Clemens. Mark Twain remains an inescapably textual character who is to be found only in solution in the fluid medium of his prose.

V

Considered as autobiography, *Life on the Mississippi* raises many of the same issues as "Old Times on the Mississippi," but with additional complications that arise from the author's return to the river. Thus, the continued narrative yields not the single image (already misleading) that memory supplies at a distance from the river but a complex double exposure—a montage of past and present, memory-image and sensory-image. Though narrator and character are often temporally and psychologically less distant from one another in the new chapters, the relationships between them are in some ways more problematic because the new chapters range more widely in time than did the old, and because their materials and techniques are more varied. Most of all, considerable self-reflexivity accrues from the fact that the author reappears on the river that furnished him with his pseudonym in the character that it designated.

At first, the relationship between the two texts seems clear. Chapter XXI, "A Section in My Biography," stitches together the two stages of the author's life—his apprenticeship as a cub and his return to the river as a writer—with a scant half-page transition. The next chapter, "I Return to My Muttons," announces the shift in perspective and procedure from the "old times" of 1875 to the new "life" of 1884. But this transition displaces, and thus conceals, the actual seam in the narrative because the last chapters of the account of the 1850s (XVIII though XX) are in fact part of the later composition. The changed vantage point of these transitional chapters is perceptible in their veering from the comic toward the tragic with Henry Clemens' death from burns suffered in a steamboat explosion. This modulation in tone belies the attempt to simulate an earlier viewpoint: the narrative "I's" do not quite match. Moreover, in passing off chapters written in 1882 as chapters written in 1875, the narrative's form denies (or defies) the passing of time—the passing away of an epoch—that is one of the book's themes. Thus, while the differing terms of the two titles evoke the key elements of conventional "life-and-times" biographies, these texts ultimately subvert the chronology and transparency of such tomes.

Once the new narrative is begun, the writer acknowledges that for his new task his pseudonymous identity may be a liability. Having escaped *into* the identity of Mark Twain, he now must flee *from* it because the success of his invention has brought with it a celebrity that interferes with the task of revisiting the river and researching his book:

> I reflected that if I were recognized, on the river, I should not be as free to go and come, talk, inquire, and spy around, as I should be if unknown; I remembered that it was the custom of steamboatmen in the old times to load up the confiding stranger with the most picturesque and admirable lies, and put the sophisticated friend off with dull and ineffectual facts (361).

His solution to his dilemma is to take refuge in an alias. Thus, a layer is added to the palimpsest, a twist to the labyrinth, and a mirror to the funhouse. The character Mark Twain is at times an acknowledged faux-naif, feigning, without really attempting to recover, the innocence of the character in "Old Times on the Mississippi" (which was already a literary simulation).

Much of the comedy of these chapters, like that of Barnum's autobiographies, has to do with mistaken identity. Like Barnum, Mark Twain takes delight both in passing himself off as another and in being found out, and he puts the failure as well as the success of his alibi to literary use. The best example of this is found in Chapter XXIV, "My Incognito is Exploded," in which the pilot-become-writer impersonates a passenger well enough to elicit from a practicing pilot fantastic "facts," including "gigantic illustrations" of the "river's marvelous eccentricities." Or so it seems: it turns out that the pilot who appears to be trying to take in an "innocent" passenger has recognized Mark Twain and is using preposterous lies to flush him from cover.

The pilot has been putting Mark Twain on in two senses, by trying to take him in and by assuming his manner. It is no coincidence that his stretcher about "alligator reefs" (373–74) reads like a parody of passages in the earlier narrative about the deceptiveness of the river's surface. The episode ends with an invitation to the traveler to resume his original Mississippi identity, with its attendant privilege and prestige: " 'Here!' (calling me by name), '*you* take her and lie a while—you're handier at it than I am' " (376–77). Thus, the failure of the writer's ploy yields an opportunity to resume the dual roles (pilot and liar) which his authorship encompasses.

When this pilot's name—"Rob Styles"—is dropped in an aside, it is clear that the reader, rather than Mark Twain, has been taken in because even though the episode poses as a story he tells *on* himself, it is of course a story he tells *by* himself: in his autobiography, just as in his fiction, he writes all the lines and plays all the parts. Characters in autobiography are functions of literary impersonation, like those in fiction and drama. When the pilot's punning name betrays the ventriloquistic nature of the dialogue, the drama collapses. Instead of the disclosure of the pseudonymous character (Mark Twain) behind his alias, we have the exposure of the apparent unmasker ("Rob Styles") as a pseudonymous self-parody. The text folds in upon itself. We are reminded that although a distinctive style might seem to signify, or even to constitute, a unique identity, it also renders that identity vulnerable to imitation, parody, and theft. These are the facts of literary life. At best, it seems, the author can deploy self-parody as a kind of preemptive strike against the forgery of his style—

and against the prospect of suffering the fate of Sellers. Thus, the narrative circles back to the ambiguous gesture of self-begetting that was the conception of Mark Twain.

While *Life on the Mississippi* in a sense deepens and extends the flow of the earlier narrative, it begins by disguising the confluence of the past and the present. Moreover, it drastically condenses an episode that "Old Times on the Mississippi" had entirely omitted but pointed toward: the author's career as a pilot. (This ellipsis anticipates Henry Adams more prominent and telling exclusion of his "life"—his career and marriage—from his *Education.*) While the motivation of this omission remains murky, it has the effect of an important evasion, like the original assumption of the pseudonym. As Louis Rubin has pointed out, "in omitting the piloting years, supposedly the most happy of his life, . . . he omits any portrayal of himself as an adult in the antebellum South . . . ."[19] Along with the Civil War, Samuel Clemens' Southern manhood disappeared within this curious crease in the text of his autobiography.

From Hannibal to Hartford, the general heading of Samuel Clemens' life, in both cultural and geographical terms, was from the Old Southwest to the Northeast. Yet nowhere in his life-writing did he retrace the overall trajectory of his career. To be sure, in *Life on the Mississippi* he identifies himself, implicitly and explicitly, as an *ex*-Southerner, and his history is laid out on a double continuum: his past lies downstream in space and upstream in time, and his present lies upstream in space and downstream in time. Even here, however the narrative does not move in a single direction. Rather, as Mark Twain, the author obscures the course of his experience by identifying himself with that American river that flows from north to south by swinging, pendulumlike, east and west. Having escaped, in a sense, from the divisive politics of the 1860s by doubling himself in literature, he sought in the 1870s and 1880s to explore but not to survey his past by voyaging recursively, in fact and in imagination, on the waters of his youth. The effect, and perhaps the intent, of the Mississippi narratives was not so much to historicize as to mythologize himself. Following the logic of his pseudonym, he characterized himself as a kind of autochthonous "author" of the river.

VI

In a sense, *Mark Twain's Autobiography* (1924) represents the end and culmination of his work. It also marks a significant departure from his earlier life-writing because the text is neither particularly humorous nor playfully pseudonymous. Its title (without a qualifying "Burlesque") distinguishes it from both the early parody and works such as *Roughing It*, *Life on the Mississippi*, and *Innocents Abroad*, which are merely autobiograph*ical*. Moreover, its posthumous publication implies what its author explicitly promised: a final authoritative self-revelation—one that might repair the evasions of the earlier texts. Indeed, the chronicler of Twain's tragic last years, Hamlin Hill, has characterized it as the product of the author's gradual emergence into the open from the cover of fiction and humor:

> Always uncertain and uncomfortable with fiction, Clemens more and more emphasized the autobiographical voice during his last years. . . . [T]he autobiography itself was the purest form of this confessional mode. It was Samuel Clemens with relatively few of the usual modifications which the comic mask of Mark Twain allowed.[20]

One of the powerful impulses behind the text does seem to have been a desire to express himself vitally, spontaneously, and directly on paper—to break decisively out of the inevitable self-reflexivity of pseudonymous autobiography.

Yet *Mark Twain's Autobiography* is neither pure confession nor definitive self-biography. After all, the text Paine published is only the partial product of a complicated, intermittent process of composition that spanned almost the entire length of the writer's career, from a few slight fragments of about 1870 to the copious dictations that began in 1906 and ended only with his death. The complexity of the project, the variety of its materials and methods, and the fragmentary and inconsistent nature of the several published versions hint at a cumulative perplexity about both of the title's terms: Mark Twain and autobiography. Of course, if Hill is right in his claim that the *Autobiography* presents its author sans mask, then its essential joke would be that its title is a misnomer. It would not do to call the book *The Autobiography of Samuel Clemens,* either, for one of its implications may be that it was no longer possible—if it ever had been—for its producer, or its consumers, to distinguish between Samuel Clemens and Mark Twain. There can be no clear title to this sprawling literary property.

Nevertheless, the issue of authority is raised by the author's announcement of his intention to speak more directly here than he had in the texts discussed earlier. Indeed, he explicitly affirmed the *Autobiography's* unique candor and authenticity, and its ability to embody genuine selfhood. The Preface states:

> I am literally speaking from the grave, because I shall be dead when this book issues from the press. I speak from the grave rather than with my living tongue, for a good reason: I can speak thence freely. . . . It has seemed to me that I could be as frank and free and unembarrassed as a love letter if I knew that what I was writing would be exposed to no eye until I was dead, and unaware, and indifferent (I, xv).

However, the notions that a writer could achieve total honesty simply by imagining himself dead and that the love letter is an inherently uninhibited mode of discourse collapse under scrutiny. According to James M. Cox, what the autobiography shares with the writer's actual love letters is not frank self-expression, but rather forceful self-repression; despite the author's claims, the contents of both prove to be quite tame (302–3).

The consensus among scholars, then, is that the book does not fulfill its promise—or threat—of candor. According to Justin Kaplan,

> It is a "true" book, in the sense that he poured into it his deflected angers and heterodoxies. . . . Speaking "as from the grave," he could tell "the truth" about some of the people he had known; he could dictate passages about God and religion which he was sure would get his heirs and assigns burned at the stake if they dared take them out of his box of "posthumous stuff" and publish them before 2006 A.D. But this was only one kind of truth. . . . Clemens . . . acknowledged tacitly that introspection and self-analysis were not his strong suit (377–78).

Similarly, Hill himself has noted the extent to which both the circumstances and the contents of the dictations protected their author from the bleak facts of his later years:

> Rejecting most of the external world, he created a preferable one from his own imagination and with his own voice. He could surround himself with loyal, salaried minions and address to them his own memoirs, insulated from truths too harsh to accept or endure (136).

In this sense, the text carried on the self-evasion of the earlier texts, though without their characteristic humor.

The first two sections offer no startling self-revelations or shocking confessions; however, they do deal, in different ways, with a process essential to his constitution as a writer: the conversion of experience into literary capital. One of the topics of the early fragments (as of the opening of P. T Barnum's autobiography) is a legacy of nearly worthless plot of land, the Tennessee acreage that Judge Clemens mistakenly believed would secure his heirs' prosperity.

Alone among the judge's children, Mark Twain derived some profit out of the land: by using the episode in *The Gilded Age,* he salvaged a fictional plot and character of some value from the worthless land. The next section, "The Grant Dictations 1885," tells of his role in the composition and publication of the *Personal Memoirs of U. S. Grant.*[21] He encouraged this project on the grounds that the general's authorship alone would create a market for the book. That the book's success rescued the general from bankruptcy was a victory for both of them.

Grant's *Memoirs* are in every way the opposite of Mark Twain's autobiographies: they are systematic, chronologically ordered, carefully documented, and factually accurate accounts of events of public record and historic significance. Indeed, they are devoted almost exclusively to the crucial national event that is so notably absent from Mark Twain's various accounts of his own life. Thus, this section of the autobiography furnishes the ironic spectacle of a pseudonymous writer who had fled the Civil War—and thus surrendered it as a literary property—urging the general who won it to write his authoritative account of his campaigns. Grant's *Memoirs* were a model that Mark Twain might have admired—not so much for their literary and historical value as for the heroism of their dictation in the face of death—but they were hardly a model he could emulate.

Insofar as this section offers an inside narrative of the book's genesis and composition, it is the authorized biography of an autobiography (Clemens' relation to Grant here in some ways anticipates Albert Bigelow Paine's later relation to him). The section also illuminates the autobiography of which it is a part. However much Mark Twain may have admired the discipline with which Grant conducted this last campaign or envied the peace it brought its author, his explicit fascination was with the portrait of Grant being simultaneously created in the form of a bust by Karl Gebhardt. Though this was done with Grant's blessing—it was thus an "authorized" portrait—it was notable, according to Twain, for its rendering of the suffering that Grant managed stoically to conceal from most observers.

Thanks to Mark Twain's intervention, Gebhardt was permitted to work in Grant's presence and even to witness his model in sleep. As a result, the bust had "in it more of General Grant than can be found in any other likeness of him that has ever been made since he was a famous man. . . . For into the clay image went the pain which he was enduring, but which did not appear in his face when he was awake" (I, 66). This story and the account of an attending minister who attributed uncharacteristically pious statements to the dying general serve as cautionary stories about the way in which celebrities were subject to the creation of likenesses outside their control. Thus, the Grant section is less valuable as an account of the life of its source than as an indication of his understanding of the ethics and aesthetics of portraiture and self-portraiture in diverse media. In particular, it reveals his awareness of the different senses in which unauthorized and "authorized" images might betray their subject—by falsifying and by overexposing it, respectively. In this way, "The Grant Dictations" furnishes a significant chapter in the autobiography of *Mark Twain's Autobiography*.

VII

In "Chapters Begun in Vienna" (1897–98), and especially in the Quarles Farm reminiscences, Mark Twain finally seems to discover his proper material, the background and sources of his best work. This section, while famous for its vivid evocation of the pastoral pleasures of his youth, is far from spontaneous and immediate. While the passages that recall the sights, sounds, and smells of the farm may seem to dissolve the boundary between past and present, they do so by virtue of highly stylized rhetorical patterns. Moreover, his famous joke here about the fallibility of his memory reminds us that "what is remembered" is as much created as recalled.

Similarly, the opposition between honesty and art in the following lines can be read as analogous to that between firsthand and vicarious experience: "I know the taste of the watermelon which has been honestly come by, and I know the taste of the watermelon which has been acquired by art. Both taste good, but the experienced know which tastes best" (I, 110). Since the writer as well as the reader acquires and enjoys the watermelon on the page by art, the passage may celebrate the self-gratification of autobiography, as well as the pleasures of childhood larceny. The pleasure of reliving one's life justifies the duplicity of autobiography.

Even more revealing of the complex motives and methods of Mark Twain's autobiography is his account of "playing bare." Here, while rehearsing naked for his role as a bear in a childhood skit, he unknowingly performs before an invisible and anonymous female audience, as well as before a male friend; the disclosure of the presence of the uninvited audience is recounted as traumatic. This anecdote, with its revelation of a deep fear of exposure and a compensatory desire to control perception of self, goes a long way to explain the double distancing of experience (by humor and by pseudonym) in the autobiographical writing of Mark Twain.

Significantly, two of the three recurrent dreams that Twain later shared with Paine also had to do with humiliation before an audience. In the first, he is compelled to resume lecturing, but finds himself "before an audience with nothing to say, . . . trying to make the audience laugh, realizing that I am only making silly jokes." In the second, he appears at a fancy party in his night-clothes or dressed as a tramp; when he tries to make himself known as Mark Twain, nobody believes him.[22] In both, he fails to engage his audience *as Mark Twain* for lack of identifying material. His fear of appearing "bare" before an audience is matched only by his fear of losing its attention. On the one hand, the dreamer depends on his pseudonymous identity both as a medium of communication and a means of disguise; on the other, he fears that excessive reliance on it may deprive him of an identity other than that of the clown or comedian.

Although a writer necessarily performs before an anonymous audience, he does so largely on his own terms. If autobiography is to some extent a matter of undressing in public, the autobiographer, far more than the dancing bear, is in control of his self-exposure. Thus, the story of "playing bare" is finally as much an example as an explanation of the writer's distancing of experience. Far from reenacting his humiliation, the anecdote retroactively redeems it: by enabling him to command the laughter, his retelling of the episode converts it to pleasure.

Still, Mark Twain remained somewhat wary even of the self-produced and stage-managed confession of autobiography, as is evident in his reconstruction of some remarks of John Hay on the inability of the autobiographer to control his text:

> And he will tell the truth in spite of himself, for his facts and his fictions will work loyally together for the protection of the reader. . . . Without intending to lie, he will lie all the time. . . . [But] the reader will see the fact through the film and know his man. There is a subtle devilish something or other about autobiographical composition that defeats all the writer's attempts to paint his portrait *his* way (I, 235–36).

Apparently, Hay (like John Sturrock) thought that autobiography's unconscious falsehoods would reliably expose the writer. Thus, he assigns to the medium a (perverse) will—and authority—of its own. In his view, autobiography is a *master,* not a slave, narrative.

The same issue surfaces in the Twain–Howells correspondence. When Mark Twain rhapsodized about the freshness and directness of his 1904 dictations to Isabel Lyon, Howells teased him:

> You always rather bewildered me by your veracity, and I fancy you tell the truth about yourself. But *all* of it? The black truth, which we all know of ourselves in our hearts, or only the whitey-brown truth of the pericardium, or the nice, whitened truth of the shirtfront? Even *you* wont tell the black heart's-truth.

Employing a grotesque but telling image, Twain replied that he would, willy-nilly:

> Yes, I set up the safeguards, in the first day's dictating—taking this position: that an Autobiography is the truest of all books; for while it inevitably consists mainly of extinctions of the truth, shirkings of the truth, partial revealments of the truth, with hardly an instance of plain straight truth, the remorseless truth *is* there, between the lines, where the author-cat is raking dust upon it which hides from the disinterested spectator neither it nor its smell.[23]

Whether resigned to, or intent on, revealing the fecal truth, Mark Twain experimented restlessly in the final stages of composition with new methods of self-expression. "The Chapters Added in Florence" (1904) first tried out the innovative, and presumably liberating, methods that would distinguish the last stages of his project: dictation, free-association, and the juxtaposition of past and present:

> Finally in Florence, in 1904, I hit upon the right way to do an Autobiography: Start it at no particular time of your life; wander at your free will all over your life; talk only about the thing which interests you for the moment; drop it the moment its interest threatens to pale, and turn your talk upon the new and more interesting thing that has intruded itself into your mind meantime.
>
> Also, make the narrative a combined Diary *and* Autobiography. In this way you have the vivid thing of the present to make a contrast with memories of like things in the past, and these contrasts have a charm which is all their own. . . .
>
> And so, I have found the right plan. It makes my labor amusement—mere amusement, play, pastime, and wholly effortless (I,193).

Similarly, in "A Memory of John Hay," he recounts his abortive attempts at autobiography over the years and blames his failure, in part, on his attempt to *write* it:

> the result was not satisfactory; it was too literary. With the pen in one's hand, narrative is a difficult art; narrative should flow as flows the brook down through the hills and the leafy woodlands, its course changed by every bowlder [sic] it comes across and by every grass-clad gravelly spur that projects into its path.
>
> ....
>
> With a pen in the hand the narrative stream is a canal; it moves slowly, smoothly, decorously, sleepily, it has no blemish except that it is all blemish. It is too literary, too prim, too nice; the gait and style and movement are not suited to narrative. That canal stream is always reflecting; it is its nature, it can't help it. Its slick shiny surface is interested in everything it passes along the banks—cows, foliage, flowers, everything. And so it wastes a lot of time in reflections (I, 237–38).

What Mark Twain seems to aspire to here is a narrative stream that would respond to the subtlest impulses of consciousness and memory, one that would avoid "signs of starch, & flatiron, & labor & fuss & the other artificialities," and one that would somehow flow directly to the reader, rather than expending its energy in reflexivity.[24] While these excerpts indicate Mark Twain's desire to make his self-proclaimed autobiography different in method and effect from earlier books like"Old Times on the Mississippi," they also suggest a desire to retain or to recapture the orality of his best work.

It is no accident that the imagery of this passage associates the flow of narrative with that of natural water courses (the setting and subject of his best work) in contrast to the more stately "motion" of a manmade canal, which "reflects" too much. The pace of his ideal narrative would be various, and its progression would be unpredictable and nonlinear. Alternating between rapids and leisurely eddies, the narrative would resist, if not negate, the chronology and teleology of life-writing that point toward the subject's death. Thus Mark Twain seems to have intended a narrative that would sacrifice iconic verisimilitude (that of a chronological record of a historical existence) to indexical verisimilitude (that of a subtle register of a responsive consciousness). The writer's past would be subordinate to his present (and presence).

In any case, the writer had difficulty finding the right voice or the right form for this unfettered and spontaneous account of himself; indeed, his persistent complaint was that his narrative tended to sound too formal—too *written.* In his letter to Howells he guessed that when he reread the earlier predictation chapters, he would want to "do them over again with my mouth," as though oral revisions would be more spontaneous than written originals. If his intentions seem confused here, there are ample explanations: decreasing confidence in his talent; ambivalence about the implications of his pseudonym and perhaps uncertainty about the nature of his autobiographical identity; fear of self-exposure coupled with a compulsive tendency to convert experience into literary capital; and increasing self-consciousness about writing (or new awareness of its inherent self-reflexiveness). It is also quite possible that Mark Twain was simply attempting the impossible—the unmediated communication of self. Whatever the causes, while his *Autobiography* promised a new directness, it tended to reenact old evasions. Instead of revitalizing his life-writing, his innovative methods threatened to lead it to premature dead ends.

VIII

One way to define the impasse in which Mark Twain found himself is to note that some of the ideas he sought to express at last in uncensored form are inimical to autobiography, at least as it had been instituted in America by Franklin—as the self-written history of a self-determined life. He was increasingly drawn to two complementary, if not logically related, beliefs hostile to the myth of individual autonomy: that American democracy was giving way to plutocracy and that all human behavior was predetermined. Both are reflected in "The Character of Man," an essay written twenty years earlier but exhumed in 1906 for inclusion in his dictations. Though its tone and sources are very different, this attack on the notion of the unique individual in some ways anticipates the recent "critique of the subject":

> There are certain sweet-smelling sugar-coated lies current in the world which all politic men have apparently tacitly conspired together to support and perpetuate. One of these is, that there is such a thing in the world as independence: independence of thought, independence of opinion, independence of action. . . . And yet one other branch lie: to wit, that I am I, and you are you; that we are units, individuals, and have natures of our own, instead of being the tail end of a tapeworm of eternity of ancestors extending in linked procession back and back—to our source in the monkeys. . . . This makes well-nigh fantastic the suggestion that there can be such a thing as a personal, original, and responsible nature in a man, separable from that in him which is not

> original, and findable in such quantity as to enable the observer to say, This is a man, not a procession (II, 8–9).

Ultimately, Mark Twain's determinism better served his psychic than his literary needs, but he seems to have believed that compulsion, or its appearance, could release him from inhibitions and thus stimulate powerful verbal performance. His reminiscence of his childhood stint as a mesmerist's subject, published in *Mark Twain in Eruption,* suggests the psychological dynamics at work here.[25] By pretending to be mesmerized, he managed to convert an entire audience, including the skeptical and aristocratic Virginian, Dr. Peake, to belief in a sham. The clincher of the sham was his spurious "vision" of a Richmond fire, the details of which he had absorbed as a negligible guest at Dr. Peake's years before. (As an appropriated eyewitness account, his "vision" was in effect a purloined autobiography.) Though his triumph was necessarily a private one, the episode suggests that he was able to unleash aggressive impulses by denying his own responsibility for them. The process, which he found intensely gratifying, is in some ways analogous to the process of composition, which he also sometimes characterized as automatic: "As long as a book would write itself I was a faithful and interested amanuensis and my industry did not flag, but the minute that the book tried to shift to *my* head the labor of contriving its situations, . . . I put it away and dropped it out of my mind" (196). Indeed, the analogy suggests that he may have embraced suspect ideas *in order to* exercise, or enhance, his powers over others; his belief in determinism may be a later, more complex version of his earlier "faith" in mesmerism.

The incompatibility of autobiography and determinism is humorously and consciously demonstrated in his late essay, "The Turning Point of My Life," published in *Harper's Bazar* in February 1910. Twain, who was one of several famous writers asked to contribute an essay under that generic title, responded by deconstructing the notions of teleology and autobiography inherent in the rubric:

> It means the change in my life's course which introduced what must be regarded by me as the most *important* condition of my career. But it also implies—without intention, perhaps—that that turning point was *itself*, individually, the creator of the new condition. This gives it too much distinction, too much prominence, too much credit. It is only the *last* link in a very long chain of turning points commissioned to produce the weighty result; it is not any more important than the humblest of its ten thousand predecessors.[26]

Here, from a standpoint outside of autobiography, he discloses the deficiencies of a notion on which much life-writing depends. The idea of a turning point arbitrarily—and thus illegitimately—privileges selected events in one's life. In a deterministic universe, *every* event is a turning point—so none is. Moreover, this popular conceit involves an illusory sense of the autonomy of the self, falsely severing one's life from those of others. Thus, as in his burlesque autobiography, but in a more controlled and subtle way, he exposes the self-flattery implicit in autobiographical discourse. In addition, he neatly exposes the power of a paradigm to shape consciousness. By tracing his career as an author back through a tenuous chain of events to an apparently absurd source—his purposely contracting a case of measles as a boy—he demonstrates that so-called turning points are themselves produced by those points at which one turns one's attention to one's past—moments at which one engages in blinkered retrospection.

In attempting to subvert the paradigm by assigning such disproportionate significance to an obscure childhood episode, he may also have unwittingly demonstrated its power. While no biographer or critic, to my knowledge, has followed this lead in explaining Mark Twain's career, one *could.* (At the very least, the perverse behavior of the boy who intentionally caught measles makes an appropriate antecedent for that of the writer who ridicules his assigned topic.) Whether because of the ineluctable truthfulness of autobiography, or because of the ingenuity of readers, his "Turning Point" can no more absolutely defy appropriation as a "true false confession" than his *Burlesque Autobiography* could. Thus, while Mark Twain can parody the paradigm, he cannot entirely discredit it or escape it; even this attempted *reductio ad absurdum* acquires explanatory power through its conformity to the model. The notion that such accounts are arbitrary and generic constructions rather than authoritative reconstructions does not entirely deprive them of interest or even truth-value. His account demonstrates, in spite of itself, the powerful appeal of the *idea* of the turning point, which makes such neat sense of chaotic lives.

Another heretical dimension of his determinism (which he seems to take less seriously here than elsewhere) is expressed in his account of the Fall, whose outcome he views as caused "Not by Adam himself, but by his *temperament*—which he did not create and had no authority over" (464). If everything is determined, then there was no Fall, or, at least, humanity need not bear responsibility for it. This remark suggests that a primary function of Twain's determinism may have been to shield him from the assaults of his Presbyterian conscience. In view of the family tragedies of his later years and his evident—and, according to Hamlin Hill, deserved (62)—sense of guilt for some of them, it must have been a soothing creed. But if there is no original *sin,* there is no originality of any kind: the theological heresy is also a literary one. Hence his joke that he had nothing to do with his eventual attainment of authorship: "none of [these details] was forseen by me, none of them was planned by me, I was the author of none of them" (462).

Thus, while a denial of individual autonomy may have assuaged his conscience—and, on occasion, paradoxically stimulated literary productivity—it ultimately and inevitably threatened his sense of his authority as a writer. Indeed, the literary equivalent, or corollary, of this determinism was his growing skepticism about the possibility of original expression. Behind his sometimes muddled accounts of his autobiographical motives and methods looms his sense—reinforced by his discovery of his unconscious theft of the dedication of *The Innocents Abroad* from Oliver Wendell Holmes—that "all our phrasings are spiritualized shadows cast multitudinously from our readings: that no happy phrase of ours is ever quite original with us" (I, 241). This skepticism about the possibility of individual authorship haunted all of his later writing but especially, perhaps, his autobiography, which he advertised as an unprecedentedly true and original work that would escape the shadow of earlier writing—real rather than artificial narrative. In the *Autobiography,* he seems to have sought to evade the predicament he mocked in "The Turning Point"—imprisonment by tradition and convention.

IX

As might be expected, various impulses came into sharper conflict in the ultimate stage of the project, the dictations begun in 1906 with the assistance of Albert Bigelow Paine, his authorized biographer. One of these impulses was an extreme manifestation of his characteristic self-possessiveness. Granted, he acknowledged the tendency of his life story—like any celebrity's—to become, in Gertrude Stein's phrase, everybody's autobiography. For example, in the *Autobiography,* he expressed some good-natured irritation at the casual way in which the public assumed proprietorship of his life, citing clearly erroneous anecdotes people told him about his own childhood. Thus, he could humorously portray his own past as a collaborative, negotiated construction:

> These episodes used to vex me, years and years ago. But they don't vex me now. I am older. If a person thinks that he has known me at some time or other, all I require of him is that he shall consider it a distinction to have known me; and then, as a rule, I am perfectly willing to remember all about it and add some things that he has forgotten (II, 4–5).

But his response to those who sought to publish, and profit by, such materials was literally forbidding. According to Alan Gribben, "he came to value every morsel, every scrap, every particle of his life, placing a mercenary price on each incident and episode as they befell him" (46). In 1900, he wrote to a Will M. Clemens (no relation), who had published one book about him in 1892 and who planned to do another: "A man's history *is his own property* until the grave extinguishes his ownership in it. I am strenuously opposed to having books of a biographical character published about me while I am still alive" (48).

His willingness to cooperate with Paine is an instance of, not an exception to, this policy because his appointment of an official biographer was part of a concerted effort to control, and capitalize on, his public image—in perpetuity, if possible. Mark Twain's sense of his own property value was particularly acute at this time. In 1906 he went to Washington (making his first public appearance in the white suit that became his sartorial trademark) to testify at Congressional hearings in favor of a stronger copyright law. In the fall of 1907 he made his name a legal trademark, registering "Mark Twain Whiskey" and "Mark Twain Tobacco" with the office of patents, and forming a prototype of the Mark Twain Company.[27] Thus, Paine's later expression of concern—in a letter of August 1, 1926, to Harper and Brothers—about Mark Twain's lasting value as a literary property was in effect a posthumous reiteration of the writer's own position:

> I think on general principles it is a mistake to let any one else write about Mark Twain, as long as we can prevent it. . . . As soon as this is begun (writing about him at all, I mean) the Mark Twain we have "preserved"—the Mark Twain that we knew, the traditional Mark Twain—will begin to fade and change, and with that process the Harper Mark Twain property will depreciate.[28]

Apparently, the collaborators were in agreement on the necessity of sustaining the literary and commercial value of the authorial identity and on the appropriate means of doing so: monopolizing his biography.

The biographical enterprise also revitalized Mark Twain's languishing autobiographical project. The new arrangements with Paine involved regular dictation and competent stenography, both of which made for consistent and satisfying productivity. In addition, Paine's assumption of responsibility for a biography freed Twain once and for all from the burden of writing a factual chronicle of his life—which in any case he was loath to do. The results are evident in the text. At this point, the manner of the narrative changes considerably: the author begins to experiment with inserted texts, zigzag more freely between past and present, and comment on current events in his own voice. As all readers beginning with Paine have realized, these dictations move the narrative further away from conventional autobiography and closer to the author's idiosyncratic sense of it.

In a way, as the young man who would perpetuate the author's name Paine became the heir that pseudonymity (and lack of a surviving male child) denied him. But in view of the Byzantine internal politics of the household (well documented by Hamlin Hill), it would have been a minor miracle had the relationship between biographer and subject, surrogate son and father, been entirely harmonious. Evidently, it was not. Though Paine ultimately triumphed in the infighting over the general management of household affairs and over access to the writer's letters (which Clemens' daughter Clara had planned to edit herself), Mark Twain was troubled by the dissension and by his own declining authority in his own home. In any case, his relationship with his in-house biographer was at times sufficiently strained that in later years Mark Twain was known to express a wish for "some Paine-killer."[29]

Nor was their collaboration without friction. In subtle but significant ways, the initiation of the authorized biography finally complicated, even threatened, the autobiographical project. The dictations, which were resumed in connection with Paine's project, were in danger of being subsumed by it—of becoming a means to an (other's) end rather than an end in themselves. Paine's dating of their relationship from their first game of billiards reminds us that it was always competitive (111, 1324–25); the image of caroming balls nicely foreshadows the contained collision of their interdependent projects.

That the symbiotic, or perhaps parasitic, relationship between their projects created confusion about which took precedence is clear in Mark Twain's first statement on subject: "My idea is this: that I write an autobiography. When that autobiography is finished—or even before it is finished, but no doubt after it is finished—then you take the manuscript and decide on how much of a biography to make" (I, 269). The conflict of interest between the biographer and the autobiographer is also evident in Paine's account of the inception of their collaboration. According to Paine, he not only initiated the biographical project, but also suggested some innovative methods of generating materials for it:

> I said that in similar undertakings a part of the work had been done with a stenographer, who had made the notes while I prompted the subject to recall a procession of incidents and episodes, to be supplemented with every variety of material obtainable—letters and other documentary accumulations (III, 1264).

At their next meeting, however, Twain modified the plan to serve his autobiographical project and defined the ground rules that would govern the production and disposition of the memoranda. The clear implication was that he should have more freedom in the process and more control over the product of the dictations than Paine might have allowed:

> He proposed to double the value and interest of our employment by letting his dictations continue the form of those earlier autobiographical chapters. . . . He said he did not think he could follow a definite chronological program; that he would like to wander about, picking up this point and that, as memory or fancy prompted, without any particular biographical order. It was his purpose, he declared, that his dictations should not be published until he had been dead a hundred years or more. . . . He wished to pay the stenographer, and to own these memoranda . . . allowing me free access to them for any material I might find valuable. I could also suggest subjects for dictation, and ask particulars of any special episode or period. . . . [W]e set to work without further prologue (III, 1266–67).

Though their disagreement was minor, and was quickly and amicably settled, it may be viewed in retrospect as the first skirmish for initiative and control over the collaborative auto/biographical enterprise.

The menace Paine posed to Mark Twain's autonomy is suggested by the extent to which Paine eventually intruded into the biography. After the narrative reaches 1906, Paine begins to employ the first-person pronoun, singular as well as plural; he even leaves his subject off stage to recount his own excursion to interview sources. Once he appears as a character in his own narrative, it threatens to become a species of autobiography—Paine's memoir, rather than his biography, of Mark Twain. Furthermore, the decline of the dictations in the last two years of Mark Twain's life and his conception of an alternative method of composition—letters to be addressed to friends, but not sent—reflect his alienation from those around him and a need to address a trustworthy audience through a more secure medium—that is, to exert more authority over his autobiography.

This, the final stage of the autobiography, was evidently composed in conscious anticipation of death: in 1906, Mark Twain spent some time planning his own funeral—including its date (Hill, 145). James M. Cox has demonstrated that the *Autobiography* would prolong the life of "Mark Twain" not just by extending his copyright, but also by assuring ample posthumous publication of new material:

> By promising a room full of forbidden surprises to readers a hundred years hence, Mark Twain was able to bestow upon himself a particular kind of immortality which would make him an actual literary competitor—a genuine publishing author—long after his death (305–6).

Obviously, the primary purpose of the biography was also to ensure his immortality; in theory, then, the two projects served the same end.

But their *forms,* which point to different versions of immortality, are implicitly in conflict. The premise of the biography, which Paine himself referred to as his "undertaking" (I, ix), was Mark Twain's imminent demise; it sought to secure Mark Twain's lasting but posthumous fame. In contrast, the autobiography aspired to confirm his enduring vitality. Insofar as Paine's chronological narrative conveyed its subject inexorably along a time line that would have death as its terminus, Mark Twain might well have resented—and wished at times to impede, thwart, or subvert—his biographer's project. In the event, both the theory and practice of the late dictations suggest that at times Mark Twain felt himself to be fighting for his Life with his biographer-in-residence.

Consider his incorporation of his daughter Susy's biography into his narrative. Here was a forerunner of Paine's authorized biography: though it was begun without his permission, or even his knowledge, it was written by an insider and, despite its subject's repeated protestations of its frankness, it gives a devoted account of him as a father and husband. Indeed, in the isolation of his last years, it served to restore his sense of the wholeness of his family and to renew his sense of his worth and status as its head: "As I read it *now,* . . . it is still a king's message to me, and brings me the same dear surprise it brought me then . . . and I feel as the humble and unexpectant must feel when their eyes fall upon the edict that raises them to the ranks of the noble" (II, 65). The appeal of Susy's biography, then, lay largely in its unquestioned loyalty and its unalloyed praise. It was unthreatening not only because it was naively written, but also because it was finished and entirely in his control. (This latter attribute derived, tragically, from the anomaly of the young biographer's dying before her subject.)

Mark Twain's salvaging of and expanding on Susy's memoir may involve a psychic withdrawal from his collaboration with Paine. His praise for her achievement may implicitly disparage the authorized biography. For example, the following remark may tacitly impugn Paine's discernment and the reliability of his book: "It was quite evident that several times, at breakfast and dinner, in those long-past days, I was posing for the biography. In fact, I clearly remember that I *was* doing that—and I also remember that Susy detected it" (II, 65–66). Mark Twain bolstered his paternal authority by incorporating Susy's biography into his autobiography even as his dictations were being consumed by Paine's.

Also, consider the sheer volume and achronology of the late dictations, which defy reduction to a simple narrative line. Unlike Grant, who marshalled his words and marched his narrative to its preordained conclusion before his death could arrest it, Mark Twain dictated prodigiously, digressed impulsively, and dallied resolutely, as if prolonging his story, in the manner of Scheherezade, would lengthen his life. He clearly relished the openness and open-endedness of his "apparently systemless system":

> It is a . . . complete and purposed jumble—a course which begins nowhere, follows no specified route, and can never reach an end while I am alive, for the reason that if I should talk to the stenographer two hours a day for a hundred years, I should still never be able to set down a tenth part of the things which have interested me in my lifetime. I told Howells that this autobiography of mine would live a couple of thousand years without any effort and would then take a fresh start and live the rest of the time (II, 246).

Far from essaying objective, let alone definitive, retrospection, his method seems designed to deny even the prospect of an ending. A notable element in Mark Twain's final dictations is his insistence that the self ultimately eludes apprehension in narrative, whether biographical or autobiographical. Even as he submitted to having his life taken by another, he implied that the real Mark Twain would not be seen whole, or clearly, through the Paine of the biography:

> What a wee little part of a person's life are his acts and his words! His real life is led in his head, and is known to none but himself. All day long, and every day, the mill of his brain is grinding, and his *thoughts,* not those other things, are his history. His acts and his words are merely the visible, thin crust of his world. . . . The mass of him is hidden—it and its volcanic fires that toss and boil, and never rest, night nor day. These are his life, and they are not written, and cannot be written. . . . Biographies are but the clothes and buttons of the man—the biography of the man himself cannot be written (I, 2).

There is a strange, even incoherent, mixture of tropes here (the volcano and the mill), but the equation of a person's thoughts with his history seems calculated to privilege autobiography over biography. The thrust of this passage, therefore, may be to defend the integrity and uniqueness of the self against the presumptive claims of biography. If Twain could not prevent his biography from being completed, he would impugn its value: authorized biography might come as close to the man as his garments, but it would necessarily disguise or obscure the naked self.

Insofar as it mimics the flow of consciousness, the narrative "stream" of the *Autobiography* would be the lava of the erupting volcano. Although the dictations would be the ultimate, most intimate verbal representation of the self, they would still be woefully incomplete:

> Life does not consist mainly—or even largely—of facts and happenings. It consists mainly of the storm of thoughts that is forever blowing through one's head. Could you set them down stenographically? No. Could you set down any considerable fraction of them stenographically? No. Fifteen stenographers hard at work couldn't even keep up. Therefore a full autobiography has never been written, and it never will be. . . . and so if I had been doing my whole autobiographical duty ever since my youth, all the library buildings on earth could not contain the result (I, 283).

Facing the end of his life, Mark Twain defined autobiography, as well as biography, in a way that would minimize its threat to his vitality.

Indeed, as he vied with Paine to have the last word on his life, he threatened to make his autobiography a kind of *anti*biography. The dictations may have been gratifying not because they came closer than biography to charting his life, but because they too predictably and necessarily failed to do so.

Remarkably, Paine managed to publish the full three-volume biography in 1912, only two years after Twain's death. In contrast, the two-volume *Autobiography* did not appear until 1924. Of course, even then it was far from complete. Mark Twain's *Autobiography* still awaits its definitive version, having now defied three successive editors. As a result of the patchwork pattern of the manuscript's editing and publication, Mark Twain's literary remains continue to be unreadable in a fundamental sense. As James M. Cox has seen, there may be a grand joke in our waiting for the revelation that the texts, quite possibly, can never deliver (305–6). Ironically, the inability of the Twain industry to produce an authoritative version in the eighty years since his death may be a measure of the success rather than the failure of Mark Twain's autobiography. The narrative's closure has proved as elusive as its disclosures.

Of course, one could press harder for revelations afforded by the texts already published. One could probe the writer's rationalization of his tendency to include trivial incidents and to exclude the traumatic events of his later years:

> An autobiography that leaves out the little things and enumerates only the big ones is no proper picture of the man's life at all; his life consists of his feelings and his interests, with here and there an incident apparently big or little to hang the feelings on (I, 288).

(The tragedies of his later life, which were naturally minimized in Paine's official biography, escaped detailed treatment until the publication of Hamlin Hill's *God's Fool* in 1973.)

One could resist the author's attempts to divert our attention from the unpleasantnesses of his family life to current events. For example, one could interpret his strange obsession with dissension among the president's staff as a projection onto the White House of the domestic tension of his own household. One might recuperate his sketch of his brother Orion as a self-portrait in a convex mirror:

> I think he was the only person I have ever known in whom pessimism and optimism were lodged in exactly equal proportions. . . . He had

another conspicuous characteristic, and it was the father of those which I have just spoken of. This was an intense lust for approval (II, 271).

One might thus attempt to correct for Twain's persistent self-evasions.

One might also ponder further the means of the final texts' production. Though the reasons may be obscure, it seems clear that Mark Twain found the act of dictation deeply and inherently satisfying; we should take his word on that. The method had its regressive dimension—after all, it involved a retreat into, and an oral performance, in bed, which was the site of childhood as well as adult pleasures. Moreover, it provided, or seemed to, a way of escaping what Mark Twain saw as the tyranny of time and penmanship—the arbitrary constraints of linear narration and the hand-held instrument. His experimental innovations (including dictation) were part of a strategy that would take him beyond conventional autobiography and enable him to play with his Life, rather than simply to replay his life.

The enterprise may have had an aggressive dimension, as well. If, as he said in "Old Times on the Mississippi," writers were mere manacled servants of the public, and if writing was, at its best, a matter of *taking* dictation from the muse, then what greater final self-gratification than to turn the tables and assume at last the role of *dictator,* with all of its political connotations. The authority Mark Twain first aspired to was that of the pilot, which differs both from the elected leader's and from the writer's (especially the humorist's) precisely because of its pure autonomy. (Subordinate to no human authority, it was subject only to the power of the Mississippi.) The imagery of natural flow in his late meditations on autobiographical narrative suggests that at least in writing his *Autobiography,* he sought the literary equivalent of the unconstrained natural forces like rivers and volcanoes. The act of speaking his life, then, must have promised a kind of supreme authorial presence: in dictating his autobiography, he may have sought an authority that had always eluded him as a writer and humorist.

Yet as a result of the unconventional, inconsistent, and intermittent process of its production, *Mark Twain's Autobiography* in some ways reinforces rather than reverses the implications of the earlier more playfully pseudonymous autobiographical writing. Perhaps the mask of Mark Twain is lowered in the final autobiography, but that is not to say that we glimpse Samuel Clemens directly. Indeed, the recession of pseudonymity in this text may suggest that pseudonymous autobiography is *not* as problematic as it might seem.

For this text, though not self-reflexively pseudonymous, is still deeply perplexed by questions of identity, as if the ludic energy that went into name- and word-play in earlier texts was here channeled into formal experiment and, occasionally, philosophical speculation. One implication of Mark Twain's entire autobiographical enterprise may be that pseudonymous autobiography merely acknowledges what conventional autobiography nominally suppresses, the sense of self-division essential to it.

The pseudonym "Mark Twain" suggests that autobiography, like humor, is always generated by—or generates—a sense of the division of the self. Because it is self-reflexive, and confesses its falseness, this pseudonym also tells a truth about all authorial names: they mask duplicity, and even multiplicity. Furthermore, Mark Twain's entire autobiographical project suggests that autobiography consists of self-impersonation in a *fundamental* way: impersonation of *a* self as well as of *one's* self. Thus, the two most remarkable aspects of Mark Twain's autobiography—its pseudonymity and its humor—may not be as anomalous as they appear, because the duplicity that underlies both Mark Twain's humor and his pseudonym is in some way necessary and essential to autobiography. By their extravagance, the humor and pseudonymity of Mark Twain's autobiographies expose what is less evident but no less true of all autobiography: it demonstrates not the identity of the author with narrator, and subject, but the distance and difference between them.

6

(En)Slave(d) Narrative: Early Afro-American Life-Writing

I

The issue of the authority of autobiography lies close to the heart of abolitionist slave narratives. More than most life narratives, slave narratives were conceived of and composed as historical testimony. At the time of their publication, however, the intense debate over race and slavery furnished obvious motives for questioning their veracity. As a result, they have been intensely scrutinized from the time of their composition to the present. Apologists for slavery reflexively denounced them out of loyalty to the institution whose immorality and brutality the texts purported to document. In anticipation of such hostile readers, the narratives' sponsors submitted them to harsh preemptive testing. Abolitionists, who were fearful of having their cause discredited by unchecked exaggeration or outright fraud, closely questioned the texts before publication. Theodore Weld advised one abolitionist writer: "Look sharp! Pass it under the blaze of a high focus, for it will be searched for flaws with *eagle eyes*, and a very little one will be seized and trumpeted as a sample of the whole argument."[1] Others, who were more disinterested, questioned the conditions they described or the literacy of the accounts themselves. As a result of their controversial content and aims, the narratives were subjected to scrutiny never applied before or since to a *class* of autobiographies. To tell the story of one's escape from slavery was to run a gauntlet of critics: the narrator's progress toward freedom, like the slave's, was hindered, if not obstructed, by the surveillance of both friend and foe.

The two major constituents of the authority of slave narrative, corresponding roughly to content and form, were veracity and authenticity. Probably the foremost issue was the question of the narratives' veracity—their truth-value as records of slavery—because they were read as "historical discourse," in Roland Barthes' sense: " . . . a matter traditionally subject, in our culture, to the prescriptions of historical 'science,' to be judged only by the criteria of conformity to 'what really happened' and by the principles of 'rational' exposition."[2] In John Searle's terms, the narratives were taken as "assertives"—statements that attempt to fit words to the world in a way that can be "literally characterize[d] . . . as (inter alia) true or false."[3] Abolitionist editors tried to maximize accuracy and credibility not only by editing skeptically, but also by appending supporting documentation. The seriousness with which truth-claims were taken had to do with the urgency of the subject, to proponents and opponents of slavery alike. In slave narrative, then, referentiality was taken as an attempt to describe, in an empirically verifiable way, an extratextual reality, and not as a merely formal gesture or a generic convention.

Given the goals of abolitionist slave narrative, this manner of reading the narratives may seem not only inevitable, but also fair; after all, in principle all autobiography is held accountable to facts. The case of slave narratives, however, is an extreme instance of autobiographers being held in a legalistic sense to an "autobiographical pact"[4] to tell the truth about the past, or at least to make statements that can be meaningfully verified. While this response may have been nondiscriminatory in principle, in fact it heightened the inherent danger of writing a slave narrative, for the very texts that asserted the narrators' freedom usually proved them to be legal chattel. (The inherent insecurity of the fugitive was both exposed and aggravated by the Fugitive Slave Law of 1850.) Some narrators, like Frederick Douglass, were bold enough to identity people and places in the real world, but others suppressed details for fear that such documentation would expose them to re-enslavement. (Some resorted to replacing proper names with initials followed by dashes [Blassingame, xxiii]; ironically, this was a convention of fiction that simulated nonfiction.) Those who dared not name names were far from paranoid: the very specificity necessary to establish the narrators' authority threatened to destroy their autonomy. Their narratives could literally "give them away."

II

As it happened, the published narratives stood up well to challenges: of the few whose particulars were questioned closely, only one or two were effectively discredited (Blassingame, xxiii–xxv). Still, their impact on the hearts and minds of mid-nineteenth-century Americans, let alone on discrete historical events, is difficult to measure. The book reputed to have had the greatest impact on the popular mind of the period was a novel—Harriet Beecher Stowe's *Uncle Tom's Cabin,* to which Abraham Lincoln reportedly assigned responsibility for the Civil War. That Stowe's novel drew powerfully on the materials of the slave narrative suggests that the narratives may have effected their end, in part, in an indirect and unintended way—by making slavery available to the fictive imagination and by buttressing the credibility of such fictions, rather than by presenting it directly as indisputable fact.

In any case, Stowe's classic demonstrates the commingling and mutual influence of the slave narrative and the sentimental novel in antebellum popular literature. Significantly, Stowe did not merely adapt the slave narrative's materials: she tried to establish her novel's veracity by retroactively pinning down its incidents to real-world events recorded in slave narratives, especially that of Josiah Henson, who thus became known as the "original Uncle Tom." In turn, Henson and others endeavored in presenting their narratives to draw on the prestige and popularity of Stowe's novel.[5] For this and other reasons, Henson's autobiography nicely illustrates some problematic aspects of the genre's authority.

According to its modern editor, Robin Winks, Henson's narrative was the most widely read, frequently revised, and influential of slave narratives (v)—largely because its association with *Uncle Tom's Cabin* assured a popularity that lasted long after the Civil War had removed the genre's original impetus. Ironically, but not surprisingly, it was also one of the least authoritative of the narratives. Its authority was compromised from the start, and Henson's exploitation of the Stowe connection inevitably eroded his narrative's veracity and authenticity. The first version (1849) was ghostwritten by Samuel Eliot, a former mayor of Boston and moderate abolitionist, yet this edition was relatively simple, accurate, and modest in its claims (vi); after all, its publication predated that of *Uncle Tom's Cabin.* In later editions, especially those ghostwritten by the Englishman John Lobb, the relation between the narrative and the facts of Henson's life became more and more tenuous, as did Henson's authority over his autobiography.

The results of the exploitation of the best-selling novel are evident in Lobb's 1881 edition of *An Autobiography of the Rev. Josiah Henson, ("Uncle Tom")*. In his prefatory note Lobb links Henson to the novel by giving a false account of the novel's genesis and by misleadingly quoting Stowe's *Key to Uncle Tom's Cabin*. In addition, he uses oral testimony elicited from Henson as a kind of unauthorized key to the novel. Characterizing Henson's narrative as the major, if not the only, source of Stowe's novel was clearly a way of enhancing the narrative's market value: the memoirs of "Uncle Tom" would command greater sales than those of a slave with a less recognizable "name." But Winks' research turned up no evidence that Stowe had met Henson, corresponded with him, or even read his narrative before writing her novel. Indeed, the flattering preface written by Harriet Beecher Stowe for the 1858 edition (and retained in the 1881 edition) studiously avoids mentioning Uncle Tom; nevertheless, Lobb did not hesitate to do what Stowe refused to do: identify Uncle Tom unequivocally and solely with Henson. Of course, Henson had every right to market his own life as literary property—and he had a greater moral claim to his own story than did Stowe—but the opportunistic efforts of his white ghostwriter to ride Stowe's literary coattails somewhat compromise the integrity of this edition.

The exploitation of the novel's popularity involves both collaborators in some odd maneuvers. For example, Lobb begins his prefatory note with the curious gesture of accounting for his subject's survival:

> Having heard that some persons have expressed doubts as to the identity of Reverend Josiah Henson with the "Uncle Tom" of Mrs. Stowe's book, chiefly because Mrs. Stowe *kills* her hero, we deem it only just to all parties to give the following explanation and corroboration (8).

Lobb explains that "faithfulness to her design and the mournful facts of slave life demanded" Tom's death in spite of the survival of his original. He does not acknowledge, however, that the logic of his form, collaborative autobiography, demanded that he take Henson's Life into his hands; he conveniently ignores the extent to which he plays Harriet Beecher Stowe to Henson's Uncle Tom.

Henson explained his outliving Uncle Tom in somewhat different terms, attributing his comparative longevity to providential protection: "Though [Stowe] made her hero die, it was fit that she did this to complete her story; and if God had not given to me a giant's constitution, I should have died over and over again long before I reached Canada" (114). Here Henson boasts of a better "constitution" than that of the fictional character. But since Stowe had claimed that *Uncle Tom's Cabin* was divinely inspired, Henson in effect asserts his *parity* with the immortal Tom—both are authored by God. In any case, the attempts of both editor and narrator to compare the origins and fate of "Josiah Henson" to those of "Uncle Tom" implicitly concede that their "Henson" is derived from a novel, if he is not himself a fictional character.

Perhaps his narrative's great popularity emboldened Henson to make the following revealing claim:

> I have been called "Uncle Tom," and I feel proud of the title. If my humble words in any way inspired that gifted lady to write such a plaintive story that the whole community has been touched with pity for the sufferings of the poor slave, I have not lived in vain; for I believe that her book was the glorious beginning of the glorious end. It was a wedge that finally rent asunder that gigantic fabric with a fearful crash (113–14).

These words are far from "humble." The suggestion that Henson may have inspired the book that started the war that finished slavery makes him, by implication, the ultimate "author" of the Civil War and Emancipation (as Benjamin Franklin's autobiography characterized him as the "author" of the Revolution). Unfortunately, Henson can make this claim only by identifying with, and accepting the name of, a fictional character invented by a white author; though he views "the title" "Uncle Tom" as honorific, it is (like a slave name) not his *proper* name. In tracing his own "title" to a popular novel, he very nearly renounces the "title" to his own Life. Unlike Mark Twain, who fought for his Life with his authorized biographer, Henson and his editor may unwittingly convey title to Henson's Life to Harriet Beecher Stowe.

In any case, Henson was no more the sole author of the narrative that made this audacious claim than he was of the Civil War and Emancipation. The coincidence of the style of the editor's note and that of the narrative indicates how completely Lobb controlled the language and gestures of this late autobiography. This is nearly acknowledged when, late in the narrative, "Henson" announces that out of gratitude for Lobb's management of his tour of England he has assigned him the book's copyright. Here, in what must be a unique moment in collaborative autobiography, the "narrator" introduces his ghostwriter and assigns him legal ownership of the narrative. Had the passage explicitly admitted Lobb's ghostwriting, it might stand as an instance of remarkable and reassuring candor. (After all, Lobb is entitled to a share of the book's copyright and its royalties.) Since it does not do so, it further obscures the text's authorship and undermines its authority.

An incident in the text nicely demonstrates the appropriation of another's memory that collaborative autobiography may involve. Long after the Civil War, when Henson visits his aging former mistress, she extracts from his retentive memory facts concerning her dead husband's service in the War of 1812—information necessary to establish her claim to a pension (161). She elicits his version of events as a way of securing her future, not as a complement to her own sense of the past. Though polite, even affectionate, she continues to exploit her celebrated ex-slave. In a similar fashion, by hiding behind Henson's persona in assigning himself the book's copyright, Lobb seems to manipulate Henson's memory for his own gain.

In his editions of Henson's autobiography, Lobb shamelessly traded on the success of the novel supposedly based on its first edition, by falsely representing the relation between the novelist and the ex-slave, the novel and the "autobiography." Thus, a process that began with the retroactive grounding of a novel in historical reality (as "transcribed" in slave narrative) ended with the valorization of an autobiography in relation to that fiction. The affiliation of novels such as Stowe's and narratives such as Henson's suggests the importance of the slave narrative in shaping the discourse of the day. As Henry Louis Gates, Jr., has suggested, the slave narrative played a major role in evoking (or provoking) the plantation novel and in stimulating antislavery literature of many types.[6] In spite of restrictions on its circulation into South, then, the currency of the slave narrative flowed freely across the border between the domains of fact and of fiction.

This mutual cross-referencing of novel and slave narrative, however, suggests that the explicit concern for the narratives' veracity may have been beside the point. If novels and narratives could authenticate each other, then authentication was not entirely—if at all—a matter of empirical verifiability. Perhaps it was more importantly a matter of who was authorized by what institutions to make what sorts of assertions about slavery. That is, credibility was as much a function of the institutional sites from which writers exerted their authority as it was of the correspondence of a textual record and an extratextual phenomenon. Needless to say, those sites were largely controlled by Northern white middle-class males.

III

With coming of the Civil War, Emancipation, and Reconstruction, the point of the slave narratives might seem to have been made, their end attained, and the issue of their veracity made moot. After all, the narratives' ultimate goal was not to document slavery definitively as a historical phenomenon but to abolish it completely as an existential condition. Yet, the question of the authority of slave testimony was inevitably raised again by historians of slavery in this century. Following Ulrich B. Phillips, many historians at first tended to dismiss the testimony of the slave narratives out of hand as biased and distorted[7]—not "history" at all, but pure propaganda. Eventually, however, revisionist historians succeeded in reassembling and rehabilitating the narratives as primary sources. Thus, history *has* repeated itself—as discourse, if not as event—for the historical controversies of the twentieth century have echoed the historic debates of the nineteenth. As Gates has pointed out,

> What had been a polemical necessity for antebellum reviewers of the narratives . . . became in the twentieth century an academic necessity among historians: these scholars had to *establish* the historical accuracy of their evidence before they could analyze it in their recreation of the slave's experience.[8]

Once again, the slave narrators won the right to be heard, but not without difficulty and not without assistance: they still depended on the authority of others to render them audible and visible.

Historians of slavery have traditionally sought to determine which narratives are authentic, and then to assess their evidence and incorporate it into a developing picture of the peculiar institution. While sensitive to the possibility of bias, they have been more concerned with the matter than the manner of presentation. Indeed, some have assumed a stance similar to that of contemporary readers, who associated a minimum of manner—of rhetoric or affect—with maximum documentary authority. Their ideal is a narrative so transparent that it effaces its own mediating effect, exposing the matter "plainly." While most historians now acknowledge that no text functions as a window, or even as a mirror, many still approach literary mediation as something to be corrected for, rather than analyzed as evidence. At least, historical analysis of slave narrative reveals a persistent impulse to look beyond or through written sources to the phenomena they depict.

For example, although John Blassingame admits that "many of the more reliable narratives contain elements [such as literary devices] that cannot be attributed to the blacks . . . ," he maintains that "a majority of [the abolitionist editors] faithfully recorded the factual details they received from the former slaves" and goes on to discuss ways of separating the editors' "rhetoric" from the ex-slaves' "sentiments"—and the "facts" from both of these more subjective elements (xxvii, xxix, xxxii–xxxiii). Yet his own description of the production of a typical narrative might arouse skepticism about the possibility of separating the constituents of such collaborative discourse:

> Generally the former slave lived in the same locale as the editor and had given oral accounts of his bondage. If the fugitive believed that the white man truly respected blacks, they discussed the advisability of publishing his account. Once the white man persuaded the black to record his experiences for posterity, the dictation might be completed in a few weeks or be spread over two or three years. Often the editor read the story to the fugitive, asking for elaboration of certain points and clarification of confusing and contradictory details. When the dictation ended, the editor frequently compiled appendices to corroborate the narrative. . . . If those among the editor's friends who first heard the story doubted its authenticity, they sometimes interrogated the fugitive for hours (xxii).

This necessarily general account is probably fairly accurate. The fact that it is based largely on editors' accounts, however, typifies the difficulties of working with such texts; available accounts of the collaborative process suffer from the same bias as the products of that process. In any case, the dynamics of the collaborative enterprises remain somewhat obscure. The account posits a kind of ur-narrative ("oral accounts") on which the written account is based, but the impulse behind these original accounts is necessarily indeterminate, as the passive voice suggests, and its audience unspecified.

Thus, Blassingame's reconstruction of the process does not enable us to ascribe initiative with any confidence to most ex-slaves. In his sketch of the ontogeny of a slave narrative, agency shifts—grammatically and otherwise—from the black informant (who "believed the white man"), to the pair (who "discussed the advisability" of publication), to the white editor alone (who "persuaded the black to record his experiences," "read the story [back] to the fugitive" for elaboration and clarification, and "compiled" supplementary documents). Moreover, the account culminates in "interrogation." This version of the protocol of composition suggests that the two dimensions of authority—veracity and authenticity—may not only be distinct, they may be in conflict. It sounds as though well-meaning editorial attempts to maximize accuracy, so as to preempt criticism, very likely diminished the authenticity of the narrative—the degree to which it issued spontaneously and unmodified from the informant. The editors' agenda inevitably intruded upon both the collaborative process and its product.

An attractively simple way of "resolving" the problem of collaborative authorship is to disqualify its products as autobiography. After all, by definition, collaborative enterprise has more than one author, and among the few essential elements of autobiography would seem to be the identity (and the singularity) of author and subject. Collaborative life-writing inevitably crosses autobiography with biography: the squeamish will shun the mongrel offspring. To do so, however, is to ban from the "most democratic province of letters" whole classes of people—various unlettered minority groups (most notably, many Afro-Americans and Native Americans) and others disinclined, though presumably able, to write their own lives (typically, this includes tycoons, politicians, athletes, entertainers, and other celebrities).

The latter group differs from the former not only in its greater degree of literacy, but also in two other crucial ways. First, the high visibility of celebrities creates a demand, or at least a market, for their narratives, whereas for anonyms, visibility depends on—though it is far from guaranteed by—the composition of an autobiography. Second, celebrities are in a better position to control the collaborative process and to profit, literally and figuratively, from its product. They are better known and more powerful than their collaborators, while the reverse is usually true of minority autobiographers. The submission by celebrities to the "authority" of their collaborators, or ghostwriters, is voluntary and thought by them to be in their interest: it saves them time, effort, and possible embarrassment, and it promises to make them rich and (more) famous.[9] In contrast, the submission of minority autobiographers to the authority of their collaborators is a function of their limited power, literacy, and access to media of communication. To rule out the possibility of collaborative autobiography is to discriminate against minorities on the basis of their disadvantage. (Insofar as the writing of autobiography produces a self, to reject collaborative autobiography is in a sense also to deny some segments of the population the right to reproduce themselves.)

This is not to say that collaborative autobiography is unproblematic. Clearly, for reasons just suggested, its authority is often deeply compromised, but it should neither be rejected automatically nor embraced naively as autobiography. Rather, cases must be scrutinized individually for the problems peculiar to each. The project for contemporary readers of autobiography should be to reexamine both those, like *Black Elk Speaks* (and perhaps *The Autobiography of Malcolm X*), that have been largely exempt from criticism, and those that have been denied status as autobiography. Indeed, the purpose of such reexamination should not be solely to decide on their status, which is usually ambiguous, but to investigate the process by which disadvantaged individuals or groups may infiltrate the realm of literature through the medium of collaborative autobiography.

IV

Not all slave narrative is collaborative, of course, but its authority is often problematic, even when the ex-slave's authorship is undisputed. Thus, in a new context and for new reasons, the authority of the slave narrative is undergoing yet another close examination. Skepticism of the referential dimension of language, suspicion of the integrity of the "I," and attention to the ideology of form all play a role in the contemporary reexamination of slave narrative. In particular, recent analysts have been critical of the authentication of abolitionist slave narratives by surrounding texts. For a long time, this extra-authorial material was ignored or looked through, as a frame: close reading focused on the narratives themselves, thought to be the only parts that deserved, or rewarded, interpretation.

Sidonie Smith's *Where I'm Bound: Patterns of Slavery and Freedom in Black Autobiography* may illustrate the kind of approach more recent critics have called into question. Her pioneering book established the primacy of slavery and freedom as the definitive poles of black autobiography, but her treatment of slave narrative too readily assumes that the act of narration is unconstrained:

> The slave narrative represented in itself a spiritual transcendence over the brutalizing experience of slavery. In the act of writing, the slave narrator could again liberate himself from slavery—in this case the spiritual slavery of the past rather than the physical slavery of the South. He achieved this spiritual liberation by giving distance to the pain of the past through the imposition of artistic form on the matter of experience, thus gaining control and mastery over it.[10]

Smith implies that due to the benevolent sponsorship of abolitionists and to the presence of a relatively open-minded audience, the slave narrator exerted a high degree of authority over his own text—such that his freedom as a narrator was nearly as complete as his lack of it as a slave. The effect of her analysis of the narratives is to drive a wedge between the debilitating experience of slavery and the autonomous act of recounting it.

If Smith contrasted the autobiographical character's suffering under slavery to the narrator's triumph over its psychological residue, more recent analysis has emphasized the narrator's continued subjection to the racism implicit in linguistic and narrative conventions themselves. Thus, contemporary readings often focus on the authority of autobiography in a narrow but crucial sense: the extent of the narrator's control over the production and consumption of his narrative. With the publication of Robert B. Stepto's *From Behind the Veil* (1979), which submitted the framing material itself to withering scrutiny, criticism of the slave narrative took a long stride in this new direction. What had been overlooked as a vestige of the oral presentation of narratives to "live" audiences at abolitionist meetings was analyzed as a symbolic gesture in its own right. Stepto characterized the enclosing of the slaves' narratives by "segregated" texts as a "race ritual." According to him, in introducing, documenting, and vouching for the slaves' narratives, white editors in effect addressed white readers over the invisible bodies of black narrators. The narrators' credibility depended on character references from white authorities; the veracity of their tales depended on extranarrative documentation; and the interpretive framework and desired response to the tale were established before the narrative voice was even heard. The narrator was granted authority at the dispensation of the sponsoring institution, and white editors often literally had the first and last words. In short, the format designed to attack the most virulent form of institutional racism in America itself enacted a form of discrimination and domination.[11]

This problem can be clearly seen in Henry Bibb's *Narrative.* The outstanding feature of its content is the extent to which it is taken up with life on the road: Bibb lives in perpetual motion, fleeing slavery in search of freedom for himself, and reentering it in quest of freedom for his family (Andrews, 151–52). The striking aspect of its presentation, however, is what Stepto has called "the most elaborate guarantee of authenticity found in the slave narrative canon" (6). Stepto has shown how the presence of the guarantors' voices in "segregated texts" diminishes Bibb's "control over the text and event of the narrative itself" (7). The very devices intended to establish the narrative's veracity tend insidiously, if unintentionally, to undermine its authenticity. Thus, the two most notable features of Bibb's narrative are in direct conflict: while his text portrays the *character* as functioning, to an extraordinary degree, as an autonomous (secret) agent operating on the margins of white institutions, its context characterizes the *narrator* not as a free lance but as a faithful and trusted laborer in the abolitionist propaganda mill. Bibb seems less autonomous as an author than as a fugitive.

The issues raised by Lucius Matlack's introduction are the usual ones, i.e., the authenticity and veracity of the narrative, but the elaborateness of their treatment makes his introduction unusually revealing of the process by which a black man was authorized to write his own life in antebellum America. Matlack begins by drawing attention to the narrative's high degree of literacy as problematic, and his first move is to parry the anticipated objection that such a literate narrative *cannot* be authentic:

> To many, the elevated style, purity of diction, and easy flow of language, frequently exhibited, will appear unaccountable and contradictory, in view of his want of early mental culture. But to the thousands who have listened with delight to his speeches on anniversary and other occasions, these same traits will be noted as unequivocal evidence of originality. Very few men present in their written composition so perfect a transcript of their style as is exhibited by Mr. Bibb.[12]

Rather than explaining or examining Bibb's acquisition of a writing style so inconsistent with his origins, the editor asserts its identity with his platform style: the authenticity of the written style is grounded in its purported transcription of an oral style presumed to be indisputably genuine. In stating that he had seen Bibb write the closing pages, the editor adds his own privileged eyewitness testimony to the widely available earwitness evidence. Finally, he states that the manuscript is available for comparison with the published text (53–54).

The basic argument here, then, is that what issued from Bibb's hand in his unique handwriting is essentially indistinguishable from what issued undeniably from his mouth on the lecture platform. But implicit in the editor's recognition of Bibb's achievement of a surprisingly "elevated style," "pure diction," and "easy flow" is a characterization of the discourse of Bibb's origins as lacking in literary, if not moral, grace. This ritual of introduction suggests that an ex-slave was licensed by abolitionists to narrate his own life on the condition of adopting a style incongruous with his origins: fugitive slaves were allowed entry to the province of autobiography only after purging themselves of some of their "slave" qualities. The editor's denial that he tampered with the narrative is a legitimate testament to Bibb's selftransformation: "no alteration of sentiment, language, or style was necessary to make it what it now is, in the hands of the reader" (53). Unfortunately, it attests less to the openness of the apparatus of publication to "other voices" than to the necessity of an ex-slave's acquiring, or hiring, an acceptably educated style. Bibb was permitted to "transcribe" his voice himself because it was already modified; had it not been, editorial intervention would presumably have been more aggressive. Thus, the guarantee of the "originality" of the voice is in effect a certification of its imitativeness.

The editor's guarantee of the narrative's veracity is notable both for the extensiveness of the documentation gathered and for the rigor of its review. Moreover, the language and procedures of authentication link the narrative to two "extraliterary" institutions. The use of terms such as *testimony* and *substantiate* establish a close link to legal discourse:

> In the Committee's opinion no individual can substantiate the events of his life by testimony more conclusive and harmonious than is now before them in confirmation of Mr. Bibb. . . . Mr. Bibb is amply sustained, and is entitled to public confidence and high esteem (55).

So does the assessment and presentation of witnesses' affidavits:

> The fidelity of the narrative is sustained by the most satisfactory and ample testimony. Time has proved its claims to truth. Thorough investigation has sifted and analyzed every essential fact alleged, and demonstrated clearly that this thrilling and eloquent narrative, though stranger than fiction, is undoubtedly true (54).

Less obvious, but perhaps more telling, is the characterization of the narrative as a kind of legal tender whose value in circulation is "backed" by a "harder" currency available on demand. The apparatus of accreditation likens the narrative to paper money—an anonymous and uniform medium of exchange one is obliged to accept by virtue of the authority of the issuing agency rather than because of its inherent value. Ultimately, the apparatus functions like a "pass" guaranteeing a slave's passage through an environment in which he would otherwise be powerless and voiceless. The elaborate prefatory accreditation of Bibb's narrative powerfully demonstrates the autobiographer's dependence on institutional sponsorship.

V

Stepto's diversion of attention from the narratives to their relationship with flanking texts underlined the way in which apparently neutral—or even positive—features of form could enact constraints on the relatively powerless. But Stepto did not present the narrators as necessarily passive or acquiescent. His analytic schema instead grouped slave narratives according to the extent to which, and the way in which, the enclosed texts commented on, played off, or reappropriated the authority of their sponsoring texts. *Eclectic narrative* "appends "segregated" documents that compromise its authority even as they purport to guarantee its veracity; *integrated narrative* manages to characterize, embody, and internalize the voices of those documents in such a way as to gain some control over them; and *generic narrative* subsumes them, mastering them sufficiently to attain the status of a genre in its own right—the slave narrative *as autobiography* (3–6).

Still, Stepto dramatically demonstrated that an antebellum black might flee the prison of slavery only to find himself in the reformatory of narrative overseen by abolitionists. Recent criticism has continued to ask whether these early Afro-American lifewriters were slaves or masters of their form, and why. Thus, once viewed primarily as documentation of slavery, the narratives are now read as testimony to a much less tractable problem, because slavery—already confined in space when the narratives were written, and then entombed in time by post-Civil War Constitutional amendments—was survived by subtle and pervasive forms of racism. In a sense, the project of much recent criticism updates the original agenda of the narratives; in effect, the narratives have recently been enlisted in a neoabolitionist mission. However admirable, this intent may involve a continued inability, or failure, to read the narratives as autobiography.

Thus, the full indictment of the form as an enslaving one demands consideration. First, as Blassingame's account of the composition process suggested, ex-slaves did not necessarily originate their own narratives. Indeed, the most highly regarded narratives (like the generally acknowledged masterpiece of the genre, *The Narrative of the Life of Frederick Douglass*) were usually written under the auspices of abolitionists. This might be because of the superiority of abolitionists as talent scouts in identifying and sponsoring able writers, rather than because of aggressive editing. Stepto has shown, however, that one consequence of their sponsorship could be loss of control over the narrative's mode of presentation. Moreover, production of a narrative under abolitionist auspices meant that it would be written, and read, as a typical rather than a distinctive story. At worst, this meant that the narratives were treated as a kind of serial petition submitted to the government of the people: the texts were more or less uniform and thus interchangeable—only the individual signatures were unique.

In any case, one apparent result of the institutional site of their composition is their formulaic content. There is no need here to rehearse the standard plot, which James Olney has pointedly called the "Master Plan for Slave Narratives,"[13] and whose unfortunate effect was to make the Lives of ex-slaves seem nearly as determined as their lives as slaves. Though the motives of slaveowners and abolitionists could hardly have been more different, the consequence of their policies was similar: they led to the suppression of black individuality.[14] An even more fundamental concern than the uniform plot is the use of what Olney has described as "florid, sentimental, declamatory rhetoric" (164). Polite language had its advantages—it appealed to the taste of middle-class readers and combatted lurking prejudice about the verbal aptitude of blacks—but its use threatened to erase rather than express black identity and experience. Moreover, insofar as they shunned the vernacular for genteel literary language, the narrators may have inadvertently sanitized a brutal, if not brutalizing, institution.

Perhaps the harshest appraisal of the linguistic and literary predicament of the slave narrator is Annette Niemztow's comment on Frederick Douglass:

> Thus, for him, the recognition that reading is an entry to freedom is not a self-conceived notion, but, like cleanliness, a standard defined by whites. Douglass conceives of a self which he will form in opposition to his master's wishes, but ironically he forms it within his master's rules. . . . Douglass's autobiography then, by virtue of its genre, unconsciously pays tribute to a definition of self created by whites . . . .[15]

Calculated to demonstrate the distance the narrators had traveled from a dehumanizing condition, their literary language could alienate them from the black culture that had nurtured their independence and will.[16]

The problem of language extends to tone as well as to dialect. Black narrators were encouraged by signals (sometimes surprisingly explicit) from editors and reviewers to adopt a neutral tone rather than a heated or extravagant tone, to dramatize by understatement, and to supply facts for white editors, readers, and reviewers to interpret and judge—in Searle's terms, to perform assertive, rather than expressive, directive, or declarative speech acts (12–19). The called-for narrator would presumably illuminate slavery by making himself inconspicuous if not invisible (Andrews, 63). Nor were the constraints on black authors limited to language or tone. Foster has noted: "The fate of the author of a slave narrative is strikingly similar to that of his protagonist. Once the protagonist achieves his freedom, the plot is finished. Once his narrative is published, the narrator's literary career is ended" (145). Though there were exceptions, most black authors were called into being by the needs of the genre, and existed only within its conventions.

James Olney has succinctly summed up the slave narrative's problematic status as autobiography:

> Of the narratives that Charles Nichols judges to have been written without the help of an editor—those by "Frederick Douglass, William Wells Brown, James W. C. Pennington, Samuel Ringgold Ward, Austin Steward, and perhaps Henry Bibb"—none but Douglass' has any genuine appeal in itself, apart from the testimony it might provide about slavery, or any real claim to literary merit. And when we go beyond this bare handful of narratives to consider those written under immediate abolitionist guidance and control, we find, as we might well expect, even less of individual distinction or distinctiveness as the narrators show themselves more or less content to remain slaves to a prescribed, conventional, and imposed form; or perhaps it would be more precise to say that they were captive to the abolitionist intentions

> and so the question of their being content or otherwise hardly entered in. (167–68)

In spite of Olney's obvious sympathy for the excruciating predicament of the narrators, he concluded that only *The Narrative of Frederick Douglass* could qualify as autobiography.

The temptation to exclude nearly all slave narrative from the domains of autobiography (and literature) can be resisted on both theoretical and practical grounds. The exclusion of black writers from the canon is a function of criteria presumed to be universal or timeless. The idea that autobiography ought to be "the unique tale, uniquely told, of a unique life" (148) seems natural enough, and it is widely shared, but as recent theory has been at pains to demonstrate, all writing is more conditioned by conventions—less original and distinctive of its authors—than we may like to think. Whether any autobiography can be the sign of a unique individual is questionable. Thus, slave narratives are different in degree rather than in kind from less constrained (mainstream) autobiographies. In any case, definitions of literary merit are ultimately grounded in extra-literary considerations: valorization of some texts as literary and denigration of others as subliterary, whether overtly or covertly, always reflects political and cultural agendas, whether conscious or unconscious. The premises of sweeping dismissals, therefore, are to be closely scrutinized.

In any case, some recent critics have rehabilitated seemingly "enslaved" narratives by showing ways in which they have resisted or subverted the "master plot." The project of these critics has been the reclamation of slave narrative as a powerful form of lifewriting, if not of autobiography narrowly conceived.[17] The most sustained and successful attempt to reassess, and reassert, the force and individuality of these narratives is William Andrews' *To Tell A Free Story: The First Century of Afro-American Autobiography.* Andrews brings to bear a variety of recent methodologies, such as reader response theory, speech act theory, and Bahktinian dialogism, in ways that again make legible the fading, but not invisible, ink of the early black lifewriters. For example, he chronicles the progression in slave narrative from simple assertives to expressives and declaratives (more aggressive speech acts that attempt to fit the world to words, rather than vice versa) and the construction of implied readers more receptive to the authors' messages than a conventional audience. Most important, he successfully distinguishes individual voices and strategies, both within and among various narratives.

Thus, while recent criticism may characterize the attempt to reach a nontextual order beyond or behind the textual one as hopeless, Andrews and others have demonstrated that slave narrators were sometimes able to assert significant individuality and autonomy within the textual order. While there may be no way to recuperate a pretextual self, ways have been suggested to throw the textual self into relief by illuminating it from new angles. If Stepto's major contribution was to point out the "framing" of the slave narrators, Andrews' has been to detail how black narrators have recognized and subverted, if not entirely surmounted, the obstacles in the way of free narrative. In particular, without denying the disadvantaged position of black authors, Andrews has demonstrated their cunning use of diverse linguistic resources to expose, diminish, or neutralize other's power over them.

The remainder of this chapter will discuss the extent to which particular slave narrators have succeeded in asserting authority in their narratives. The examples are chosen to illustrate a range of responses to their predicament rather than to argue for or against the authority of slave narrative on the whole.

VI

Judging from its title, one might expect that *Twelve Years a Slave: Narrative of Solomon Northup, a Citizen of New York, Kidnapped in Washington City in 1841, and Rescued in 1853, From a Cotton Plantation Near the Red River, in Louisiana* would be the supremely authoritative slave narrative. As a free, literate, and relatively prosperous black living up North, Northup might seem ideally equipped to offer a masterful account of life as a slave. In fact, in the early chapters he cites his credit in the white community as an index of his narratorial authority, portraying himself as one *restored* to the intellectual and emotional world of his readers, rather than as one entering it as a fugitive from a world elsewhere:

> Having all my life breathed the free air of the North, and conscious that I possessed the same feelings and affections that find a place in the white man's breast; conscious, moreover, of an intelligence equal to that of some men, at least, with a fairer skin, I was too ignorant, perhaps too independent, to conceive how anyone could be content to live in the abject condition of a slave.[18]

While his conversion into a slave was disorienting, his previous freedom enabled him to frame this alien condition in a perspective accessible to his readers—just as he could retrospectively identify the site of his initiation into slavery as a slave pen within sight of the Capitol (42–43).

Thus, before Northup was a slave, he already possessed one aspect of autobiographical consciousness: a sense of his individual worth and significance. His abduction into slavery supplied him with another: a sense of a rupture in his life. This is one implication of a statement that foreshadows his kidnapping:

> Thus far the history of my life presents nothing whatever unusual—nothing but the common hopes, and loves, and labors of an obscure colored man, making his humble progress in the world. But now I had reached a turning point in my existence—reached the threshold of unutterable wrong, and sorrow, and despair. Now had I approached within the shadow of the cloud, into the thick darkness whereof I was soon to disappear, thenceforward to be hidden from the eyes of all my kindred, and shut out from the sweet light of liberty, for many a weary year (27).

His legacy of literacy and freedom meant that he entered slavery aware both of the perspective of abolitionism and of the narratability of his ordeal. Once rescued, therefore, he should have been equipped to write and publish a narrative with a high degree of autonomy and authority.[19]

The same factors that predisposed Northup to be an autobiographer, however, also set him apart from other slaves and peculiarly inhibited the autobiographical impulse while he remained among them. Ironically, his distinction from the others was self-reinforcing: Northup was psychologically isolated by his fear of divulging the most important fact about himself—that he had been borne, rather than born, into slavery. However much material he stored up for later recounting, he did not dare to share his distinctive story with his fellow slaves, much less to declare his difference to his masters. This may help to account for the extensive passages of documentation in his narrative. In place of the greater introspection (and perhaps self-pity) one might expect from a narrator kidnapped into slavery, his text offers detailed descriptions of the externalities of Southern customs.

Northup explicitly deprecates outside or secondhand testimony as dangerously inaccurate:

> Men may write fictions portraying lowly life as it is, or as it is not—may expatiate with owlish gravity upon the bliss of ignorance—discourse flippantly from arm chairs of the pleasures of slave life. . . . Let them know the *heart* of the poor slave—learn his secret thoughts—thoughts he dare not utter in the hearing of the white man; let them sit by him in the silent watches of the night—converse with him in trustful confidence, of "life, liberty, and the pursuit of happiness," and they will find that ninety-nine out of every hundred are intelligent enough to understand their situation, and to cherish in their bosoms the love of freedom, as passionately as themselves (206–7).

The clear implication here is that Northup's account of slaves' thoughts is authoritative because he *has* sat with them.

But while he undeniably experienced slavery firsthand, the narrator's perspective sometimes regrettably resembles that of Northern travelers, who, regardless of their sympathies, could only view slavery as having nothing to do, essentially, with themselves. Perhaps viewing slavery as an aberration in his life helped make Northup at times an *eye*witness rather than an *I*-witness to it, to use William Andrews' distinction (65). In any case, in addition to his indignation at monstrous acts of oppression, and in contrast to his assertion of a universal love of freedom among slaves, he also expressed a surprising degree of tolerance for the slave's lot: "I think of [Master Ford] with affection, and had my family been with me, could have borne his gentle servitude, without murmuring, all my days" (103–4). Moreover, his claim to an inside perspective on slavery is belied by the stereotypical and patronizing portraits in this account of Christmas festivities:

> They seat themselves at the rustic table—the males on one side, the females on the other. The two between whom there may have been an exchange of tenderness, invariably manage to sit opposite; for the omnipresent Cupid disdains not to hurl his arrows into the simple hearts of slaves. Unalloyed and exulting happiness lights up the dark faces of them all. The ivory teeth, contrasting with their black complexions, exhibit two long, white streaks the whole extent of the table. All round the bountiful board a multitude of eyes roll in ecstasy. . . . Cuffee's elbow hunches his neighbor's side, impelled by an involuntary impulse of delight; Nelly shakes her finger at Sambo and laughs, she knows not why, and so the fun and merriment flows on. (215–16)

Even as the narrator purports to demonstrate the humanity of slaves, he reduces them to catalogues of cliched and undifferentiated parts—flashing teeth and rolling eyes. His attempt to establish their full membership in the human race metaphorically dismembers them.

As it happened, the testimony of this self-styled faithful witness of the slave was mediated by a white amanuensis whose prefatory remarks make a similar claim of intimacy with, and fidelity to, his source: "Unbiased, as he conceives, by any prepossessions or prejudices, the only object of the editor has been to give a faithful history of Solomon Northup's life, as he received it from his lips" (xvi). Thus, while Northup's narrative shows an admirable impulse to document the torments of others as well as his own, it also displays alienation from them and a disturbing readiness to turn his Life over to another.

The fact that Northup's freedom was regained by rescue rather than escape affects the narration as well as the plotting of that crucial episode of the slave narrative. Like Harriet Jacobs, he attempts to write his way out of his predicament—to "author" his own salvation; however, his letters are a good deal less autonomous than hers. As we shall see (in section VIII), her security after her escape depends on her skill as literary trickster: her goal is to disguise her actual whereabouts from her letters' white readers, whom she attempts to befuddle. Northup's problems, and his achievement, are less rhetorical than technical or logistical. Excluded from the apparatus as well as the channels of written communication, he has to steal or manufacture his own materials. Moreover, his goals are not to confuse his master, but to smuggle a letter past him, not to dupe his letter's reader but to enlighten him, and not to disguise his whereabouts but to disclose them to someone who can help to relocate him. Whereas Jacobs' letters create a kind of freedom for her, Northup's report his illegal enslavement and summon liberators. Moreover, like his narrative, the letter that led to his rescue was written for him—in this case, by an anomalous Southern abolitionist named Bass: "He subscribed my true name, but in the postscript intimated I was not the writer" (275).

Thus, even though Northup entered slavery by way of the world of P. T. Barnum—the world of "Ventriloquism and Legerdemain," according to one page heading—he escaped it by way of official institutional intermediaries: judges, governors, senators, and sheriffs. This puts him in a peculiar predicament as a slave narrator. Escape is usually a slave narrative's symbolic as well as narrative climax because the successful plotting of one's deliverance is the supreme demonstration of autonomy. In addition, the details of flight are typically the ultimate autobiographical secret divulged by the ex-slave. (Or not divulged: Frederick Douglass made a compelling argument against disclosure.) Having played a relatively passive role in his escape, Northup also found himself dependent on his benefactors for the particulars of its accomplishment. This anomaly is marked in chapter XX by a shift in the narrative's viewpoint and a break in its chronology. A line of asterisks is followed by this transitional statement: "Having now brought down this narrative to the last hour I was to spend on Bayou Boeuf—having gotten through my last cotton picking, and about to bid Master Epps farewell—I must beg the reader to go back with me to the month of August; to follow Bass' letter on its long journey to Saratoga; to learn the effect it produced . . . " (288).

The next chapter, much of which is told in the third person, traces the legal steps taken to free Northup. In it, the narrator condemns the system that ruled Northup's testimony inadmissable on grounds of his color and thus failed to convict his original purchaser. In the face of this defeat, he appeals to a supreme authority: "A human tribunal has permitted him to escape, but there is another and a higher tribunal, where false testimony will not prevail, and where I am willing, so far at least as these statements are concerned, to be judged at last" (319). Insofar as the autobiography is the first (rather than the supreme) court of appeal—in which Northup is plaintiff and witness, and the reader is the judge and jury—Northup succeeds in transferring his case to a more favorable venue. Still, his dependence on the legal system to rescue him from the plantation tends inevitably to affirm the legitimacy of slave laws. As Northup well knew, his predicament was rare, and the legal machinery that procured his freedom did nothing to alter the condition of his fellow slaves. Indeed, his rescuers met as little resistance as they did from Southern officials precisely because cases like Northup's were atypical: freeing the "falsely" enslaved served to legitimize slavery rather than to undermine it. Through no fault of Northup's, his story is not so much one in which an individual created his own freedom as one in which freedom was finally recognized where it had always existed. Insofar as Northup depends on intermediaries to rescue him, to write his narrative, and to guarantee it, the narrative's authority is located outside of itself and beyond Northup's immediate control.

VII

The language of the legal pass Northup is given in New Orleans, which is transcribed in his narrative, begrudgingly authorizes him to "pass unmolested, he demeaning well and properly" (311). The latitude allowed him in transit is analogous to that generally extended to slave narrators, whose decorum was also carefully gauged. One possible authorial response to such close circumscription, however, was the thematization and dramatization of white control over black discourse. For example, Frederick Douglass illustrates the dangers of honest assessments of masters by their slaves, and concludes:

> [S]laves, when inquired of as to their condition and the character of their masters, almost universally say they are contented, and that their masters are kind. . . . They suppress the truth rather than take the consequences of telling it, and in so doing prove themselves a part of the human family.[20]

Such open indictments of masters' attempts to control slaves' voices may function as covert indictments of editors' control of ex-slaves' voices—a way of disarming or exposing even the most benevolent form of censorship.

Silence as well as self-expression may play a role in the assertion of authority over one's narrative. One of the devices used in slave narrative is what we might call the rhetorical figure of inexpressibility—the assertion of a subject's ineffability in such a way as, paradoxically, to say something important about it. Henry Bibb, for example, declares right at the outset of his narrative: "[N]o tongue, nor pen ever has or can express the horrors of American Slavery. Consequently I despair in finding language to express adequately the deep feeling of my soul, as I contemplate the past history of my life" (65). Similarly, William Wells Brown comments on seeing his sister for the last time, after she was sold: "I cannot give a just description of the scene at that parting interview. Never, never can be erased from my heart the occurrences of that day!"[21] Slavery's inexpressibility is identified as another of its horrors: the institution's violation of the slave's soul is aggravated by the impossibility of adequately describing that transgression, and thus of fully indicting it, or venting the emotions engendered by it. While the unspeakable may seem ineradicable, however, the very assertion of its inexpressibility may afford some psychic relief. It may also function as an ultimate and self-authorizing condemnation of slavery. By construing slavery as unutterably evil, the trope serves to discredit certain tests of veracity: believable utterances are *inherently* inadequate. This figure, which is superficially an admission of verbal impoverishment or disenfranchisement, can play a role in validating ex-slave discourse and in recuperating power in slave narrative.

If one kind of eloquent silence results from the (apparent) inability to articulate something, another results from the unwillingness to do so. If the trope of inexpressibility can powerfully express vulnerability, secrecy can assert and signify invulnerability, as, for example, when Frederick Douglass declines to spell out the details of his escape on the practical and moral grounds that "such a statement would most undoubtedly induce greater vigilance on the part of slaveholders." His assertion that he is not "at liberty" to "gratify a curiosity, which I know exists in the minds of many" reminds his audience that he is more closely bound to his brothers in slavery than to his readers (137). Moreover, his flouting of expectations by withholding details of the narrative's climactic event vigorously affirms his control over the contents of his text.

The value of secrecy is also made clear by William Wells Brown, whose mistress inquired into his love life and then purchased a woman in whom he had confessed some interest. Though unable openly to resist her inquiries, he sensed that her curiosity was a form of surveillance:

> But the more I thought of the trap laid by Mrs. Price to make me satisfied with my new home, by getting me a wife, the more I determined never to marry any woman on earth until I should get my liberty. But this secret I was compelled to keep to myself, which placed me in a very critical position (213).

He resolved not only to avoid marriage but also to avoid confiding anything further of substance to his mistress—to lie, if necessary. Of course, Brown does confide this "secret" to his readers. This may be viewed as reflecting his greater trust in them, his reduced sense of vulnerability as an ex-slave, and his greater control of the circumstances of this confidence. It may also be regarded as inducing an obligation in his readers. That is, instead of passively positing virtuous readers, the narrator may be actively constructing them in a desired image by providing a cautionary model of reaction to a slave's confidence. When Edmund Quincy, the editor, states in his preface that "a man must be differently constituted from me, who can rise from the perusal of your Narrative without feeling that he understands slavery better, and hates it worse, than he ever did before" (176), he presumably means that one would have to come *to* the text with a different makeup from his own to come *away* with a different reaction. We can also think of Brown as trying to *constitute* his readers in such a way that they would all respond as sympathetically as Quincy.

In any event, Brown's narrative thoroughly dramatizes slaves' wariness of masters' discourse. For example, it is an important dimension of the incident in which he cunningly deflects a beating intended for himself onto a free black. Brown's master gives him a note to take to the jailer: in effect, its message is, give the bearer a sound thrashing. Though illiterate, the suspicious and self-protective Brown has the wit to have the note read to him by a disinterested party. He then cons an innocent man into carrying the note to the jail and taking the beating. This evasion of punishment depends on, and exposes, racist aspects of the note, which assumes that its bearer is as lacking in ingenuity as he is in literacy. Brown cleverly exploits this assumption, as well as the inability of white officialdom to distinguish among individual blacks, slave or free; it is, after all, only because the note fails to *identify* him that Brown is able to send a substitute for himself. (The ploy also exposes the impotence of free blacks against white authority.)

William Andrews has pointed out that Brown's explicit condemnation of his own act here is somewhat disingenuous; the tone and manner of his account betray his lingering sense of pleasure in his triumph. Andrews argues that in this incident the voice of "Sandford," the unreconstructed con man, eludes the censorship of Brown as well as of his white editor (148–50). The effect is to give the narrative a dimension foreign to more tightly controlled texts; here, as elsewhere, the reader is admitted to the amoral world of the trickster slave. When Brown gets home, he wets his cheeks, simulating the expected emotion in order to "sell" his master. As Andrews has noticed, Brown's appended moral is belied by his handling of the incident, and the sentiment "expressed" in the moral may be as fake as the slave's tears. This gesture, which by itself might seem to undermine the sincerity of the narrative, may be part of a strategy that implies the reader's responsibility for honest communication, for if the reader is constructed here as a master to be "sold" when the narrator's feelings might be unacceptable, then the very form tests the reader's readiness to accept an uncensored narrative.

The story of Brown and his prying mistress may also be read as a gloss on the process by which slave narratives are produced. In this process the intentions and interests of narrator and editor/publisher never quite coincide, the relation is never one of equals, and the confidences of the former may be exploited by the latter. Thus, the episode's conclusion may be cautionary. The slave's lie to his master, an expression of distaste for free states, has "the desired effect": allowed to enter free territory, Brown makes his escape (214). What begins with the mistress's manipulation of the slave into a confidence she can abuse ends with the slave's manipulation of his mistress into a state of confidence the slave can exploit to ease his way to a state of autonomy.

VIII

Attempts of slave and master to manipulate each other with words are at the heart of Harriet Jacobs' *Incidents in the Life of a Slave Girl,* and the intimate nature of her self-revelation complicated the entire process of negotiating the narrative's publication. To begin with, the delicate nature of the material to be confided—Jacobs had escaped the sexual advances of her master by entering a sexual liaison with another white man, who fathered her children—made her hesitate a long time before undertaking to narrate her life. When she finally did, she felt compelled to veil her identity with a pseudonym, "Linda Brent." The story of how the narrative reached print (which is unusually well documented) forcefully demonstrates the risks of self-disclosure for the slave narrator as autobiographer.

At first glance, the apparatus that authenticates Jacobs' narrative may seem to follow a fairly conventional pattern. In her "Introduction," the editor, Lydia Maria Child, vouches for both the veracity and the authenticity of the narrative, attributing its literacy to Jacobs' "quick perceptions" and "favorable circumstances," rather than to her own editing.[22] Jacobs' prefatory remarks also contain standard elements: apologies for the text's lack of polish, assertions that "this narrative is no fiction" but rather an understated account of her life, and attempts to deflect the readers' attention from her suffering to that of "two millions of women at the South, still in bondage" (1–2). Testimony appended as documentary confirmation of the narrative's factuality illustrates one of the unwritten rules of the slave-narrative code—events should be illuminated by a neutral, white light:

> This narrative contains some incidents so extraordinary, that, doubtless, many persons, under whose eyes it may chance to fall, will be

> ready to believe that it is colored highly, to serve a special purpose. But, however it may be regarded by the incredulous, I know that it is full of living truths. I have been well acquainted with the author from my boyhood. The circumstances recounted in her history are perfectly familiar to me (205).

The diction here illustrates the "Prejudice against Color" inherent in the language itself, as well as in the official aesthetic of the slave narrative (title of Chapter XXXV).

In some ways, this narrative is presented as a typical abolitionist slave narrative—as objective antislavery testimony, not as subjective life-writing. Other aspects of the authentication, however, deviate significantly from the race ritual of "segregated texts." The narrative proper is bracketed by two pairs of documents: the inner pair is supplied by Child and Amy Post, and the outer pair by Jacobs and George W. Lowther. Thus, the book's first words are those of the author, a free black woman, while its last words are those of Lowther, a free black man. Moreover, the two appended testimonials were solicited by Jacobs.[23] The supporting documentation, then, breaks the usual pattern of the authorization of slave narratives by white males, thereby subverting the hierarchy of race (and gender) characteristic of authentication.

Furthermore, because the names of places and individuals are disguised, the apparatus relies more on a chain of interpersonal trust (i.e., the editor's in her narrator and, in turn, the reader's in the editor) than on a series of reinforcing documents. The narrative's guarantee is intimate and personal rather than formal and legalistic. The narrator's sole attempt to authenticate her narrative internally is consistent with the editor's gestures: to verify the most fantastic aspect of her tale—her seven-year confinement in a tiny garret (three feet by nine feet by seven feet)—she refers the incredulous reader not to an appended affidavit but to the (inaccessible) testimony of her family and that of her body, which she claims still manifests the crippling effects of her painful ordeal.

The most remarkable of the accrediting documents is the appended letter from the Quaker abolitionist Amy Post, to whom Jacobs apparently first told her tale "in private confidential conversations." It emphasizes Jacobs' original reticence and the courage required by the process of composition and publication:

> Even in talking with me, she wept so much, and seemed to suffer such mental agony, that I felt her story was too sacred to be drawn from

> her by inquisitive questions, and I left her free to tell as much, or as little, as she chose. Still, I urged upon her the duty of publishing her experience, for the sake of the good it might do; and, at last, she undertook the task (204).

The letter displays a rare, if not unique, sensitivity to the slave narrator's predicament vis-à-vis her audience, immediate and remote, present and future. Torn between her sense that Jacobs should be "free" not to divulge her story and that she was morally obliged to do so, Post tried to elicit her narrative without violating her privacy. Her letter comes closer than any similar document to doing justice to the emotional, moral, and political complexities of the collaborative production of slave narratives.

Indeed, as William Andrews has observed, "It is very likely that Post and Child embodied demonstrably the kind of implied reader who Jacobs needed to believe was out there in the white world ready to listen empathetically to her story."[24] Child's foreword and Post's afterword not only help to validate the narrative, they also help to construct readers in their image—a rather different image from the vengeful readers generally implied by male abolitionist editors. In particular, when considered as an authenticating text, Post's letter implies that the narrative's value (its sacredness) is proportional to its extreme delicacy: its authority lies in the risk and trauma of its divulgence, not in its relation to empirically verifiable fact. Thus, the presentation of the narrative operates on somewhat different principles and assumptions than those of most abolitionist narratives.

Despite its careful authentication and respectful reviews in the abolitionist press, the narrative has until recently been considered suspect by most twentieth-century scholars because of its literary sophistication, its employment of novelistic conventions, and its pseudonymity. At best, the narrative was thought to be the product of Child's pen; at worst, it was termed an antislavery novel in the guise of a slave narrative, like *The Autobiography of a Female Slave,* which was written by a white Southerner, Mattie Griffiths, and published four years earlier. Jean Fagan Yellin's sustained and resourceful research, however, has definitively established Jacobs' authorship and verified many of the narrative's details. The correspondence between Jacobs and Child not only confirms Jacobs' literary skill; it also indicates that she worked on the project alone for long periods—keeping it secret from her employer, N. P. Willis, who she suspected was proslavery—and exerted an extraordinary amount of control over the collaborative process of editing and publishing the manuscript.[25]

In some ways, Yellin's account of the narrative's genesis corresponds to Blassingame's generalized version. Although Jacobs was initially reluctant to tell her story, she was urged to divulge it—first by Bishop Daniel A. Payne of the African Methodist Episcopal church on her arrival in the North in 1842, and later by the Quaker abolitionist Amy Post, with whose family she lived in 1849. In 1853, when Jacobs first considered publication, her intention was to give an oral account to a white author. Had she been successful in arranging such a collaboration, the narrative's mode of production would have conformed to Blassingame's generic model, in which initiative and control pass gradually from black ex-slave to white editor.

When Jacobs' initial impulse was blunted, however, a different process eventuated. She had aspired, perhaps too ambitiously, to collaborate with the most renowned of antislavery writers, Harriet Beecher Stowe. But when Post broached the idea by sending Stowe a sketch of Jacobs' life, the novelist's response was devastating. Rather than considering Jacobs' story worth a book of its own, Stowe proposed including it in her *Key to Uncle Tom's Cabin.* Worse, to verify Post's account, she sent it to Jacobs' employer, Cornelia Grinnell Willis, to whom Jacobs had not confided the troubling details of her sexual life. Thus, Stowe not only condescendingly suggested appending Jacobs' obscure Life to her own famous fiction, she also violated the confidence on which any collaboration would have to depend.

At this point, Jacobs assumed responsibility for producing her own narrative. (Thus, Stowe served unwittingly and ironically as her muse.) Like Benjamin Franklin, but at a much later age, Jacobs undertook a self-imposed literary apprenticeship; like him as well, she acceded to authorship by submitting anonymous articles to newspapers. The circumstances of her life and work as a domestic, however, as well as her need to hone her literary skills, impeded progress on her narrative, and the manuscript was not completed until 1858. It was not published for another three years: while she could train herself as a writer, she could not recommend herself to book publishers. She failed to find a publisher in her travels to England, and the necessity for sponsorship by a white writer or editor remained a hindrance.

In lieu of Stowe as her amanuensis, however, she eventually

obtained Child as her editor through abolitionist connections. Unlike Stowe, Child proved respectful of her manuscript. Although she reorganized what Jacobs had supplied, asked for elaboration of some episodes, and suppressed a final chapter on John Brown, her editing was not particularly aggressive—it apparently involved no major changes of substance or style. Had Jacobs not been suddenly called upon to deliver Mrs. Willis' premature baby, she would have been on hand to discuss the final version with Child; ironically, she served as midwife to another woman's baby rather than to her own book.

Child was also scrupulous about rights to the manuscript and to the proceeds of publication: although she signed the contract, she was careful to assign the rights and royalties exclusively to Jacobs. The last hitch was the sudden failure of the publisher after the contract had been signed and the plates made. The result of this apparent disaster was in a way appropriate: Jacobs somehow managed to purchase the plates and have the book published independently "for the author."[26]

The extent to which Jacobs was able to assume and maintain control over her narrative was probably exceptional. Ironically, it was also a function of a system that very nearly banned the self-written lives of minority women: Jacobs exercised such authority over her manuscript only because of the failure of the white authorities on whom she at first depended. Thus, the process by which her Life came to print illustrates the peculiar constraints under which minority autobiography is usually produced. So does the process of its recent validation, because in effect Jean Yellin has recapitulated the process by which slave narratives were originally authenticated. Indeed, her scholarly edition surrounds the text with a documentary apparatus that exceeds even that of Henry Bibb's *Narrative*. The already authenticated narrative is bracketed once more, this time by state-of-the-art scholarly documentation: an authoritative introduction and endnotes, Jacobs' correspondence (photographed as well as transcribed), a photocopy of her owner's advertisement for the runaway slave, a detailed chronology, maps, and even architectural drawings of the garret. Though the rehabilitation of the narrative is a welcome result of energetic and committed research, its inevitable effect is to document the narrative in the legalistic fashion that it may have purposely eschewed.

Despite the establishment of Jacobs' authorship, her narrative's reliance on the conventions of sentimental fiction has continued to be a source of controversy—including the charge that it is inauthentic. Essentially, the objection is that novelistic conventions, especially those of sentimental fiction, are inappropriate to autobiography, which is essentially a kind of nonfiction, despite its fictive elements. This position has been strongly expressed by Annette Niemtzow who, while aware of the rhetorical appeal of these conventions, argues that Jacobs' distinctive style and self finally disappear into trivial and irrelevant generic stereotypes (105–7). This apparent surrender to feminine stereotypes, however, may function instead as a critique of the implicit masculine bias of the conventional slave narrative. Indeed, a generous view of her narrative would credit Jacobs with keeping her distance from the conventions of either genre. Her conscious divergence from her sentimental models seems quite clear in occasional narratorial comments, and her divergence from standard slave narrative conventions is implicit throughout her tale.

An example of the first phenomenon is her pointing out how her ending departs from the sentimental formula:

> Reader, my story ends with freedom; not in the usual way, with marriage. I and my children are now free! . . . The dream of my life is not yet realized. I do not sit with my children in a home of my own. I still long for a hearthstone of my own, however humble. I wish it for my children's sake far more than for my own. But God so orders circumstances as to keep me with my friend Mrs. Bruce. Love, duty, gratitude also bind me to her side (201).

Niemtzow has seized upon this longing for hearth and home as evidence of a desire to be completed by acquisition of a husband. In doing so, however, she misreads a statement of fact as a confession of failure: the thrust of the whole narrative has been to establish a nonpatriarchal home on the memorable (and memorialized) model of her grandmother's. Jacobs wants not a husband but freedom from a life of service in a white home.

Her narrative strategies also seek to establish an autonomous zone outside of male control. Significantly, she begins by defining her audience as female. Her story also differs from the standard (masculine) model in shape as well as in tone and incident. Indeed, the title itself, which characterizes it not as an integral "narrative" but as "incidents" in her life—may suggest its departure from the linearity of masculine tales. In any case, "escape" takes on a distinctive form in her text. Instead of lighting out for free territory, she secretes herself within slave territory, accepting claustrophobic self-incarceration as the price of maintaining contact with her family. Her goal in escaping is less to elude others' designs on her than to sustain maternal authority over her children. Thus, her narrative's turning point is not her liberation from her master or her (much deferred) flight to and arrival in free territory; rather, it is the sale of her children (contrived by her and her grandmother) from her master to their father.

Throughout, her fundamental means of averting and subverting her master's authority is a curious experiment in authorship. In slave narrative, accession to literacy is generally portrayed as a crucial triumph over the system. Literacy, itself a form of psychic liberation, is useful in achieving physical freedom, and is indispensable in recounting its attainment. One of the distinctive features of Jacobs' narrative is its anomalous treatment of literacy. For her, the advent of literacy is associated with vulnerability: rather than enabling her to assert or express herself, it provides her master with another medium through which to insinuate himself into her privacy. Thus, her literacy is at first merely another avenue of violation (31).

Dr. Flint uses writing as an instrument of domination both in his intimate letters to her and, later, in his advertisement of her as a fugitive, which she transcribes into the narrative:

> $300 Reward! Ran away from the subscriber, an intelligent, bright, mulatto girl, named Linda, 21 years of age. Five feet four inches high. Dark eyes, and black hair inclined to curl; but it can be made straight. Has a decayed spot on a front tooth. She can read and write, and in all probability will try to get to the Free States (97).

This notice reduces her to lost property identified by a few salient characteristics that are mostly physical. Letting her master supply the narrative's only description of her effectively forces her readers to assume, momentarily, the viewpoint of a betrayed owner. The abrupt shift from a subjective to an objective point of view and from expressive authorial to possessive proprietorial language convincingly indicates the power of slavery to commodify people. By conveying the threat her master's writing posed to her autonomy, this passage underscores the relationship between political and literary authority.

Once Jacobs has managed to appear to disappear, however, she turns her literacy aggressively against her master. By having letters mailed to her master from the North, she drafts him as a character in an epistolary novel whose plot she controls. She employs writing to imply her absence rather than to assert her presence, thereby throwing her pursuers off the scent and locating herself linguistically beyond reach in free territory. To an extraordinary extent, her narrative concerns her perpetration of an elaborate written hoax. More than any other fugitive slave, her "escape" depends on her inventing and sustaining a desperate fiction while exposing those of her master. Indeed, the latter half of the narrative is largely an account of a war of words—a campaign by correspondence.

On one occasion, Dr. Flint substitutes a letter of his own for one she has had mailed to her grandmother, in care of him, as part of the pretense that she had fled (130). In her master's forged letter, "Linda" apologizes to her family for running and admits that it has been a mistake. The ploy fails, of course, because her family is in on the hoax, and the master's phony letter merely indicates that he has been "sold" by his legal chattel; the usual hegemony of discourse is here disrupted. A failure at writing as well as at reading her letters, Dr. Flint only thinks he controls the exchange of texts; in fact, he takes his slave's name in vain.

At another point, Jacobs transcribes and comments on a letter, purportedly from Dr. Flint's son, that entices her to return "home":

> This letter was signed by Emily's brother, who was as yet a mere lad. I knew, by the style, that it was not written by a person of his age, and though the writing was disguised, I had been made too unhappy by it, in former years, not to recognize at once the hand of Dr. Flint (172).

Here, by detecting her master's authorship, she undercuts his authority and foils his plot. Once again, his fraud not only fails, but signals her success in throwing her voice, making it seem to emanate from a free space she does not in fact occupy.

The connection between her writing as a fugitive slave and as a slave narrator is implied by a chapter entitled, "What Slaves are Taught to Think of the North." Without endorsing the myth of a non-discriminatory North—a heaven as well as a haven for fugitives—Jacobs counters slaveholders' propaganda and impugns their credibility:

> Slaveholders pride themselves upon being honorable men; but if you were to hear the enormous lies they tell their slaves, you would have small respect for their veracity. I have spoken plain English. Pardon me. I cannot use a milder term. When they visit the north, and return home, they tell their slaves of the runaways they have seen, and describe them to be in the most deplorable condition (43).

Here, Jacobs reenacts as a narrator what she has done as a character: she exposes and discredits masters' "slave narratives." She explicitly denounces their stories as hoaxes that pretend to record past events while seeking to shape future ones. She implicitly improvises a narratorial ethic and aesthetic: compared to the systematic and deliberate deception of masterly discourse, her implausible narrative is "plain English."

The narrative's pseudonymity remains a problem. "Linda Brent" was not a transparent, let alone a playful, pseudonym like "Mark Twain"; rather, it served to protect Jacobs from possible embarrassment by masking her authorship. It thus threatens to undermine the narrative's authority as autobiography, if not as testimony against slavery. Indeed, her use of a pseudonym damages her self-authentication in the "Preface by the Author": "I have concealed the names of places, and given persons fictitious names. I had no motive for secrecy on my own account, but I deemed it kind and considerate towards others to pursue this course" (1). The opposite is closer to the truth: her concern for secrecy probably had less to do with consideration for others than with residual uneasiness about disclosing the specifically sexual form of her exploitation. Her expression of a desire to protect others, while sincere, also served to deflect attention from her use of a pseudonym as a shield for herself.

One could argue, however, that in the case of slave narrative, distinguishing between pseudonymous and nonpseudonymous autobiography is always problematic. Most slave names are improper names, imposed or assumed on false premises, as Jacobs (whose paternal grandfather was white) notes in connection with the naming of her daughter: "What tangled skeins are the genealogies of slavery! I loved my father; but it mortified me to be obliged to bestow his name on my children" (78). Insofar as slave names are false names, all slave narratives are in a sense pseudonymous.

There is an important distinction between "Linda Brent," on the one hand, and "Frederick Douglass" and "William Wells Brown" on the other; however, it is not a simple distinction between "false" and "true" names. Which of the males' names are true: the given names they bore as slaves or the surnames they chose on reaching free territory? Insofar as they combine elements passively received and freely selected, reminiscent of slave childhood and symbolic of free manhood, representative of continuity and of disruption in their identities, the names "Frederick Douglass" and "William Wells Brown" —like their autobiographies—defy classification as simply, or proportionally, true or false. For our purposes, the crucial difference between these names and "Linda Brent" is that the former are names by which the authors were known outside their texts, while "Linda Brent" was entirely a literary phenomenon that reflected Jacobs' conflicting desires to give public testimony and to retain her privacy. "Brent" is in a different category from the other characters in her text not for the reason she gives in her preface—because they need secrecy more than she does—but because their names were known to be fabricated, while hers was not.

Thus, Jacobs' use of a pseudonym, while understandable, seems inconsistent with autobiography, whose essence after all involves self-identification—if not a pact binding the author to tell the truth about her historical existence. As with the distinctive authenticating strategy of this narrative, however, a gender difference may be relevant here. Perhaps authentic authorship of one's Life need not entail aggressive self-assertion and naked self-display. (The text itself suggests that women and men may define and experience autonomy differently in a chapter entitled "The Slave Who Dared to Feel Like a Man." In it, her uncle Benjamin acts out a male scenario of self-assertion—a solo escape attempt—while Jacobs sketches out a female one: "The war of my life had begun; and though one of God's most powerless creatures, I resolved never to be conquered. Alas, for me!" [19]) Like the rhetorical figure of inexpressibility, perhaps pseudonymity, apparently a form of self-concealment or self-effacement, can make a legitimate and powerful autobiographical statement. One might pursue this possibility by noting that, as a slave woman, one of Jacobs' greatest fears was of physical and psychic violation. By her own analysis slavery peculiarly endangered black women, by depriving black men of the power to protect them: "Some poor creatures have been so brutalized by the lash that they will sneak out of the way to give their masters free access to their wives and daughters" (44). White men were thus able to use black women's bodies to produce children who increased their property holdings: they could simultaneously beget children and "author" slaves.

The apparent source of Jacobs' reticence is her lingering uneasiness about eluding her master's sexual advances by entering a fruitful sexual relationship with another white man:

> [T]o be an object of interest to a man who is not married, and who is not her master, is agreeable to the pride and feelings of a slave, if her miserable situation has left her any pride or sentiment. It seems less

> degrading to give one's self, than to submit to compulsion. There is something akin to freedom in having a lover who has no control over you, except that which he gains by kindness and attachment (54–55).

Whatever the rationale for her sexual conduct—and modern readers are likely to endorse it—it represents only a modest self-empowerment. Although she thus managed to select the father of her children, she did so at the cost of her chastity and her grandmother's respect, if not her self-respect.[27] Despite her self-assertion, authority and paternity remain closely linked: Jacobs knew from experience that the "freedom" to select her children's father did not entail the freedom to acknowledge him publicly: "My master was, to my knowledge, the father of eleven slaves. But did the mothers dare to tell who was the father of their children? No, indeed!" (35). In such circumstances autonomy came to mean the preservation of the integrity and safety of her family to Jacobs, not the assertion of self.

What lies behind her pseudonym, therefore, is the sexual vulnerability of black women in a racist, patriarchal culture—and her clever but costly strategy for self-protection. The narrator's self-camouflage mimics and extends the ruses resorted to by a slave desirous of preserving her integrity. Ultimately, her role as narrator recapitulates an earlier scenario. In this role, she gives up a literal hiding place (the garret) for a figurative one (her pseudonym); she once again (or still) writes from under cover.

Although this gesture may seem to diminish her authority, or to disqualify her book as autobiography, it may be viewed instead as what William Andrews calls "a mode of deauthorizing." Andrews has observed that as slave narrative developed in the antebellum period it became "novelized"; that is, it increasingly assumed characteristics—such as extensive use of dialogue—that were associated with the novel and thus thought to be inconsistent with nonfiction. He argues that such devices are part of a progressive questioning, on the part of emerging black authors, of the legitimacy of authority as conventionally conceived (269–72). Like Douglass' withholding of the details of his escape, and like William Wells Brown's punning on "will" in the name he retains from his days as a slave, Jacobs' use of pseudonymous narration may be a way both of asserting some control over the relationship between her and her anonymous readers and of reminding her readers of the perverse shapes authority sometimes assumed. After all, virtually the last act recorded in the narrative is Jacobs' purchase—without her permission and against her will—by a benefactor. Taking refuge in a pseudonym not only protects her from the criticism of a possibly insensitive public, it also dramatizes her continued need for protection from others' designs on her.

IX

Perhaps *The Narrative of Frederick Douglass* best illustrates both the obstacles to authoritative lifewriting by slave narrators and the strategies for surmounting them. According to Stepto, its two introductory texts are less overpowering than most because the first, William Lloyd Garrison's preface, vouches for the impact rather than the veracity of Douglass' narrative, and the second, Wendell Phillips' letter, addresses Douglass as an equal.[28] Still, these authenticating texts illustrate the challenge posed even to the most skilled and resourceful of narrators. Their high ambitions for slave narratives in general, and Douglass' in particular, threaten to subsume the individual black author's distinctive voice.

Both Garrison and Phillips characterize the missionary function of the genre—its prophetic impulse—in terms of a kind of authoritative writing that the ex-slave's text should evoke or stimulate, but not *be.* Garrison concludes his hortatory preface by calling on his readers to "inscribe on the banner which you unfurl to the breeze, as your religious and political motto—'No compromise with Slavery! No union with Slaveholders!' " (42) He depicts the ultimate goal of Douglass' writing as the transcribing of Garrisonian mottoes on his readers' ideological banners. Though more moderate in tone, Phillips concludes by exhorting Douglass:

> Go on, my dear friend, till you, and those who, like you, have been saved, so as by fire, from the dark prison-house, shall stereotype these free, illegal impulses into statutes; and New England, cutting loose from a blood-stained Union, shall glory in being the house of refuge for the oppressed . . . (46).

He sees Douglass' writing as inducing a revision of the legal code tantamount to the re-constitution—and hence the redemption—of New England, if not the nation.

The term *stereotype* is used here in the printer's sense—to reproduce from a one-piece cast plate. Phillips hopes that the narrators' fugitive impulses will help mold a monolithic legal discourse. While Garrison and Phillips are eager to grant Douglass' impulses the highest legal and moral authority, they view his writing as subordinate to the cause, and Douglass and other black narrators are urged to underwrite abolitionism's agenda rather than freely and fully to develop idiosyncratic ones. In effect, Garrison and Phillips seem to regard slave narrative as an expedient—and thus disposable—genre with little, if any, standing as lifewriting, let alone literature.

As we have seen, one response of the slave narrator to his constraining circumstances was to expose them by analogy or implication in his narrative. Douglass' text is particularly candid and thoughtful in its treatment of the problematic nature of his authorship and verbal authority. For one thing, it clearly registers his alienation from the official discourse of his time: he begins his narrative by noting that he had never seen "any authentic record" of his age (47) and ends it by confessing the peculiarly racial anxiety of authorship that accompanied his first speech before a white audience: "The truth was, I felt myself a slave, and the idea of speaking to white people weighed me down" (151).

Moreover, his analysis of slave songs implicitly characterizes the form of authorship most accessible to slaves as antithetical to personal writing: anonymous, oral, collective, spontaneous—indeed, only partially verbal:

> They would compose and sing as they went along, consulting neither time nor tune. The thought that came up, came out—if not in the word, in the sound;—and as frequently in the one as in the other. They would sometimes sing the most pathetic sentiment in the most rapturous tone, and the most rapturous sentiment in the most pathetic tone . . . (57).

Far from patronizing slave songs, Douglass views them as potentially the most authentic and compelling form of antislavery testimony: "I have sometimes thought that the mere hearing of those songs would do more to impress some minds with the horrible character of slavery, than the reading of whole volumes of philosophy on the subject" (56). But the formal parallelism of the style with which he describes the songs indicates his distance from this mode of composition.

He admits that he had not fully appreciated the songs' import while a slave, and he acknowledges that the signifying codes that made them safe to sing in the master's hearing also made them vulnerable to misinterpretation by the uninitiated:

> I have often been utterly astonished, since I came to the north, to find persons who could speak of the singing, among slaves, as evidence of

> their contentment and happiness. It is impossible to conceive of a greater mistake. Slaves sing most when they are most unhappy (58).

Even as his discussion of slave songs renders them more legible—or audible—to his readers, it implies that slave narrative must employ a more widely understood language than the hermetic one to which his birth entitled him (and threatened to limit him). Slave narrative would necessarily involve a different form of authorship from slave song.

The acquisition of literacy plays a large role in Douglass' escape from slavery—psychologically, if not practically. One of the narrative's impressive features is its tracing of the complex connections among literacy, autonomy, and authority. His achievement of literacy had two complementary elements: the concealing of his own incipient handwriting inside the household and the covert consumption of "outside" authors. Both required great ingenuity and self-discipline. In the beginning, Douglass used his physical surroundings as a slate on which he scrawled crude letters, like graffiti: "During this time, my copy-book was the board fence, brick wall, and pavement; my pen and ink was a lump of chalk." Later he refined his script by tedious imitation: "When left [alone] thus, I used to spend the time in writing in the spaces left in Master Thomas's copy-book, copying what he had written. I continued to do this until I could write a hand very similar to that of Master Thomas" (87). Thus he learned to write invisibly—in the times and spaces left empty by his master. His behavior was at once autonomous and imitative, at once defiant of, and constrained by, white authority.

The ability to read brought access to discourse not entirely controlled by masters, to texts written figuratively as well as literally outside slave territory. Thus, he found autonomy not beyond language, but in discourse (such as abolitionist speeches) that crystallized, confirmed, and sanctioned inchoate ideas that seemed to issue from within himself:

> These [speeches] were choice documents to me. . . . They gave tongue to interesting thoughts of my own soul, which had frequently flashed through my own mind, and died away for want of utterance. . . . The reading of these documents enabled me to utter my thoughts, and to meet the arguments brought forward to sustain slavery. . . . The more I read, the more I was led to abhor and detest my enslavers. . . . As I read and contemplated the subject, behold! that very discontentment which Master Hugh and predicted would follow my learning to read had already come. . . . (84).

His master could foresee, but he could not forestall, the effect of his slave's learning to read.

Here Douglass acknowledges the extent to which his identity was shaped by texts. Though he attests that he did have thoughts of freedom before reading abolitionist tracts, he admits that they were stillborn; therefore, in a sense these "choice documents" chose *him*. By giving his deepest impulses stable, objective, and lasting form, abolitionist literature made them accessible to his mind and to his tongue. He does not seem concerned with laying claim either to original discourse or to unprecedented behavior: he admits being created, in a sense, by others' writing. One reason why his initiation into the abolitionist movement provides a fitting conclusion to his narrative is that this event represented Douglass' dedication of himself to the propagation—and enrichment—of the discourse that had liberated and shaped him.

More than any other slave narrator, Douglass seems to view slavery as a "gross fraud," as well as a system of horrors or terrors (115). He uses his hard-won literacy to deconstruct the codes and conventions at the core of slavery's fraudulent discourse. For him, self-liberating lifewriting involved the use of verbal devices, tricks and tropes, that turned the system's strength against itself. These gestures are complementary to his decoding of slave songs: the latter seeks to legitimize folk discourse, while the former attempts to delegitimize official discourse. For example, Douglass attacks the discourse of oppression by redefining Christmas "liberty" as "a dose of vicious dissipation, artfully labelled with the name of liberty" (116). Similarly, to choose a minor but revealing example of verbal judo, his pun on a master's name "deauthorizes" a system that gives a virtual monopoly on landownership and freedom to Southern whites: "But by this time, I began to want to live *upon free land* as well as *with Freeland*" (122). By bisecting the proper name and lowering its case, he rescues its common meaning from his master's exclusive proprietorship.

Even when he appears most contained by official discourse, there is often a discordant subtext. For example, consider the marriage certificate he transcribes into his narrative:

> "This may certify, that I joined together in holy matrimony Frederick Johnson and Anna Murray, as man and wife, in the presence of Mr. David Ruggles and Mrs Michaels.
>
> "James W. C. Pennington
>
> New York, Sept. 15, 1838" (145)

This text would seem to exemplify and signify the author's accession to official discourse, which identifies and locates him in its coordinates of space, time, custom, and law. Moreover, insofar as it represents a felicitous speech act binding him to a chosen partner, it would seem to function as an internal authenticating document.

But its language does not quite circumscribe the narrator. A footnote explains how, and why, "Frederick Johnson" became "Frederick Douglass": Douglass gave up the name "Johnson" because it proved too common in New Bedford, while he retained "Frederick" in order "to preserve a sense of my identity." The discussion of his names establishes "Frederick Douglass" as the latest and last in a chain of signifiers reaching back to the birth of a slave called "Frederick Augustus Washington Bailey." By declaring his commitment to his new name, Douglass marks its acquisition as a decisive change in his status: "From that time until now I have been called 'Frederick Douglass'; and as I am more widely known by that name than by either of the others, I shall continue to use it as my own" (147).

The value of the new name resides in two considerations. The first is that it was chosen by a black friend and benefactor, Nathan Johnson; it is thus a name given by a proper father figure. The second is that it is "widely known"; it is thus a "name" in the sense of "fame" or "reputation"—one he can claim to have *made* for himself through his escape, his abolition lectures, and lastly his narrative. With its allusion to Scott's *Lady of the Lake,* its tentative status, and its mixed ancestry, the name "Frederick Douglass" reflects his complex relation to genteel literature, official institutions of the North and South, and black culture. In important ways, however, it also signifies a self-authored identity produced by his own words.

In his appendix, Douglass makes two final moves that bear on the authority of his narrative. First, he feints toward an accommodation with established religion—"I have, in several instances, spoken in such a tone and manner, respecting religion, as may possibly lead those unacquainted with my religious views to suppose me an opponent of all religion"—only to launch a direct assault on all churches, South or North, implicated in slavery:

> What I have said respecting and against religion, I mean strictly to apply to the *slaveholding religion* of this land, and with no possible reference to Christianity proper. . . . [I] hate the corrupt, slaveholding, women-whipping, cradle-plundering, partial and hypocritical Christianity of this land. Indeed, I can see no reason, but the most deceitful one, for calling the religion of this land Christianity. I look upon it as

> the climax of all misnomers, the boldest of all frauds, and the grossest of all libels (153).

Here the misnomer is not the name of a former master, Mr. Freeland, but that of a religion that invokes divinity to abuse humanity: "He who proclaims it a religious duty to read the Bible denies me the right of learning to read the name of the God who made me" (154).

The significance of the gesture, for my purposes, is that it represents an authorial attempt to control the consumption of his narrative. Though his self-interpretation is more or less consistent with those of Garrison and Phillips, it is notable that Douglass warns against complacent misreading in his own (after)words. Having been prefaced and introduced by white authorities, he himself occupies the book's final space and uses it to establish the way his text—and the Bible—should be read. Standing outside his own narrative, he calls attention to its location outside fraudulent discourses in which literacy, liberty, and Biblical interpretation are privileges reserved to whites.

Having thus grounded his narrative in his own reading of Scripture, Douglass concludes with a travesty of the conventional validation of slave narratives. His parting shot is to "certify" a satirical poem about slavery by a Northern preacher who had lived in the South. He makes essentially the same claims for it that were typically made for the slave narrative: that it lacked bias, was based on reliable eyewitness testimony, and was "true to life." This final gesture, a prime example of "deauthorizing," both expropriates and mocks the apparatus of authentication.[29] It concludes a process by which Douglass sought to wrest control of his own narrative from those who presumed to authorize it.

X

Two passages in the narrative itself—the young slave's apostrophe to ships on Chesapeake Bay and his forging of a pass—particularly illuminate the complex legacy of literacy for Douglass, and by extension for any slave turned writer. Though he introduces his apostrophe as a distillation of a series of impulsive outbursts inspired by the sight of the ships, it is no "rude" outpouring of his "soul's complaint," but rather a carefully crafted set-piece. It begins with a series of antitheses, modulates into a prayer, and then subsides into a soliloquy in which the speaker resolves on and plans his escape (106–7). While no one doubts that Douglass wrote this passage, it is obvious, despite his remark to the contrary—"Thus I used to think, and thus I used to speak to myself"—that the slave boy could not have expressed himself in anything like these terms. Thus, although both Phillips and Garrison responded favorably to it—indeed, Garrison calls it "the most thrilling [passage] of them all" (39)—the apostrophe is problematic. At best, it is implausible in the mouth of the character, and its formal language illustrates the potentially alienating effect of a genteel style.

Jonathan Culler has characterized apostrophe, the signature trope of the ode, in terms that illuminate its use here in a very different context. According to him, apostrophe constitutes the speaker as a visionary by willing a world responsive to the speaker's words and wishes.[30] In light of the fact that the slave's world grants him little if any autonomy or discursive authority, Douglass' apostrophe both explains and epitomizes his lifelong endeavor to use language as a lever on the world. Though apostrophe was almost certainly not part of the slave boy's linguistic repertoire, its attribution to him at once expresses his intense yearning for power and enacts the fulfillment of that desire: apostrophe instantaneously rewrites the world, and reconstitutes the self as authoritative. Since, as Culler suggests, apostrophe is itself a discursive event rather than the representation of one (152–53), it offers a verbal shortcut to the future promised and prophesied by both Garrison and Phillips, in which ex-slaves and abolitionists would revise the nation's laws and thus prescribe its history.

Culler's most interesting observation indicates why this passage stands out even in such a formal and rhetorical narrative: "[Things apostrophized] are immediately associated with what might be called a timeless present but is better seen as a temporality of writing . . . a time of discourse rather than story" (149). It is because apostrophe violates narrative reconstruction of a temporal sequence of events that this passage floats free of the text (like the one that describes the death of Douglass' grandmother in the present tense—as an ongoing, rather than a historical event [93]). The passage thus involves two very different kinds of anachronism. The first is the attribution to a fifteen-year-old of an impossibly "literary" monologue. The unsuitable language undercuts the narrator's attempt to re-present his earlier self; its implausibility reveals how irreversible Douglass' flight has been. Not only is his new self the product of recently mastered literary conventions, but Douglass is either unable or unwilling to recross the linguistic frontier between his present and his past self.

The second, more fundamental, anachronism is the expression of a persistent and radical impulse to escape from the constraints of time and history altogether—to achieve a kind of discursive authority that transcends rather than engages historical forces. (The longing here for escape from historical contingency seems as much the narrator's as the slave's.) Because apostrophe seeks to establish the speaker's authority immediately and unconditionally, it is fundamentally inconsistent with the historicity and circumstantiality of the slave narrative. Just as it tends to sidestep the whole laborious process of authentication and verification, apostrophe disrupts narrative and threatens to annihilate referentiality. Working against generic expectations of documentary objectivity, it is a powerfully self-authorizing gesture.

A very different, but related, fruit of Douglass' difficult apprenticeship as a writer is the "protection" he wrote for himself and others in his first attempt at escape:

> "This is to certify that I, the undersigned, have given the bearer, my servant, full liberty to go to Baltimore, and spend the Easter holidays. Written with mine own hand, &c.,1835.
>
> William Hamilton"

It is hard to conceive of a more literary method of escape than the composition of this tiny, tricky text. Here what began in laborious and slavish imitation of the master's script is subtly transformed into the subversion of the master's language: this facsimile of an authentic pass functions as a kind of self-emancipation proclamation.

The ironies of this text are many and, given the failure of the ploy, they are its point. The pass's privileging of the undersigned master over the anonymous "bearer" reflects the rigid hierarchy of slave culture; however, its failure to identify its bearer also renders it—like Brown's master's letter to the jailer—vulnerable to misuse. Practically speaking, the utility of passes depends less on the distinctiveness of particular masters' signatures than on the general illiteracy of slaves; hence, the assumption of the power of the master's pen depends more on the impersonation of a generic master—the ability to reproduce, with authority, the phrasing of a white slaveowner—than on the counterfeiting of Hamilton's handwriting or signature (which a functional illiterate might conceivably accomplish). Just as the slave's attainment of ironically "full liberty" in this case required the successful simulation of masterly discourse—the erasure of any self-identifying mark of tone or style—the "liberty" of the black autobiographer might also at times depend on his disguising, if not suppressing, his distinctive voice or style. (This was at least the implication of Lucius Matlack's preface to Henry Bibb's narrative.)

Despite its failure, the protection serves as a model of an ultimately, if prematurely, self-licensing text that attempts to enact its author's "liberty" simply by declaring it. If it met the requirements for a felicitous speech act, it would stand as a prototype of a self-liberating slave narrative. (Of course, Douglass' "pass"—like the Emancipation Proclamation—did not meet conditions for a valid declaration. Just as Lincoln lacked the authority to effect the emancipation of slaves in rebel territory, no slave had the authority to write his own pass—or to travel without one.) Despite its fraudulence, however, the pass written in 1835 shares a powerful impulse with the apostrophe written ten years later. Both gestures manifest Douglass' extreme impatience with limitations on his discourse—whether his outright exclusion from privileged forms of it as a slave or his limited access to them as a narrator. With the pass, the slave breaks the rules of hegemonic discourse in quest of individual autonomy; with the apostrophe, the narrator deploys the conventions of poetic discourse to (re)constitute himself as authoritative. Both of these masterly gestures arrogate linguistic authority to effect *immediately* the freedom his narrative, and others, were encouraged to seek with somewhat more deliberate speed. That is, both gestures bypass the mechanisms by which authority, political or literary, is customarily granted—or denied—to blacks.

Although the slave narrative is not usually considered a self-reflexive form, many narratives devote a disproportionate amount of space to what one might call "meta-discourse"—writing about the discursive disadvantages of blacks, slave or free. (This is perhaps especially true of abolitionist narrators, who were probably both more strictly constrained than other narrators and more conscious of imposed limits.) The controls, both implicit and explicit, that were placed on black narrators sometimes deflected their energy from narrative of individual experience into commentary on those limitations. Rather than simply or straightforwardly writing autobiography as "the unique tale, uniquely told, of a unique life," ex-slaves sometimes felt bound to disclose and subvert the obstacles to their doing so. "Autobiography" in the narrow sense was displaced by analysis of its difficulty, or impossibility—the autobiographical impulse might be spent in a preparatory clearing away of obstacles to its expression.

An analogous situation occurs in *Walden,* whose long first chapter is devoted to exhibiting and razing false constructions and setting out the principles by which a proper life is to be led (and a proper Life written). Too many slave narrators, however, never get beyond the proto-autobiographical gestures of what we call the slave narrative. Unfortunately, rather than narrating life freely, slave narrative sometimes merely prepares the way for the *living* of a life that might be—but rarely is—idiosyncratically narrated (without the necessity of authentication and documentation and the obligation of representativeness or typicality). What this process yields is perhaps not autobiography as conventionally conceived; however, by dramatizing the difficult process of their own composition, these texts qualify as powerful and authoritative forms of lifewriting.

Douglass' apostrophe and his pass, which seek to cut through constraints all at once, remind us of the extraordinary limitations on early black autobiographers. These narrators were not allowed the ludic license of a Franklin, or a Barnum, let alone the playful pseudonymity of a Mark Twain. They were not encouraged to joke with their narratives in ways that suggested their utter control over their written lives: too much was at stake—and too little could be presumed of their audiences—for such self-indulgence. Minority autobiographers generally have had to fight harder for their Lives. This may involve subversion of prevailing or imposed conventions, but it also means insisting on (and accepting help in) buttressing the authority of their own narratives, rather than playfully undercutting it.

Ultimately, the situation of slave narrators is different in degree rather than in kind from that of majority autobiographers. The restraints on slave narrators remind us of the checks on all autobiographers—and of the reasons for them. Both common readers and many theorists would insist that some notion of empirical verification is essential to all autobiography, whether or not it is acted upon. It is precisely because all autobiography threatens to be a self-written "pass" that the idea of an autobiographical pact is so appealing. Douglass' pass may thus stand for a kind of outer limit of falsely self-authenticating lifewriting that no autobiographer, whether black or white, majority or minority, collaborative or solo, is encouraged to transgress. While the writing of Douglass' pass was morally justified, the writing of its autobiographical equivalent would represent an act of illegitimate self-authorization in which autonomy is achieved at the expense of authenticity and veracity. Thus, the special constraints on slave narrators remind us that, because the notion of its authority is both important and uncertain, autobiography is always a metaphorically manacled form of writing.

7

Mary Boykin Chesnut: Secession, Confederacy, Reconstruction

> As long as women remain silent, they will be outside the historical process. But, if they begin to speak and write *as men do,* they will enter history subdued and alienated.
>
> SIDONIE SMITH[1]

I

The circumstances of Mary Boykin Chesnut's life could hardly have been more different from those of Harriet Jacobs'. Chesnut was born into a prominent South Carolina family, and married into another; Jacobs was born a slave. Chesnut had an excellent formal education; Jacobs was essentially self-educated. Chesnut married but had no children; Jacobs had children but never married. Chesnut, though critical of slavery, was deeply implicated in it and the way of life it made possible; Jacobs managed only after much suffering and anxiety to escape from slavery and reunite her family. In short, Chesnut was among those Jacobs considered her oppressors. (Indeed, rather than sympathizing with the sexual vulnerability of slave women, Chesnut seems to have resented their corrupting influence on the morals of Southern gentlemen.) These two Southern women seem to have lived on opposite sides of an unbridgeable cultural and political divide.

The one apparent similarity between them is that both were devoted, artful, and idiosyncratic lifewriters. Also, although they were divided by race and class, they were both marginalized by gender. Both composed in secrecy or semisecrecy, and both of their books were long delayed in reaching print—in part because of the need for editorial assistance and sponsorship. Most important and revealing, both books have been accused of inauthenticity. Thus, like the controversy over Jacobs' narrative, the dispute over Mary Boykin Chesnut's account of her Civil War years raises fundamental questions about the authority of women's autobiography.

If Jacobs' narrative offers an account of life at the bottom of the Southern hierarchy, Chesnut's offers a unique account of life at the top as the South seceded, organized a war effort, fought a long and losing campaign, and finally surrendered to the Union Army. By virtue of her marriage to James Chesnut, Jr. (a U. S. senator and, after secession, a key aide to Jefferson Davis), Mary Chesnut had ready access to the center of political power and military intelligence. Thus, she was in a position to record at first-hand the pulse of the Confederacy from its birth to its death-throes. Along with glimpses of plantation life, her diary offers a running account of the administration of the Civil War and insights into Confederate politics, as well as a sensitive register of the War's daily impact at its epicenter—the circle of elite Southern families. Gossip about courtship and marriage, news of lives lost in battle, reports of homefront morale, speculation about the course of the War, an incisive and candid critique of its conduct, and analysis of the shortcomings that hindered her region in its bid for autonomy are all elements that combine to make the diary fascinating reading.

Still, her book did not see print in any form until 1905—fifty years after the War's end—when it was published in an abridged version as *A Diary from Dixie.* It was not until 1962 that Edmund Wilson's praise of the 1949 edition (also abridged) as "an extraordinary document—in its informal department, a masterpiece"—effectively established it in the Civil War canon.[2] It was twenty more years before C. Vann Woodward edited and published a full scholarly edition, under the title *Mary Chesnut's Civil War.*[3] Greeted with critical acclaim and awarded the 1982 Pulitzer Prize for History, Woodward's edition bestowed further prestige on the book. His editing, however, revealed that what had been published in 1905 and in 1949 as a diary dating from the war years had in fact been revised and greatly expanded by its author, in two intensive efforts, over a twenty-year period.[4] Seizing upon this revelation, Kenneth Lynn, in a review-essay in the *New York Times Book Review,* flatly condemned the Chesnut diaries as a hoax.[5] Like the skepticism about *Incidents in the Life of a Slave Girl,* the denunciation of Chesnut's "diaries" lends support to Sidonie Smith's assertion that "the contributions of women to the genre have traditionally been perceived as forms of contamination, illegitimacies, threats to the purity of the canon of autobiography itself" (43).

Exploiting the troublesome fact of the book's revision, Lynn accused Chesnut of sanitizing her text to exploit the growing taste, after Reconstruction, for Southern apologias of the sort written by Thomas Nelson Page and Thomas Dixon, Jr. Similarly, he charged Woodward with conspiring to misrepresent a racist Southern belle as a progressive (a covert abolitionist and feminist). According to Lynn, Mary Chesnut's revisions betrayed not only her own devoted slaves, but also their entire race: "Is it any wonder that she left out of her manuscript the most troubling conduct of white masters and mistresses toward their slaves which she had recorded two decades earlier? . . . She tailored its contents to fit the emerging literary fashion" (57). Indeed, to him, her entire account of the Confederacy was finally as suspect as her liberal credentials:

> As a young woman, Mrs. Chesnut did not respond to her husband's deceptions either by leaving him or by becoming a crusader for women's rights. In her later years, though, she herself became a deceiver, albeit not in the realm of sexual infidelity. She wrote a novel about the South during the Civil War and called it a diary (59).

Lynn's accusations are generally unfair—as the tenor of the last quotation suggests—but, by questioning the book's authority, he raises issues relevant to the concerns of this book. The first, and most easily resolved, is whether the "diary" was carried out as a hoax—like Clifford Irving's "autobiography" of Howard Hughes or the more recent "Hitler diaries." In answer to Lynn's charges, Woodward has pointed out, first, that Mary Chesnut never titled her work a "diary" and made no effort to hide her revisions, and second, that he himself has carefully and openly chronicled the manuscript's evolution.[6] Clearly, neither Chesnut nor Woodward contrived to deceive the public. If anyone is guilty of fraud, it is the editors of *A Diary from Dixie,* who neglected to acknowledge either the twenty-year gap in composition or their own aggressive editing of the text. Still, the accusation of fraud, like the controversy over the bestowal of the Pulitzer in History, reminds us of the powerful expectation that life-writing ought to be more factual than artifactual. Though Mary Chesnut's social position could hardly have been more different from that of an ex-slave, the controversy stirred up by Lynn makes it clear that, as with slave narrative (and for some of the same reasons), the political stakes here are too high to permit toleration of "literary" play.

The issue of the authority of the text is of course bound up with the question of what it is—how we read it depends on its genre. At the Reynolds Conference on South Carolina Women Writers, in October 1975, where Woodward first publicly explained his editorial decisions and procedures, this issue was raised but never resolved. According to Woodward, what began as a journal—a day-by-day record, written daily—"became more and less than that." He thus hinted at, but passed over, the anomalous nature of the diary as a genre: unlike a novel, a tragedy, or an autobiography, a diary becomes something else when revised. Just what this text became Woodward declined to say. Rather than labeling it, he described it as "a genre of her own, a kind of art form to embody her experience of the greatest historical drama of her time."[7] The other discussants were largely in agreement that the later version, at least, is a work of conscious literary art, but no one seemed ready to pronounce it a novel—apparently out of a sense that to do so would be to denounce it, as Lynn later did. (Apparently unaware of the lapse of time in its composition, Edmund Wilson had cited the *Diary's* novelistic quality as an asset: "[T]he diarist's instinct is uncanny. Starting out with situations or relationships of which she cannot know the outcome, she takes advantage of the actual turn of events to develop them and round them out as if she were molding a novel" [280].)

In a more recent discussion of the text, Woodward has expressed continued perplexity over "questions regarding the nature of diaries, the historian's expectations of them, the distinctions we draw between diaries and memoirs, the classification of the one as primary and the other as secondary sources, the reliance upon memory as a source, and the ambiguities of memory itself," as well as the overarching question of when "art" enters into writing.[8] A crux of the problem seems to be our sense that daily, or nearly daily, composition is the essential feature of a diary—as the term's etymology implies—and that this mode of production precludes hindsight. Woodward wonders "how many diaries live up to the abstract concept":

> Diarists' own diaries are often their favorite reading, and as they pore over them later, sometimes years later, they may often be tempted to delete, correct, supplement, smooth out, bring up to date, revise. . . . It often happens that the nightly session with the diary has to be postponed, sometimes for weeks . . . and reconstructed when there is

> time. In such experiences . . . opportunities for the introduction of hindsight are not lacking (206).

Woodward's remarks here seem to imply that the "dailiness" of the diary—the immediacy and discreteness of each entry—may be regarded more as a generic convention than as a fact of its composition.

Indeed, one trend in current thinking about the diary as a literary form is to challenge the conventional distinction between diary and autobiography. Thus, in a recent book on English diaries, Robert A. Fothergill questions the

> assumption that [the diary's] defining characteristic is an unpremeditated sincerity. . . . [For] when this quality is made out to be the essential attribute of the species . . . an ethical standard is coming into conflict with literary considerations and asserting a rigid and unrealistic scale of merit. To endeavour to write well, to consider the formal structure of the book one is writing, to address oneself to a putative reader or think of publication, to edit or rewrite one's own entries—all these practices must appear to corrupt the pure spontaneity of utterance that should mark the "true" diary.[9]

Critical of the Romantic cult of the "spontaneous" or "immediate" record, Fothergill argues for recognition of the diary as a self-conscious literary form whose most mature version may become what he calls "serial autobiography."[10]

Fothergill's term may be useful, but because of Chesnut's wholesale revision it suits her text no better than "diary" on the one hand or "novel" on the other. (What Chesnut produced in the 1880s is perhaps best described as a novelized chronicle in diary format.) Still, Fothergill's critique of the aesthetic of immediacy is salutary for readers of Mary Chesnut's "diaries." Similarly, what poststructuralists in general—and historians like Hayden White in particular—have had to say about the ways in which all narrative constructs reality seems to militate against any absolute or easy distinction between "primary" and "secondary" sources. Nevertheless, Woodward declined to follow where his own argument seems to be taking him—toward reconceiving this distinction as a difference in degree rather than in kind and toward a more powerful probing of the way in which all written "sources" are mediated by literary conventions. Rather, he emphasized the fidelity of Chesnut's revision to her original, despite the lapse of time between the two versions. Indeed, as if to demonstrate this faithfulness, he and Elisabeth Muhlenfeld soon published Chesnut's wartime journal as *The Private Mary Chesnut* (1984).

Ironically, however, this may ultimately serve to damage rather than to enhance the authority of the revised manuscript because—contra Fothergill—many will view the "original" manuscript as the *truer* diary, in two mutually reinforcing senses of that phrase: it will seem more *trustworthy* because it is more *immediate* in its composition. In any case, most scholars who have discussed the problem of the Chesnut texts—in reviews as well as at the 1975 conference—have tended to take the 1860s version at face value, even though a long section of it is avowedly a "memoir" written after a considerable passage of time, and although Woodward confesses uncertainty as to whether the entries' dates refer to the moment of composition or to the events recorded.[11]

These last considerations remind us that, like all diaries, even the first version of Chesnut's was inevitably informed by hindsight. As Woodward acknowledges, the dating of Chesnut's entries may elide or suppress a significant gap between the events recorded and the event of their recording. In any case, entries are necessarily retrospective since events are never recorded as they are happening. Moreover, each entry after the first is written with awareness of those that precede it; as entries accumulate, this self-consciousness (a form of hindsight) accrues and inevitably shapes new entries. There is also a sense in which there is no history unless and until it is recorded—both for the diarist, who in some sense acquires a past only in writing it, and for the reader, to whom gaps between entries remain voids.

Because the hindsight thought by some to compromise the integrity of the revision is also present, in more subtle forms, in Chesnut's 1860s journal, the tendency of some scholars to refer to the first version as the "original" is dangerously misleading: it risks assigning the journal a value it does not—and could not—possess. It also encourages the use of the first version as the standard against which the later ones should be measured—or even as a guide to what they mean—thereby obscuring the fact that *all* versions are retrospective textual constructions of a history that, insofar as it is unwritten, may be irrecoverable. Still, some scholars seem to believe that Chesnut's revisions could, and did, effectively recreate her earlier responses to the Civil War. For example, in reviewing *Mary Chesnut's Civil War,* Nancy F. Cott endorsed Woodward's claim "that the twenty years intervening [did not give] the polished version any altered cast of mind or ideology" and went on to generalize: "Indeed, his conclusion that Mrs. Chesnut in the 1880s remained true to her persona of the 1860s suggests how dominant and immutable that Confederate persona was in her life, and perhaps similarly in the lives of her kind."[12]

Even if one concedes that there was no substantial shift in Chesnut's explicit ideology, there are several questionable assumptions here. The first is that earlier experience can be reproduced from verbal cues. The elaboration of condensed diary entries twenty years later can no more recapture original responses than the addition of tap water to canned concentrate can truly reconstitute the original fruit juice. Another is that one can argue from text directly to life, as though continuity in the text automatically reflects immutability in life. As the use of the word *persona* indicates, neither Woodward nor Cott means to say that Chesnut did not change in the twenty years following the war. Assuming that she did change (as she must have), the persistence of an immutable "persona" in the diary would characterize her revision as the literary equivalent of self-embalming. As it happened, Chesnut did not merely re-sign herself to her wartime diary. Instead, she effectively transformed it. Nor did her "persona of the 1860s" endure immutably and inertly into the 1880s; as we shall see, her revision of her earlier text significantly altered—reinvented—her persona. In any event, the idea that such elaborate revisions could be effected without "an altered cast of mind" is implausible: it is based on naive notions of memory, of history, of writing, and of the relations among them.

Of course, Woodward's and Cott's primary concern is to establish that Mary Chesnut's 1880s views on such key issues as slavery, race, and women were not retrospective creations, but were characteristic of her "mind or ideology" in the 1860s. If one thinks of ideology as consciously held and explicitly articulated beliefs, then that is true. There seems little doubt that Chesnut was opposed to slavery in the 1860s, when she began to keep a journal, and was so possibly as early as the 1840s: the antislavery sentiments voiced in the text are evidently not a function of post-Civil War selfreconstruction. At the same time, as Woodward acknowledges, she seems to have thought of blacks as an inferior race. Indeed, one of Chesnut's strongest denunciations of slavery (omitted from the 1880s version) seems motivated by disgust at sexual intercourse between slave women and their masters—not out of sympathy for exploited black women (like Harriet Jacobs), but rather out of a sense that miscegenation mocked the honor of women of her class:

> I wonder if it be a sin to think slavery a curse to any land. Sumner said not one word of this hated institution which is not true. Men & women are punished when their masters & mistresses are brutes & not when they do wrong—& then we live surrounded by prostitutes. An abandoned woman is sent out of any decent house elsewhere. Who thinks any worse of a Negro or Mulatto woman for being a thing we can't name. . . . Like the patriarchs of old our men live all in one house with their wives & their concubines, & the Mulattoes one sees in every family exactly resemble the white children.[13]

(While she does not explicitly judge slave women here, her diction—"prostitutes"—implicitly blames the victims for the crime against them.) Thus, as Cott shrewdly points out (128), the keystone of Chesnut's politics was neither abolitionism, nor feminism, nor racism, but veneration of aristocratic Southern women: "[A]gain I say, my countrywomen are as pure as angels, tho' surrounded by another race who are the social evil" (PMC 43).

The suppression of this passage in revision does not necessarily confirm Lynn's charge that Chesnut defended slavery in the revision. In addition, although Michael Johnson argues that her racism may be somewhat more pronounced in the 1880s version, the changes in Chesnut's comments on race do not seem sufficiently thorough or programmatic to reflect conscious exploitation of a changing climate of opinion.[14] In any case, a writer who worked as hard and published as little as Chesnut did is not very vulnerable to charges of pandering to shifts in taste. While the core of her "ideology" does persist in her revision, its emphasis and tone do change. As the purging of this passionate, nearly incoherent outburst demonstrates, time did alter her cast of mind.

Woodward's claim that Chesnut's revisions are essentially "faithful" to her wartime journal fails to convince for other reasons as well. First, there are vast stretches of *Mary Chesnut's Civil War* that cannot be traced to, or from, the surviving journals from the 1860s because of the large gaps in them. Second, even where both versions survive, the revised entries are often so much more extensive and elaborate than the originals that they defy comparison. As Muhlenfeld puts it, "In every case where we have a portion of the original diary, as it was recorded day by day, corresponding to the later version as it was revised in the 1880s, the latter version bears no more than a close family resemblance to the former."[15] Of course, the two overlap considerably: both purport to record the same crucial episode of her life, which she knew early on was her essential literary subject. However, the two versions are products of separate eras in her life. Moreover, the twenty-year interval between them was in effect a literary apprenticeship, during which she investigated various genres, both fictional and nonfictional. The 1880s versions may have been changed more by literary craft than by historical hindsight, but it is transformed nevertheless.

Thus, there is another troublesome assumption here that is shared by Woodward, Cott, and Lynn: that "ideology" is a matter of attitudes on key issues as registered more or less explicitly in particular comments or anecdotes. To treat ideology—like factual content—as essentially independent of form is to neglect the political implications of genre itself. In the case of Mary Chesnut, as in that of the slave narrators, it is especially perilous to ignore the ideology of form. Her restless revisions in the two decades after the Civil War transformed an already noteworthy narrative into a more complex and distinctive form of lifewriting. More importantly, they also manifest a certain frustration with conventional sex roles and the limited authority to which women of her era could aspire. To adapt the title of Woodward's *Yale Review* essay, Mary Chesnut in search of a genre is also a woman in search of a literary gender.

II

Mary Chesnut's narratives may be read in the context of a larger problem, that of the authority of women's lifewriting. To begin with, for women, as for slaves, the crucial identicality of author, subject, and narrator in autobiography is complicated by the lack of a proper name:

> For women in our culture . . . a proper name is at best problematic; even as it "inscribes" her into the discourse of society by designating her role as her father's daughter, her patronymic effaces her matrilineage and thus erases her own position in the discourse of the future. Her "proper" name, therefore, is always in a way *im*proper because it is not, in the French sense, *propre,* her own, either to have or to give.[16]

With women autobiographers writing under their "real names"—as with Mark Twain, Black Elk, "Linda Brent," and most slave narrators—the simple gesture of referring to the writer under consideration becomes complex.[17]

The distinctive "anxiety of authorship" faced by women writers takes on a particular intensity for women lifewriters because autobiography involves an assertion of one's significance and autonomy traditionally reserved for men in patriarchal societies.[18] Indeed, Sidonie Smith has recently claimed that "autobiography"—the quotation marks are part of a deconstructive strategy—is a kind of male "plot," in a couple of senses:

> In privileging the autonomous or metaphysical self as the agent of its own achievement and in frequently situating that self in an adversial stance toward the world, "autobiography" promotes a conception of the human being that valorizes individual integrity and separateness and devalues personal and communal interdependency. . . . [T]hat conception of selfhood is decidedly male-identified (39).

"Autobiography" contrives to exclude or silence women by conflating male patterns of individuation and development with the real, the narratable, and the auditable.

Even cultures considered conducive to lifewriting have not necessarily encouraged it in women; certainly in America, autobiography (in a narrow sense) has been underpopulated by women. Thus, women life-writers have been engaged in an enterprise in which gender and genre have seemed to be inherently at odds—as though the phrase "woman autobiographer" were an oxymoron. Indeed, Smith argues that

> women who do not challenge . . . gender ideologies and the boundaries they place around women's proper life script, textual inscription, and speaking voice do not write autobiography. They may write autobiographically, choosing other languages of self-writing—letters, diaries, journals, biography. Even so, their stories remain private, their storytelling culturally muted, albeit persistent (44).

The challenge for women lifewriters, then, is to engage in lifewriting without implicating themselves in, and subordinating themselves to, patriarchal plots, characters, and tropes—to invent forms that validate women's experiences on their own terms. Recent feminist criticism has had no trouble identifying patterns that seem to characterize or distinguish women's lifewriting: a preference for private confessional forms, such as the diary, rather than for more public forms of autobiography; a tendency to focus on the private sphere of home, family, and friends rather than the public sphere of power, career, and accomplishment[19]; a tendency, within narratives of public life, to undercut rather than to aggrandize the self (Spacks, 131–32), and even within the private forms to assume a supporting rather than a leading role (Fothergill, 87); a tendency to write narratives that seem discontinuous, fragmentary and nonlinear, in comparison with those of male prototypes (Jelinek, 17, 19); and to discover and disclose the self with reference (but not necessarily deference) to some other presence or consciousness (Mason, 210). (A classic instance of deference would be the coupling of a wife's memoirs with her biography of her husband [Mason, 211].)

Many of these patterns, however, seem to reflect, rather than to resist, patriarchal constructs. Hence, theories of women's autobiography built on such differences threaten to perpetuate rather than to eradicate essentialist concepts of what it is to be male or female, trapping women in a discourse not entirely of their own creation. Thus, the critic of women's lifewriting must beware of a version of the double-bind that constricts women lifewriters: to ignore the role of gender ideologies is to overlook a powerful constituent of autobiography, but to require women's lifewriting to transcend such historical conditioning may be to ask too much, and thus to consign it to inevitable failure. One risk run by contemporary feminist criticism is that it will perpetuate a pattern of male condescension: working from assumptions diametrically opposed to those of patriarchal critics, feminist critics will nevertheless speak of women's lifewriting "as men have done" (i.e., they will define it out of existence).

Mary Chesnut could not have entered public discourse without some compromise with its male biases. Still, there is evidence that she was aware of the complexity of her predicament and groped her way toward a solution. Her intense reaction to the published letters of Jane Carlyle certainly reveals the difficulty of establishing the value of female experience on its own terms:

> He is a better fellow than his wife. Wailing and howling—to ones family and friends—easier than writing the "French Revolution"—difference between a man's sense—and a clever woman's hysterics—when she cut old Carlyle as with a two edged sword—*I was there*—but when it is all—head aches—stomach aches—*maids* (whom *she* kisses!)—*bugs*—house-cleaning which she piles on ad nauseam. I feel—"people read all of this—because she is old Carlyle's wife". . . . She had two motions—the one around her Sun—or brilliant husband—is delightful—the harder she hits him—the better fun—but when she turns on her own axis—and thrusts her homely details under our noses by the guise—she is a bore.[20]

This letter, written to Varina Davis in June 1883 reveals a good deal more than what Muhlenfeld calls Chesnut's "horror of being a bore." An elaborate code that endorsed the writing of men and denigrated that of women is evident in the distinctions between Thomas Carlyle's subjects (the French Revolution) and his wife's (her husband, her house-cleaning, and her ailments), between the nature of his mental state (sense) and hers (hysterics), between the difficulty of his writing (great) and hers (small), and between his audience (the public, posterity) and hers (family, friends, and—thanks only to the eminence of her husband—the public). This conventional division privileges the public, the outer, or the rational—the "masculine"—over the private, the inner, or the emotional—the "feminine."

Chesnut's attitude toward this code is not altogether clear. Her response to Jane Carlyle's letters seems to envision no escape from the double-bind in which women writers find themselves: while she relishes the correspondent's criticism of her husband, she scorns her attempts to assert her independence of him—to "turn on her own axis." Chesnut seems to allow Jane Carlyle no valid subject of her own; at best, the tedious household details are tolerated because of the importance of its male occupant. The effect is to confine her to his orbit. Still, the letter unmistakably registers Chesnut's shocked recognition of her own predicament as the wife of a "great man." Had Chesnut been the wife of a famous *writer,* her identification with Jane Carlyle might have been complete. As she well knew by the time she wrote this letter, however, she was her husband's superior as a writer. Moreover, her marriage to him provided her with a privileged vantage point from which to observe firsthand the historic cataclysm that she could make *her* literary subject. If the Civil War was analogous to the French Revolution as a world-historical event, then Mary Boykin Chesnut could emulate Thomas rather Jane Carlyle. Although she may have conceded the difficulty, if not the impossibility, of establishing the value of a woman's experience on its own terms, she may also have seen that she had another course open to her; thus, the letter hints at how she overcame the anxiety of authorship—by establishing her authority as a witness to, and a participant in, events of unquestioned significance.

Her diary should be read then in the light of her particular predicament as a woman and a writer. As the daughter of one prominent state politician and the wife of another, Chesnut participated vicariously in public life and became what her biographer calls "a superb player of a kind of universal parlor game" of flirtation and gossip (MBC, 102). Still, she lacked adequate outlets for her energy and talent, and she chafed under the constraints on her (113). Because she was childless, she lacked one time-honored occupation (46, 62). She also clearly resented the imposed leisure of life at her in-laws' plantation, Mulberry, which was headed by her patriarchal father-in-law, and where domestic affairs were managed by Chesnut women "senior" to herself. During the Civil War, one of her constant fears was that her husband's failure to advance himself would result in their forced rustication on the plantation—next to Union victory, she most dreaded being condemned to Camden. In any event, her acute and critical awareness of the limits placed on women in her culture is evident in her journal, especially in her comparisons between slavery and marriage (PMC, 21; MCCW, 15, 735), in her direct expressions of a yearning for power and authority, and in her harsh criticism of the ineffectual leadership of the Confederacy, which tended to waste its energy on infighting. (At one point she quips that what began as a War of Secession was becoming a War for the Succession of Places [PMC,49].)

The evolution of her ambition is best understood in the context of her marriage. All the evidence suggests that James Chesnut had difficulty living up to his wife's high expectations (and that these were modeled on the achievements of her father). In particular, the following passage from the 1870s version (interpolated in MCCW) suggests that his career was occasionally an issue between them—and that he at times suspected her of undermining him:

> J. C. and I had a most uncalled-for row. I reminded him of how I laughed when years and years ago I saw his name among the list of distinguished citizens. He grew angry and said my levity had ruined him, had effectually prevented his being anything, &c&c, all before Harriet Grant. I grew absolutely hysterical with rage and mortification, and he sulked the rest of the evening and did not sleep the whole night. Very odd. Such an unexpected turn to a small joke. Poor me. The mirth must be innate and constitutional that Sandy Hill and Mulberry could not drown out long years ago, and constant snubbing I live under. Thank God it is *irrepressible* and I will laugh at the laughable while I breathe (MCCW, 645).

Her intense interest in her husband's prospects would seem inconsistent with any conscious sabotage, but her characterization, in the wartime diary, of his failure to be elected to the first Confederate Congress as "an end of JC's political life" (PMC, 212) suggests that she was tempted to write him off as a failure. Apparently, Mary Chesnut was at times prone to view herself as a kind of political widow.

As Woodward has pointed out, the crisis of war—disastrous though it was—appeased some of her emotional needs:

> She feared and dreaded the war, but she embraced its demands with all the fierce passion of her nature. It meant outlet for many frustrated impulses and energies dammed up within her. It meant being involved, challenged, needed, wholly committed, and totally absorbed. It also opened doors of escape from dullness and boredom and self-absorption (MCCW, xxxviii; cf. MBC, 73).

What has not been adequately recognized is the role of her diary-writing (and rewriting) in the gratification of her ambitions. Indeed, the argument over her politics has been carried on almost without reference to her literary form, which is inevitably and inextricably tied up with the politics of gender, at least. What requires attention, then, is the way in which her writing may express a kind of feminism through its very existence and its evolving shape.

In the 1860s manuscript, her ambition was expressed explicitly in terms of her involvement in, and disappointment with, her husband's career. By contrast, in the 1880s version it seems to have been channeled—sublimated—into the work of revision itself. Indeed, Muhlenfeld's description of James Chesnut's role during the Civil War quite nicely fits the role assumed by his wife as narrator of her revised journal: "[H]e would be the fact-finder, the official observer, the carrier of news, the center of attention only when he was speaking of someone else's exploits" (MBC, 105). Unlike the *ideal* performance she seemed to expect of him, his *actual* role of observer and reporter was one that she could emulate as a writer, after a self-imposed apprenticeship and many drafts. Her long, if intermittent, engagement with her journal may therefore be seen as her own vicarious political career. By dint of the hard work of rewriting, over many years, she finally attained a genuine literary power that was eventually (posthumously) recognized. Thus, in her long literary campaign, she sought, and to some extent achieved, a kind of authority denied to most women in her time.

III

After the war Mary Chesnut might have fulfilled her literary ambition in a number of ways; indeed, she tried her hand at a number of quite different projects. For example, in the early 1870s, she made extensive, though ultimately abortive, efforts to convert her girlhood and her war experience into genteel fiction (MBC, ch. 6). According to her literary biographer, however, "she had little respect for writers of sentimental fiction, and she knew that she had no talent for poetry" (137); evidently, she had little taste or aptitude for the most popular "feminine" literary forms. Thus, her shift from a fictional to a nonfictional genre in the mid-1870s, when she first revised her journals, may involve a shift in gender roles as well.

It proved a temporary aberration, however; she soon dropped the journals to revert to a traditional woman's form—a biographical sketch of her husband. Commissioned for a series of "Sketches of the Lives of Leading and Prominent Men of our State, from 1861 to 1865," this piece was clearly an essay in Southern hagiography. (In view of her husband's disenfranchisement, her literary rehabilitation of him was also implicitly a counter-Reconstruction project.) But in addition to the deference to her husband inherent in the form, there may have been an element of covert self-portraiture in some of what she wrote:

> With his great power of reasoning, his accomplishments and learning he is, as he always was, inclined to stand back, and let the world flow by him.
>
> His friends urge upon him the necessity of recording what he has personally known in these last forty years of American life.
>
> He has amassed documents and letters invaluable as material for "memoires pour servir." His style is clear and correct and he has the gift of telling his story so as to interest all hearers (MBC, 171).

In any case, when Mary Chesnut returned to her own account of the Confederacy in the early 1880s, she not only assumed a "masculine" role, she also specifically assumed a prerogative she herself had assigned to her husband.

Hence, we may read her revised narrative as the resourceful response of an ambitious and talented woman to a literary and historical double-bind. She evidently had no desire to publish her 1860s journal, with its domestic focus and its raw expression of her personal concerns. Though her prominence might have facilitated her access to print, would it have militated against indecorous self-exposure at the same time. Had she made her husband the journal's center, she would have transformed it into a kind of memoir of an important Confederate, but that would have meant resigning herself to orbiting around his axis, and thus succumbing to the Jane Carlyle syndrome. As it turned out, her revision of her journal produced neither unguarded private confidences nor a deferential memoir of her husband's career but rather a collective autobiography of the embattled Confederacy that was also an idiosyncratic form of self-life-writing.

The broader focus of the revision was achieved at the cost of considerable self-effacement, but this was not necessarily a function of feminine self-deprecation in acquiescence to patriarchal values—it may have had to do with a complex literary ambition. At first glance, both the keeping and the revision of the "diary" would seem to be the acts of the wife as confederate, as well as Confederate. While her gender disqualified her from repelling military invaders, she often apostrophized and exhorted the troops, like an officer, in the first version of the diary: "Proud Carolinians—you must conquer on your own soil" (PMC, 59; cf. 67, 115). Similarly, as a diarist she could (and did) counterattack such literary enemies of the South as Ralph Waldo Emerson, Harriet Beecher Stowe, and William Howard Russell, the London *Times* reporter. Moreover, the inclusion of political and military intelligence in the wartime diary—side by side with home-front news—dramatized her life and validated her writing: if the diary's acquisition by the enemy would be costly to the Confederate cause, then its protection was important. In time of danger, burning it would be the kind of patriotic sacrifice that the childless wife of a noncombatant was ordinarily denied.

The patriotic motive certainly dominates the first full entry of the 1860s journal. Written during the war years (but not, apparently, as early as its date—February, 18, 1861), it was probably consciously and retrospectively composed as an introductory entry:

> I do not allow myself vain regrets or sad forebodings. This southern Confederacy must be supported now by calm determination and cool brains. We have risked all, and we must play our best, for the stake is life or death. I shall always regret that I had not kept a journal during the two past delightful and eventful years. The delights having exhausted themselves in the latter part of 1860 and the events crowding in so that it takes away one's breath to think about it all. I daresay I might have recorded with some distinctness the daily shocks—"Earthquakes as Usual" (Lady Sale). But now it is to me one nightmare from the time I left Charleston for Florida, where I remained two anxious weeks amid hammocks and everglades, oppressed and miserable, and heard on the cars returning to the world that Lincoln was elected and

> our fate sealed. Saw at Fernandina a few men running up a wan Palmetto flag and crying, South Carolina has seceded. Overjoyed at the tribute to South Carolina, I said, "So Florida sympathizes. . . ."[21]

Several traits of the initial entry typify the 1860s version, including her enthusiastic submission to the cause, both as woman and as diarist, (in the 1860s draft she notes that, as the daughter of a Nullifier, she was a "rebel born"); the resolute suppression of doubt and foreboding (coupled with the implicit confession of fatalism—"our fate sealed"); the literary allusion (and the detachment its understatement affords); the mixture of summary compression ("one nightmare") and vivid vignette (the raising of the "wan Palmetto flag"); and the interplay between prospect and retrospect. (They are also qualities that, when enhanced by the two-stage revision, would help to account for the power of the 1880s version.)

Though not uncritical of the Confederacy, she remains loyal to it throughout her "diary." Revising it over a twenty-year period, and reliving the war in the diary format, was thus a way of perpetuating a vital cause and of salvaging textual order, at least, from the disorder of defeat. Indeed, some obvious bits of revisionism in the 1880s version—for example, her suppression of the tensions, early in the war, between her and Varina Davis—strengthen her portrayal of herself as a loyal wife and patriot. What self-reconstitution her revision effects is certainly not a concession to Reconstruction: insofar as it dramatizes and elegizes the fall of the once-proud Confederate elite, Mary Chesnut's revision, like her sketch of her husband's life, is a counter-Reconstruction project. Writing and rewriting the journal were important ways of participating in the communal crisis, and of validating herself as a partisan.

But her writing also asserted her autonomy as a wife and as a woman, as if in emulation of the masculine prerogative of those who seceded in order to reconstitute prevailing political institutions to their own specifications. The journal offers substantial evidence, both direct and indirect, of Mary Chesnut's efforts to resist her husband's authority or to achieve some independence from him. According to Muhlenfeld, late in 1860—well before she began to keep a journal as such—Chesnut wrote in a commonplace book what proved to be the seed or germ of the Civil War diary:

> November 10th 1860
> James Chesnut Jr
> resigned his seat in

the Senate of U.S.A
alas I was in Florida
I might not have been
able to influence
him—but I should
have tried

Sometime after she began her formal journal in February of the following year, she inscribed a subtly different version of this primal entry on its flyleaf: "November 10th 1860 James Chesnut Jr resigned his seat in the U.S.A. Senate—'burnt the ships behind him' The first resignation—& I am not at all resigned."[22]

The second version's epic allusion not only adds a strong intimation of war, it also makes the passage more self-consciously literary. The tenses—and thus the tone—are significantly different, too. In the former, "might not have" and "should have" sound tentative and wistful—reluctantly submissive, perhaps. In the latter, the firm "am not . . . resigned" explicitly denies her acquiescence. In any case, this entry establishes the coincidence of her signing on (or up) with her husband's signing off. The two acts—his termination of his career as senator and her initiation of hers as diarist—are linked in subtle tension. Her act complements and compensates for his: as he ceases to be a public representative, she begins to be a private one.

Another entry (which she suppressed in revision) delineates differences between husband and wife that may have encouraged her journalizing:

> Mr. Chesnut hurt because Mr. Hill said he kept his own counsel. Mr. C, thinking himself an open, frank, confiding person, asked me if he *was not.* Truth required me to say that I knew no more what Mr. C thought or felt on any subject now than I did twenty years ago. Sometimes I *feel* that we understand each other a little—then up goes the Iron Wall once more (PMC, 32).

This suggests that she lacked a confidant even when he was at home. The journal, which met a need he could not, quite literally became a husband surrogate. It both expresses and enacts her desire for independence. To a degree, then, *keeping* a journal (from her husband) in the first place was a kind of silent secession.

Despite her avowed devotion of herself and her journal to the Confederate cause, the first full journal entry hints at her sense of exclusion from privileged forms of discourse:

> When we arrived in Charlestown, my room was immediately over a supper given by the city to a delegation from Savannah, and Colonel Bartow, the Mayor of Savannah, was speaking in the hot, fervid, after-supper Southern style. They contrived to speak all night and to cheer &c . . . (MCCW, 4).

The militant oratory of Southern men reached her in her upstairs room as sound and fury, signifying everything she believed in, but nothing she could emulate in her writing. Thus, from the start, her diary problematizes the position of the woman writer as Confederate.

Though such stylized masculine rhetoric was obviously not accessible to her, the pressure of events demanded some modification of her discursive practice. The 1860s journal expresses her nostalgia for innocent, antebellum uses of discourse: "I cannot write in this book without thinking of the happy days when I sat & read & heard the scratching of my darling Mary Stevens' pen as she scribbled her love nonsense in a red book like this" (PMC, 12). While she did not entirely give up escapist reading—in the revised version she rather guiltily notes, "How much I owe of the pleasure of my life to these much reviled writers of fiction" (MCCW, 10)—she increasingly supplemented it with memoirs of wars, invasions, and revolutions in search of historical perspective and literary precursors. When the exigencies of her situation encouraged her to expand her repertoire beyond the narrow limits of the conventionally feminine, she ventured boldly onto masculine literary turf.

Chesnut was proud of her taste for literature considered disturbing by most women of her class and region. Thus, in contrasting her own taste with that of her mother-in-law, she distanced herself from the gentility associated with Victorian women readers and writers. The old

> Mrs. Chesnut set her face resolutely to see only the pleasant things of life and shut her eyes to wrong and said it was not there. The most devoted, unremitting reader of fiction I ever knew . . . would not tolerate Thackeray. . . . She lived in a physical paradise and made her atmosphere a roseate-hued mist for her own private delusion.

In contrast, the diarist herself admired "the laying bare the seamy side—going behind the pretty curtain of propriety we hold up" that she found in Shakespeare (*Lear*) and Thackeray (MCCW, 761–62). Implicit in the diarist's expressions of her literary preferences are scorn for tenderminded readers and writers, and admiration for hard-headed ones.

The precedent cited in the introductory entry is ominously appropriate: in 1843, the wife of a British officer, Lady Florentia Sale, had published *A Journal of the Disaster in Affghanistan [sic], 1841–1842.* (Lady Sale's laconic refrain, "Earthquakes as Usual," probably inspired Chesnut's, "A few more men killed" [MCCW, 769].) Chesnut found other helpful models among the British memoirs of the Revolutionary War:

> Those Tarleton memoirs, Lee's memoirs, Moultrie's, Lord Rawdon's letters—self is never brought to the front. I have been reading them over and admire their modesty and good taste as much as their courage and cleverness. That kind of British eloquence takes me. Soldats—marchons—gloire? Not a bit of it (September 18, 1861, MCCW, 194).

As a woman and a wife, she was more or less confined—during the war, at least—to private discourse in the form of letters and diary entries. If she could not deploy the combative male oratory of her day, she might emulate the more subdued eloquence of retired (British) officers: she found in their memoirs a culturally validated version of the sort of self-restraint that her gender imposed on her. By appropriating such literary vehicles, Chesnut made her civilian account of the war a record that would be read long after the official oratory of her day was only a faint memory.

IV

As even the earliest entries suggest, the journal was never merely a receptacle for spontaneous outbursts—the urge to revise was evident from the outset. Examination of the differences between the 1860s and the 1880s versions reveals that the revision was generally away from conventionally "feminine" qualities and toward "masculine" ones; from the lyric impulse toward the epic and dramatic. The manner of the early diary tends to be cryptic: entries sometimes read like a kind of narrative stenography—like notes for anecdotes, rather than complete, let alone linked, stories. Its miscellaneousness and discontinuity at times characterize the diarist as so rushed or overwhelmed by events as to be incapable of thoughtfully digesting her experience (in terms of her discussion of the Carlyles, the effect is that of "a clever woman's hysterics").

In contrast, the selection and elaboration of material in the revision yields an impression of continuity and coherence—the effect of "a man's sense." Both the parts and the whole remain highly diverse in content, but more elaborate development, more careful juxtaposition, the foregrounding of certain materials, and the linking of entries give the effect of serial narrative (perhaps influenced by Chesnut's consumption of serial novels) rather than of hasty jotting.

In a sense, the revision's effect of utter *composure* is no more artifactual than the hectic impression of the first. Both versions were conditioned by the very different circumstances of their composition, but their contrasting effects are ultimately produced by formal qualities: in the first, they are produced by cryptic fragments, in the second, by extended and shapely scenes. While the diary format implies the contemporaneity of event and record, however, the serene manner of the later version belies its contents: the events in question would not seem to have allowed for such elaborately composed entries. One somewhat ironic effect of the revision is to make Mary Chesnut's war more civil—more cultivated, polite—than it could possibly have been. While the pervasive composure of the revision reveals its actual perspective (and its employment of hindsight), its retention of the diary format is implicitly a counter-Reconstruction gesture insofar as it effectively denies the passage of the intervening twenty years.

The revision retains the original's relatively informal style, but it more frequently and self-consciously uses puns, allusions, and tropes. Typically, the tropes are mock-heroic—often at the expense of women or other civilians:

> And so we took Fort Sumter. Nous autres. We—Mrs. Frank Hampton &c, in the passageway of the Mills House between the reception room and the drawing room. There we held a sofa against all comers. And indeed, all the agreeable people South seemed to have flocked to Charleston at the first gun. That was after we found out that bombarding did not kill anybody. Before that we wept and prayed—and took our tea in groups, in our rooms, away from the haunts of men (MCCW, 51).

She satirizes both sexes, sometimes simultaneously. Here, she mocks face-saving military euphemism and her husband's imperiousness, disguised as solicitousness:

> Mr. Chesnut held up his watch to me warningly and intimated, "It was late indeed for one who had to travel tomorrow."
>
> So as the Yankees say after every defeat I "retired in good order" (MCCW, 185–86).

Here her primary target is the feckless exertions of the Ladies Aid Society:

> Small war in the Ladies Aid Society. Harriet president, Sue Bonney V.P.—and already secession in the air—a row all the time in full blast.
>
> At first there were nearly a hundred members—eighty or ninety always present at a meeting—now ten or twenty are all that they can show.
>
> The worst is, they have forgotten the hospitals, where they really could do so much good, and gone off to provision and clothe the army. A drop in the bucket—or ocean (MCCW, 195).

As the "secession" analogy makes clear, the women are criticized in part for mimicking the infighting and ineffectuality of the Confederate government, which was run by men.

Chesnut's wit sometimes casually undermines conventional gender roles: "I will bid farewell for a while, as Othello did, to all the pomp and circumstance of glorious war. And come down to my domestic strifes—and troubles" (MCCW, 53). On one level, Chesnut seems to take for granted the hierarchy that privileges glorious war over domestic strife—the "masculine" sphere over the "feminine"—but the very gesture of invoking the tragic hero as she makes a narrative transition in her diary threatens to collapse the distinction between the epic and the domestic. Her targets vary considerably, but her tropes often cut two ways at once. On the one hand, they serve to keep in perspective the kinds of homefront concerns that threatened to monopolize women's attention and energy during the war. The effect is that of viewing the home front through the wrong end of a military telescope: the domestic scene is seen in sharp focus, but is reduced in scale. On the other hand, her tropes humorously deflect or defuse the dangers of war. On the whole, then, the tropes suggest Chesnut's ironic distance from her immediate circumstances, characterizing her as the narratorial equivalent of a good officer, at once involved in and detached from the action.

In a reversal of the usual perspective, one trope views the war through domestic lenses: "We separated because of incompatibility of temper. We are divorced, North from South, because we hated each other so. If we could only separate—a 'separation a l'agreable,' as the French say, and not a horrid fight for divorce" (MCCW, 25). This passage is especially interesting in light of Chesnut's appropriation of diplomatic terms for a marital crisis in her wartime journal: "[I] have refused to accept overtures for peace and forgiveness. After my stormy youth, I did so hope for peace & tranquil domestic happiness" [PMC, 41].) Mary Chesnut's ability to see the parallels between national and marital politics, and to construe each in terms of the other, may owe something to her sense, confessed directly in the early journal, of the anomaly of her own life: "My experience reverses all others—private life is wrangles & rows— & strife & ill blood & neighbourhood & family snarls. *Public* life has been peace & happiness, *quiet* & comfort" (PMC, 146).

The traditionally feminine sphere, domestic life, had been her combat zone, whereas the traditionally masculine sphere, public life, had been her sanctuary. In any case, the effect of her tropes, like that of the revised journal as a whole, is to assume a perspective from which the relation of the homefront with the war front may be viewed in an unconventional and illuminating way. Not willing to confine herself to the woman's sphere, nor to consign herself to the woman's auxiliary, she annexes diplomatic and political territory to her turf. Cumulatively, then, the tropes characterize a subject who questioned or defied certain conventional patterns and gender categories. Expanding her diary's scope to take in more public dimensions of the communal cataclysm was a way of raising her voice as a woman and inscribing a more assertive subject in her text.

The literal infrequency of the "I" in the 1860s diary is misleading. The typical entry begins with a verb of which "I" is the implied subject, and the diary's first version is a highly subjective document in a "feminine" mode. In it, the diarist frequently expresses her personal anxieties and frustrations, records marital tensions and social gaffes, and accuses herself of moral and spiritual failings. The tone and purpose of the 1880s version are significantly less confidential and confessional than those of the 1860s version. There (as befits her *actual* perspective), she assumes a more reflective stance, that of the collective consciousness of the Confederacy.

This effect was deliberately and painstakingly achieved. In an 1883 letter to Varina Davis, Chesnut said, with regard to the revision of her journal, that she had been "two years over looking it—copying—leaving myself out."[23] While this comment grotesquely understates the nature and the extent of her revision, it does hint at a paramount design of the project: the downplaying of her private fears, frustrations, ambitions, and jealousies. In her diary, as in her life, Mary Chesnut struggled to avoid "subjectivity," a state she associated with vulnerability to hysterics and humiliation. At least, this is the implication of an early entry in the wartime diary, which conflates a public scene with an obscure private crisis:

> Yesterday on the cars we had a mad woman raving at being separated from her daughter. It excited me so, I quickly took opium, & *that* I kept up. It enables me to retain every particle of mind or sense or brains I ever have, & so quiets my nerves that I can calmly reason & take rational views of things otherwise maddening. Then a *drunken* preacher began to console a "bereaved widow." He quoted more fluently scripture than I ever have heard it—the beast! My book (*after* the opiate) I read diligently. He misses in attempting to describe Yankee character after an elaborate trial, & his women are detestable failures. Still, it made the time *glide* rapidly for me. Here I am for Sunday << & have refused to accept overtures for peace & forgiveness. After my stormy youth, I did so hope for peace & tranquil domestic happiness. There is none for me in this world. "The peace this world >> cannot give, which passeth all understanding." . . . I have written to Kate that I will go to her if she wants me—dear, dear sister. I wonder if other women shed as bitter tears as I. They *scald* my cheeks & blister my heart. Yet Edward Boykin "wondered & marvelled at my elasticity. Was I always so bright & happy, did ever woman possess such a disposition, life was one continued festival." . . . Much they know of me—or my power to hide trouble.[24]

Rarely does the diary portray her in such a frantic and confused state. Significantly, this passage was drastically shortened in her revision, from which she omitted all but the description of the mad woman and the "bereaved widow." The result is to distance the diarist somewhat from the madwoman, thereby substituting sympathy for the empathy apparent in the earlier version. In effect, then, the process of revision accomplishes retrospectively what the opium had done at the time: it quells her "feminine" response and restores her to a more "masculine" state of reason. At the same time, in restoring her deceptive public mask, it affirms her strength—her power to dissimulate, if not to shrug off tribulation.

To the extent that her wartime diary allowed her to express and thus to discipline her "subjectivity," it served her private purpose of self-improvement. Toward the beginning of it, she periodically accuses or exonerates herself of self-absorption: "What nonsense I write here—however, this journal is intended to be entirely *objective*. My subjective days are over. No more *silent* eating into my own heart—making my own misery when without these morbid phantasies I could be so happy" (PMC, 33). Later in the same entry, she confesses: "I think this journal will be disadvantageous for me, for I spend time now like a spider spinning my own entrails instead of reading as my habit was at all spare moments" (PMC, 34). Unlike Emily Dickinson, for whom a spider could represent a woman's capacity to create a fragile and evanescent yet autonomous and precious art, Chesnut uses the spider as an image of unhealthy female self-absorption, even self-abuse.[25] In her implicit aesthetic, words needed to be anchored to substantial, external, "objective" reality.

Thus, even though Chesnut retained the format of a diary, many features of the revision resist the constraints and implications of that form. In terms of gender, the thrust of the later version is to combine traditionally female traits with male ones. In form, the text is implicitly private and confessional, but in focus it favors the public sphere, opening up to include the most historic events of the day. Significantly, the wartime version characterizes itself as a locked diary to which only the diarist had access, whereas the revision represents itself as a document open to the household to read. (Apparently, as she revised for a public audience, Chesnut inserted references to the openness of the journal.)

In a discussion of secrecy in Harriet Jacobs' *Incidents,* William Andrews has written:

> The bearing of the male secrets may render a woman honorably discreet in male-dominated society, but it will leave her pathetically discrete from women's community. . . . Secretiveness, discreetness, discretion—all tend toward the creation of a discrete, or separate and potentially secret, thing. The question . . . was, would a woman allow herself to become a discrete, isolated entity, dependent on men, for the sake of bearing male secrets with discretion?[26]

Whereas for Jacobs, male secrets—such as the insinuations of Dr. Flint's letters—were an insult and a violation, for Chesnut, they were a trust that lent significance to her life and diary-keeping. These state secrets did not originate with her, however, nor could she responsibly pass them on—being entrusted with them meant guarding one's discourse. In Chesnut's belated effort to prepare her diary for publication, one senses the pressure of having borne male secrets in silence for so long. At the very least, to publish the diary meant to gain recognition for her earlier discretion. Ideally, it meant more: to liberate her hitherto private discourse from quarantine and to establish her credentials as an authoritative chronicler of a communal crisis.

Chesnut was not alone in this enterprise. A number of women's accounts of the war—mostly diaries—were published around the turn of the century. Predictably, since the war was fought mostly on Southern soil, most were written from the Confederate point of view. (Predictably, too, most of these narratives were published only after officers on both sides had their say.) Among the Confederate women's accounts of the war, Chesnut's was anomalous in its literary quality, its criticism of slavery, its outspokenness on political issues, and in its refusal to focus exclusively on the feminine sphere, the homefront, not in being so long delayed.[27] Despite these distinguishing characteristics, the publication of her account established her as one of a community of hitherto silent women who witnessed and wrote the war from a new and previously neglected perspective.

Part of what Chesnut meant by leaving herself out of her revised manuscript was the consistent, conscious suppression of the subjectivity that inevitably characterized her initial journals. While the revision erases subjectivity in this blatant—and, to her, objectionable—form, it also incorporates or reinscribes it in subtler forms, for insofar as subjectivity is a linguistic phenomenon, her expanded literary repertoire permitted more complex manifestations of it. In revising, Chesnut did not passively re-sign her earlier entries: as if to consolidate her control over the text, she actively overhauled it from her new perspective.

Steven Rendall has claimed that the diary's distinguishing feature is its inevitable dialogism. Because " '[k]eeping a diary' means overcoming the temptation to suppress what one has written," the diarist's "voice" is inescapably plural—it is a somewhat discordant chorus rather than a single tone.[28] In revising her diary, Chesnut erased its inherent dialogism, but the revision achieves its own form of multivocalism. It results from the projection of Chesnut's voice onto others, or her invention of voices to converse with her own, not from letting previous entries stand untouched. Thus, at the same time that it blended the discrete voices of the original entries, the revision endowed the text with a more literal and literary form of dialogism. For the dialogism of the diary, which constructs a deferred and self-differing subjectivity, Chesnut substituted that of the novel, which constructs a more diffuse but not necessarily a more deferential subjectivity.

Her mouthpieces are sometimes identified, like her young friend Isabella Martin, to whom Chesnut attributed some of her own sentiments in revision. At other times, however, they are anonymous:

> "So we whimper and whine, do we? Always we speak in a deprecating voice, do we? And sigh gently at the end of every sentence—why? Plain enough. Does a man ever speak to his wife and children except to find fault? Does a woman ever address any remark to her husband that does not begin with an excuse? . . . Does she set up for strong-minded? So unwomanly—*so unlike his mother.* So different from the women of his family, the women he was accustomed to at home. Do you wonder that we are afraid to raise our voices above a mendicant's moan?"
>
> "And yet, they say our voices are the softest, sweetest, in the world."
>
> "No wonder. The base submission of our tone must be music in our masters' ears."
>
> "Female rebellion she is preaching." (MCCW, 735).

This passage both implies and enacts the aesthetic of the revision, for the revised diary achieves its musical tone deceptively, not by submitting to male domination but by distributing authorial assertions among other characters. By effacing her self as a character and expressing opinions anonymously and dialogically, Chesnut succeeded in making her point without risking retribution. In part, then, her strategy was similar to that of Harriet Jacobs. The ex-slave took refuge from masters' vengeance in pseudonymity, while the slaveowner's wife took refuge from patriarchs' disapproval in anonymity—and, on a larger scale, in pseudomorphism. What she presented as a journal was in a sense her carefully camoufaged military memoirs. Her sly novelizing was thus perhaps a form of deauthorizing—it claimed value for her testimony without exposing her to embarrassment. Inevitably, Chesnut yielded somewhat to the code that dismissed a woman's personal narrative, even of war, as no account. But in mastering more sophisticated techniques of characterization and plotting during her twenty-year apprenticeship, Chesnut also earned a degree of independent power and authority that validated her story.

Although she did suppress her inner life, Chesnut did not limit herself to orbiting around her husband's axis. The shifting of emphasis away from her self and marriage to the fortunes of the Confederacy, while loyal to the sectional cause, resulted in a narrative less dominated by any single individual—male or female—or by a single prominent point of view. It also permitted the assertion of a powerful critique of the administration of the war. The exclusion of self also facilitated a more inclusive chronicle of crisis: the revision issued in a collective autobiography of the embattled Confederacy from a woman's perspective. In addition, as Joan Lidoff has reminded us, "Using a collective voice—that is, a voice that defines itself through speaking for others, or that tells its own story as interwoven with others—is one narrative strategy that has been enabling for woman writers."[29] Though Chesnut's self-effacement was part of her absorption in Confederate history, it also, paradoxically, licensed an assertion of her own autonomy.

V

Although most of the war's casualties—like its heroes—were men, Mary Chesnut was sensitive to the distinctive ways in which war could victimize women:

> Women who come before the public are in a bad box now. False hair is taken off and searched for papers. Pistols are sought for [under] "cotillions renversés." Bustles are "suspect." All manner of things, they say, come over the border under the huge hoops now worn. So they are ruthlessly torn off. Not legs but arms are looked for under hoops. And sad to say, found. Then women are used as detectives and searchers to see that no men come over in petticoats.
>
> So the poor creatures coming this way are humiliated to the deepest degree. << I think *these* times make all women feel their humiliation in the affairs of the world. . . . Women can only stay at home, and every paper reminds us that women are to be violated, ravished, and all manner of humiliation. >>[30]

While recognizing that the threat of female spies—and male spies impersonating women—was quite real, she nonetheless resented the general suspicion of women in wartime and their vulnerability to humiliation. Her own response to the war was mixed. In a sense, in writing her journal, she stayed indoors. In revising it, however, she prepared to go "before the public" by adopting various forms of literary camouflage—such as rendering scenes dramatically rather than in first-person narrative. Indeed, her use of such devices in some ways approached a kind of literary cross-dressing. While her writing retained the superficial appearance of a private and, in that sense, feminine form of discourse, it permitted her to venture into, and exercise authority in, traditionally male spheres.

However, since Mary Chesnut did not complete the revision, much less oversee its publication, the authority of her text, in a couple of senses, inevitably passed into the hands of others. In 1885, she left the manuscripts with a friend, Isabella Martin, with the request that she publish them in the event of her death (MBC, 214–15). Martin had been a young friend of Mary Chesnut's during the war, and Chesnut projected the growing strength of their post-war friendship back onto the war years by substantially expanding Martin's role in the revised diary. This gesture not only helped to efface the author's subjective presence (since the character "Isabella" sometimes spoke for her), it may also have served to cultivate the real Isabella as a future editor. In turn, Martin enlisted the help of another woman experienced in editing Civil War memoirs, but the 1905 edition was apparently prepared largely by an in-house editor at Appleton, Francis W. Halsey. In addition to annotating and indexing the manuscript, and then dividing it into chapters and titling them, Halsey drastically shortened the work and brought it into greater conformity with the post-Reconstruction myth of the Old South (MCCW, xxviii).

Further liberties were taken with the text by the editor of the 1949 edition, the New England novelist, Ben Ames Williams. (Like its predecessor it bore the misleading and unauthorized title, *Diary from Dixie.*) Having become an ardent admirer of Mary Chesnut on the basis of the 1905 edition, Williams had used her as the model for a prominent character in his romance of the Civil War, *A House Divided* (1947). When he gained access to the manuscripts of the 1880s journal, he decided to bring out an expanded edition. In preparing it, he sometimes changed dates, deleted and altered entries, rewrote narrative as dialogue and vice versa, and even wrote the passages with which the narrative began and ended (MCCW, xxix). In suffering these two successive editorial encroachments, the manuscript obviously lost some of its integrity, for in addition to obscuring Mary Chesnut's own extensive revisions, the editors disguised their own. In an important sense, then, Mary Chesnut was not the (sole) author of either edition of *Diary from Dixie.* Indeed, in the Williams edition, the persona of the diarist, having passed through the crucible of his Northern novelistic imagination, was to some extent his own reconstruction of Chesnut.

Thus, the belated publication of her manuscript ironically fulfilled Mary Chesnut's fear of the violation of "women who come before the public." Indeed, despite her secure position within the Southern elite, despite her literacy, and despite her initiation and careful revision of her manuscript, its fate has much in common with that of the narratives of ex-slaves, especially those who published under abolitionist sponsorship. Like their manuscripts, Chesnut's came under the aegis of editors whose benevolent intentions encouraged rather than deterred the taking of liberties with the text—liberties she was not in a position to resist.

Her narrative's lot also anticipates that of Black Elk's life-story, which is the subject of chapter 8 in this book. As literary archeologist and restorer of her manuscripts, C. Vann Woodward is analogous to the anthropologist, Raymond J. DeMallie, who recently published the transcripts of Black Elk's dictations. Both of these contemporary academics attempted to restore the integrity of appropriated life-writing through responsible scholarship and scrupulous editing, but neither is completely successful. The transcripts of Black Elk's narratives are in English—even the most scrupulous editing cannot restore the oral Lakota original. Despite the abundance of Chesnut manuscripts, Mary Chesnut's editor also lacks a single complete, finished, or authorized draft among the fragments. In any case, the eclecticism of Woodward's edition, which selectively supplements the 1880s text with passages from others, creates a kind of hybrid version, eliding rather than illuminating the differences among the various manuscripts.

Moreover, like DeMallie, Woodward cannot escape the implications of his role. In order to restore a compromised text, the scholar-editor must function either as validator or as emender, or as both; in any case, he inevitably assumes authority over another's Life. (As literary sponsor, he is always in danger of becoming patronizing and proprietary.) Woodward's consciousness of his dilemma is clear in the remarks he made at the Reynolds Conference:

> I'm in the curious role, as editor—my first duty will be partially to destroy Mary Chesnut's reputation as a diarist. That's lamentable. My second duty, it seems to me, as historian, is to preserve such integrity as her diary has, not to forfeit it or to destroy it. But when I inform my fellow craftsmen that what they've been reading is a bunch of fiction, well—[31]

As a historian, he has qualms about the integrity of the text. At the same time, his intimacy with Chesnut's writing has given him a personal interest in her reputation, which at times conflicts with scholarly neutrality: Is it lamentable to destroy her reputation as a diarist if its basis is false? Clearly, he would like to admit her to the fraternity of historians; however, unable to do that, he will make appropriate allowances and salvage what authority the revision retains.

In his "Introduction" to *Mary Chesnut's Civil War,* he does this less equivocally than he had at the Conference:

> The editor . . . began in a spirit of skepticism, with misgivings that it would become his duty to expose inconsistencies, anachronisms, distortions, hindsights, and special pleadings that would raise doubts about the worth and integrity of a famous book and its author. Well before the completion of the long task, however, a growing respect for the author and the integrity of her work began to replace the original misgivings. Given the kind of liberties she took in revising and expanding the original Journal . . . Mary Chesnut can be said to have shown an unusual sense of responsibility toward the history she records and a reassuring faithfulness to perceptions of her experience of the period as revealed in her original Journal. It would be a regrettable and most ironic outcome of this effort to reveal the true nature of her work and an accurate text of what she wrote if it all resulted in lowering the esteem in which her work is held (MCCW, xxvii).

(There is an interesting parallel here between Chesnut's revision of her first diary and Woodward's modification of his "original misgivings" about her project; in both cases, the amended versions are presented as correct and "responsible.")

Despite Woodward's good intentions (and his formidable job of editing), there is, inevitably, a trace of condescension here: that of the present toward the past, the professional toward the amateur, and, possibly, the male toward the female. In effect, in vouching for Chesnut's integrity, Woodward is defending her honor against the sort of attack that Lynn eventually launched. In any case, his defense is based on assailable assumptions. He mentions the "liberties" she took with her "original"—as though she had no more authority over her manuscript than her later editors. Furthermore, in reassuring the reader that on the whole Chesnut was responsible toward "the history she records" and faithful to her earlier "perceptions" and "experience," Woodward may be projecting his own historian's ethic on her. To his credit, Woodward has firmly defended Chesnut's right to choose, or invent, her genre, but requiring fidelity to her "original perceptions" infringes on that right. Indeed, in obliging her to be faithful in her revision to the spirit, if not the letter, of the earlier text, he may be asking the impossible of her—the "reconstitution" of "original" experience.

Unconsciously, then, Woodward in effect binds her to her first rather disorderly and claustrophobic textual space. The apparent thrust of her revision, however, was to break out of the clutter and the self-absorption of the earlier draft. In her revision she sought to assume a more authoritative stance on a broader stage. If its objectivity is an illusion, it is by and large a convincing and hard-earned one that she never tried to pass off as spontaneous. The flawed authority of the *Diary from Dixie* lay not in the liberties *she* took with her original, but with those taken by her editors, not the least of which was the concealment of her new narrative viewpoint. In any case, if contemporary readers (like William Andrews) are legitimizing the novelizing techniques of the later slave narratives as essential to their telling of a *free* story, then the same license must be granted a writer like Mary Boykin Chesnut; to do otherwise is reverse discrimination.

VI

Mary Chesnut wisely made no explicit claims that her account of the War was historically accurate. On the contrary, she repeatedly commented, directly and indirectly, on the unreliability of wartime intelligence:

> JC adds always: "It is dangerous to repeat what you hear. In military circles there is envy, slander, backbiting, jealousy, &c. Military jealousy is the worst form of that bad passion" (July 10, 1862, MCCW, 411).

> Conflicting testimony. Young Wade Hampton says Hood lost 12,000 men in the battles of the 22nd and 24th. Brewster says not *three* thousand at the uttermost.
>
> Now here are two people strictly truthful who tell things so differently. War? In this war people see the same thing so oddly—one does not know what to believe (August, 14, 1864, MCCW, 635).

> Met there a young person from Tennessee. She was an ardent partisan of Joe Johnston. And in this wise she stated her case—and backed them.
>
> "So I was told—and my authority? Oh, high up as a major general. He said, says he, 'Miss —.' " (Dec, 3, 1864, MCCW, 684)

> Now, remember, I write down all that I hear, and the next day, if I hear that it is not so, then I write down the contradiction, too. (June 4, 1862, MCCW, 360)

> Isabella still calls me Cassandra and puts her hands to her ears when I begin to wail. Well, Cassandra only records what she hears—she does not vouch for it. For really, one never nowadays feels certain of anything (Nov 25, 1864, MCCW, 676).

The young partisan of Joe Johnston understandably but naively treats authority as a function of rank. In the patriarchal South, it was perhaps even more a function of gender. Consciously or not, in revising her diary Mary Chesnut was recasting her experience in terms of characteristics associated with masculine discourse and authority in her culture; ultimately, she turned a private confessional form inside out to comprehend a public, communal crisis. Of course, to do so was to side step the sexism that underwrites such a dichotomy, not to challenge it directly. Her tactic is perhaps analogous to the assumption by many nineteenth-century women writers of male pseudonyms, which sloughed off improper names and appropriated male prerogative at the cost of denying, by disguising, their gender.

In returning to and thoroughly revising her first manuscript, however, Mary Chesnut attained a kind of authority denied most of her peers. The result of her long labors was a kind of idiosyncratic narrative that retained certain traditional features of "feminine" discourse while it annexed traditionally masculine subjects. As a "diary," the text is implicitly private, confessional, and immediate, but this one opens up to include the most historic events of the day. Though Chesnut retained the format of a diary, many features of the revision subtly resist the constraints and implications of that form. In making her journal a less private and confessional and a more public and communal narrative, Chesnut assumed a viewpoint aloof from the male power structure to which she was literally wedded. Although she could not ignore or entirely transcend nineteenth-century conventions, she managed, I think, to renegotiate gender/genre boundaries in her account of her life as a Confederate. Woodward's title for his scholarly edition—*Mary Chesnut's Civil War*—is thus doubly appropriate. Though Chesnut is less central, as a character, to the revised journal, the war it recounts is emphatically *hers,* in two senses: First, it is hers in the sense that the account of the conflict is more consciously shaped and thus more in her control than it had been earlier; second, it is hers in the sense that its subtext is an inner civil war that manifests a secessionist impulse of a potentially more subversive order.

8

Black Elk Speaks *With Forked Tongue*

> Autobiography . . . expresses a concern peculiar to Western man, a concern that has been of good use in his systematic conquest of the universe and that he has communicated to other cultures; but those men will thereby have been annexed by a sort of intellectual colonizing to a mentality that was not their own.
>
> GEORGES GUSDORF[1]

> Traduttore, tradittore.

I

Alone among similar books, *Black Elk Speaks, Being the Life Story of a Holy Man of the Oglala Sioux,* as told through John G. Neihardt (1932),[2] has enjoyed both popular and critical acclaim. Since the 1960s, it has been something of a cult classic, and until quite recently, scholars and critics extolled it as an authentic and authoritative Native American autobiography—indeed, perhaps the only one. Euramerican critics set it apart from the narratives gathered by anthropologists on the basis of its literary merit. It was also cited respectfully by prominent Native Americans: William Least Heat Moon paid homage to it in his bestseller, *Blue Highways* (1982), and it was invoked in the mid-1980s by Sioux attempting to regain control of sacred lands from the federal government. Its status was such that Vine Deloria not only published an edition in 1979, but declined, in his introduction, to inquire into the problems of its genesis, authorship, and editing.[3] It was virtually canonized, then, both as aboriginal autobiography and as Lakota prophesy.

Several reasons were advanced for its unique status. First, unlike most "native informants," Black Elk was a holy man; as a result, his testimony was thought to possess particular authority. Second, he exercised a rare degree of initiative in proposing the narrative, in choosing his collaborator, and in arranging the time and circumstances of the dictations. Third, John Neihardt was thought to be a uniquely qualified collaborator. As an amateur historian of the West, he was knowledgeable about Native American history and religion; as a mystic, he felt a spiritual affinity with Black Elk; and as a regional epic poet, he was equipped to translate the dictations into compelling narrative. Finally, Black Elk's ritual adoption of Neihardt was seen as endowing their collaboration and the text it produced with unimpeachable authority.

The notion of the text as one that offers a valid, even invaluable, insight into Lakota culture rested for a long time on Neihardt's own account of the collaboration—first offered in his preface to the book and later supplemented in interviews with scholars—and on a reading of the text in isolation from the transcripts. Given the book's reputation as a paragon of Native American autobiography and of bicultural collaboration, its inability to stand up to recent scrutiny is particularly distressing. Despite Neihardt's talent, empathy, and good intentions, *Black Elk Speaks* has proven to be not nearly as reliable as it appears, or was made out to be. In it, we see Black Elk not face to face, but through the gloss of a white man—a translation whose surface obscures Black Elk by reflecting the culture of his collaborator.

II

To read the recently published transcripts is to be impressed by the sheer scope and complexity of Neihardt's task and the ingenuity and care with which he undertook it. Before enumerating the book's failings, then, it is only fair to acknowledge the considerable efforts Neihardt made to honor Black Elk's narrative. For example, sensing that the narrative's meaning resided in its ritualized conveyance as well as in its discrete message, he conscientiously rehearsed the transaction that produced the book. His preface explains the circumstances of his meeting Black Elk and of their arranging to record the story. The first chapter is devoted to the ceremony by which Black Elk adopted him and renamed him Flaming Rainbow (and through which the narrative was initiated). A postscript later returns the book from narrative to prayer and benediction. Similarly, the book acknowledges its doubly collaborative nature: whole sections are spoken by older tribe members who are present to verify the narrative and to supplement it with stories of events Black Elk did not witness.[4] Their constant presence and their intermittent contributions give the narrative tribal sanction and endow it with a communal dimension. Though the narrative as a whole is introduced and vouched for by a Euramerican, this internal verification counteracts the "race ritual" of the authentication of minority autobiography (as seen most dramatically in abolitionist slave narrative).

Moreover, various shifters periodically remind us of Neihardt's presence and of the immediate surroundings, grounding the book in a particular spatial and temporal framework, and in the dynamics of oral narrative, which addresses a proximate and palpable audience. Black Elk's "asides"—for example, "[W]hen you look about you can see what it was they wanted"—not only incorporate the editor into the very performance he is "transcribing," thereby reminding the reader of the transaction that produced the narrative, they also locate the narrative in a particular (and sacred) landscape. Neihardt is attentive to the way in which an oral culture treats words as events, and narration as performance, rather than as conveyers of information.

Finally, the language of the narrative is impressive—simple but dignified, detailed but concise. Neihardt apparently sought to retain its mythic dimensions by using Lakota names (translated into English: e.g., "Moon When the Cherries are Ripe") for months, years, and places. Other details of the translation also simulate a Native American point of view. For example, whether or not "yellow metal" literally translates a Lakota term for "gold," the phrase effectively demystifies the substance and induces a Euramerican reader momentarily to view it from outside his cultural perspective. The popularity and prestige of the narrative over the years obviously stem in large part from its stylistic distinction: it *sounds* the way most readers believe a Lakota holy man would, or should, sound in translation.

III

The problems that remain, however, severely compromise the book's authority and authenticity. Not that we should blame Neihardt: the book's failures were largely unavoidable, and were determined by cultural forces beyond any editor's control. Nor should we condemn the book or bemoan its existence, for as David Brumble has pointed out, bicultural documents like this one can teach us much about "the effects of cultures in collision, the effects of literacy, the history of autobiography, literature, and literary theory."[5] *Black Elk Speaks* is best read then as a text that illustrates, and illuminates, a series of interesting problems inherent in the process through which members of oral or tribal cultures enter that "most democratic province of letters," the domain of autobiography.

The difficulty of rendering a Lakota narrative into English is complicated by the problem of transforming oral into printed materials. Dennis Tedlock has argued that the performative qualities of oral literature—gesture, tone, timing, and sound effects—can be suggested, in freshly recorded narratives, by means of typographical effects,[6] and Dell Hymes has shown how oral literature can be recuperated from transcripts.[7] Neither of these ingenious attempts to recreate oral forms in print helps much with *Black Elk Speaks,* however, because of its complicated ontogeny. Black Elk's Lakota was first translated into idiomatic "Indian English" by his son, Ben Black Elk. In turn, that translation was rendered into standard English by Neihardt, and recorded stenographically by his daughter. Later, at a geographical (and cultural) distance, Neihardt revised and edited the transcripts. The final text is so many removes from its source that the original language and gestures are irrecoverable. Thus, a scholar interested in assessing the accuracy, or faithfulness, of Neihardt's "translation" soon reaches an impasse: one cannot compare Neihardt's prose to the original Lakota, which vanished upon utterance.

Neither could Neihardt. Since he spoke no Lakota, and Black Elk spoke no English, the language of *Black Elk Speaks* was produced without being checked either against the original or by its originator. Thanks to Raymond J. DeMallie, however, one can now compare Neihardt's text to the transcripts.[8] A look at them reveals the extent to which Neihardt is responsible for the readability and the dignified and consistent tone of *Black Elk Speaks*—confirming Dell Hymes's argument that literal translations of oral materials are generally most valuable, since "literary" patterns are more often imposed on, than discovered in, native materials (38–39). The transcripts reveal that Neihardt was editing in terms of white preconceptions about what Lakota "longhairs" *ought* to be sound like. Even DeMallie, who claims that Neihardt's free translation is likely to be "more faithful to the intended meaning than a strictly verbatim recording," concedes: "In a sense, Neihardt was already 'writing' Black Elk's story by rephrasing his words into English" (32). For this project, Neihardt's vaunted poetic talent may have been a liability rather than an asset.

As was his mysticism, perhaps. Neihardt's belief in his spiritual affinity with the holy man was no doubt sincere, but the danger implicit in such a belief is apparent in a letter he wrote to his publisher, William Morrow:

> There was a very peculiar merging of consciousness between me and Black Elk, and his son, who interpreted for me, commented on the fact. Very often it seemed as though [Black Elk] were only repeating my thoughts or my own poetry although he knows no English and is utterly unaware of the existence of literature. . . . Once he said, "This man could make an ant talk" (DeMallie, 41).

The publication of oral materials clearly involves much more fundamental questions than those of the "accuracy" or "faithfulness" of the "translation." It involves the distortion or contamination of the originals by the assumptions of literate cultures. As Krupat has noted, the status and reception of American Indian discourse "have always been tied to its presumptive anonymity, its lack of named authors." Native American culture valorizes an authority of augmentation, rather than of origination.[9] Both meanings are implicit in the etymology of the word *author,* but literate cultures tend to exalt the latter at the expense of the former, conceiving of verbal creations as individually "authored" and privately possessable. According to Marshall McLuhan, this new sense of authorship reaches maturity when the printed book makes possible, on the one hand, the close identification of an individual with a fixed text, and, on the other, the dramatic spatial and temporal extension of that individual/text.[10]

Writing and printing, then, entail phenomena alien to oral cultures: transcription and publication inevitably import these phenomena into oral materials, thereby profoundly transforming them. This bears directly on *Black Elk Speaks,* whose bicultural production involved conflicting ideologies of authorship. As we shall see, in participating in the production of a book, Black Elk attained authorship in the Euramerican sense—the spatial and temporal extension of a text identified with him—only at the cost of relinquishing a large measure of control over his vision—the sole source of his authority as a Lakota holy man. In addition, the commission of his narrative to a permanent printed form had unanticipated, and troublesome, consequences for him.

Another phenomenon characteristic of literate cultures but alien to oral peoples is a sense of history. According to Jack Goody, history, as opposed to communal memory of the past, begins with writing. Unlike myths or genealogies stored in the memory for oral reconstruction, texts are linear and static; as a result, contradictions and inconsistencies are easy to detect. Documents encourage conscious correction, verification, and rationalization.[11] Thus, when Black Elk's oral narrative was written down and printed, it did not merely pass from one language to another, it passed from myth to history—from one mode of understanding the universe and organizing experience to another. The irreversibility of this process is demonstrated by the fact that DeMallie's edition of the transcripts is, in some ways, further removed than *Black Elk Speaks* from the (ab)original utterance it seeks to recuperate. For DeMallie cannot revoke Neihardt's poetic license and retroactively cancel its effects; at best, he can devote his scholarly skills to the recovery of the *historical* Black Elk from the distortions of Neihardt's translation and editing. Of course, this necessitates correcting Black Elk when his narrative gets events "out of order" or confuses one with another. DeMallie's attempt to "restore" the narrative inevitably surrounds it with extensive annotation and embeds it in scholarly apparatus. The narrative is further textualized—or intertextualized—when DeMallie pins down events with cross-references to published sources. We should, of course, welcome such editing, for we can understand the narrative—can grant its reality—only by inscribing it within our own history. We must acknowledge, however, that between the mythic world of Black Elk and our world remains a gulf that is created—not bridged—by printed texts. The problem is far from "academic": the relationship between oral and written agreements (promises, treaties) is one of the most vexed issues in the history of Indian–white relations.

A question related to the transformation of oral into printed materials is that of the genre and its genesis. It has been claimed that, at its best, American Indian autobiography offers a "penetrating insight into the private world of the subject. . . . Nowhere else is such direct and intense contact possible as in the works that issue from recorded autobiography."[12] But the assumption of a division between public and private selves and the supposition that the genre can afford "direct and intense contact" with individual tribe members are disturbingly ethnocentric because the very medium is profoundly at odds with the culture it purports to express, or exhibit. Autobiography depends on the privacy and introspection encouraged, even required, by literate cultures; in contrast, orality tends to foster "communal and externalized" personalities not given to self-analysis.[13] As Robert F. Sayre has put it, "Autobiography, as any editor thinks of it himself, depends on European and American concepts of *life, self,* and *writing*. The Native Americans obviously had no such thing."[14] For this reason alone, autobiography necessarily misrepresents the life of a member of an oral, tribal people.

The implications of the historical and collaborative processes that produced Native American autobiography have only recently begun to be explored. Clearly, the idea of autobiography involves an equation between a life and a book that is alien to oral cultures. Indeed, the suggestion by a Euramerican that autobiography is possible, and the questions that elicit its contents, normally *create* the very kind of self-consciousness that is conventionally thought to generate the genre.[15] (In such cases, at least, the poststructuralists appear to be right: autobiography produces self-conscious selves rather than vice versa.) Moreover, as Krupat points out, the first American Indian autobiographies were produced quite literally by "Euramerican pressure" (21). The specific impetus was the final push toward confinement on western reservations:

> [W]ith few exceptions Indian texts did not begin to be produced until the 1830s, when the eastern tribes were forcibly removed west of the Mississippi. It was then that Indians, still popularly believed to have no culture of their own and so no capacity for cultural contribution, were accorded a history—one which began when a particular tribe resisted white encroachment (5–6).

Implicit here is a significant difference from black autobiography: abolitionist slave narrative, at least, began as an attempt to correct historical injustices and to enable a minority group to participate in mainstream history, but Native American autobiography began, at the initiative of Euramericans, as an attempt merely to amend the historical record as Indian tribes were physically shunted aside to make way for mainstream culture. The idea was to precipitate textual relics of a culture perceived as doomed to irrelevance, if not to extinction.

Krupat provides a subtle and incisive account of the genre's complex biculturalism. On the one hand, he points out the disadvantaged position of the Native American in its collaborative production. Since "defeat is the enabling condition of Indian autobiography," Indians enter into autobiographical discourse at first literally as prisoners-of-war (48). In addition, he exposes the role played by Native American autobiography in the discourse of self-justification required by white conquest: native testimony confirmed the inevitability of the supplanting of "barbarism" by "civilization." On the other hand, he notes that of the several forms of literary discourse about the Indian, autobiography alone required contact with a living individual or recorded his voice (48–52): "[I]t is in its presentation of an Indian voice not as vanished and silent, but as still living and able to be heard that the oppositional potential of Indian autobiography resides" (35).

Even in Krupat's account of the genre, its "oppositional potential" is more potential than oppositional. Despite his shrewd analysis of the interplay of cultural values on the discursive frontier of autobiography, his notions of "contact" and "voice" remain problematic. Is the voice of the Indian really heard if it is attended to only when it concedes the inevitability of its eventual silencing—that is, when its discourse confesses, under duress, that aboriginal culture is doomed, and hence somehow inferior? (As we shall see, Neihardt may have twisted Black Elk's words into such a confession.) The closer one looks at Native American autobiographies, the more they seem to be, in an ironic sense, narratives of Indian captivity.

IV

The genesis of individual texts is as tricky to assess as that of the genre as a whole. For example, consider Neihardt's assertion that Black Elk initiated the idea of conveying his power vision and life story to him at their very first meeting:

> I was about to break the silence by way of getting something started, when the old man looked up to Flying Hawk, the interpreter, and said: "As I sit here, I can see in this man beside me a strong desire to know the things of the Other World. He has been sent to learn what I know, and I will teach him" (viii).

For a long time, this version of the text's origins was thought to distinguish and legitimize the collaboration. In 1981, however, David Brumble expressed his suspicion of it, implying that it may have owed more to Paul Radin's introduction to the autobiography of Crashing

Thunder than to the facts. Indeed, regardless of its source, Brumble faulted it for helping to make a self-serving claim—that "the *Indian* is eager to have the god-sent white man preserve the Indian's sacred knowledge"—a convention of white-assisted autobiographies (29).

But Clyde Holler has recently rehabilitated this crucial passage. According to Holler, Neihardt's account of the narrative's ritual initiation corresponds closely with other accounts of the transmission of tribal wisdom. Since Neihardt had approached Black Elk in the traditional manner, by offering tobacco, Black Elk was likely responding with the customary greeting of a Lakota holy man to a supplicant. Thus, the very details that make Neihardt's account of their first meeting seem, to some, too good to be true are apparently rooted in Lakota traditions. (The interview's anomaly lay not in Black Elk's "foreknowledge" of Neihardt's visit, but in his use of a traditional welcome with a nontribe member. Neihardt, apparently unaware of these conventions, interpreted his reception as evidence of Black Elk's supernatural powers.)[16]

That evaluation of a crucial feature of the narrative—the degree of the informant's initiative—may require such anthropological reconstruction of its context suggests the difficulty of understanding the dynamics of the collaboration as a whole. Even if Black Elk did initiate the transaction, as Holler argues, he did so in response to a man who arrived with his own agenda: scholars (including Holler) have increasingly acknowledged that Black Elk and Neihardt had different notions of, and objectives for, the dictations that resulted from their meeting. For example, according to DeMallie, "Neihardt conceived of the project as writing Black Elk's life story, whereas Black Elk conceived of it as making a record of the Lakota religion" (62). The white writer envisioned the end result as autobiography, whereas the Lakota visionary saw it as communal or sacred history. As Holler is at pains to point out, Black Elk was intent on giving sacred instruction to Neihardt in the hope of resuming his own traditional role and benefiting his tribe (26). Neihardt's decisive, costly misstep was his failure to honor—perhaps even to understand—this motive.

Comparison with slave narrative may be instructive here. On the one hand, a non-English-speaking Native American is further removed from, and at a greater disadvantage with respect to, mainstream culture than even an illiterate slave narrator. On the other hand, Black Elk, at least, had cultural resources at his disposal that could serve to bind him and his collaborator in a relation of mutual responsibility: he could attempt to offset his own submission to "white" discourse by ritually initiating his collaborator into tribal culture. Unfortunately, Neihardt seems to have viewed his adoption by Black Elk as licensing, rather than restricting, him. Ultimately, his disposition of Black Elk's narrative violated the ritual context in which it began.

In addition to the problems inherent in bicultural collaboration, there is the perplexing visionary dimension of *Black Elk Speaks*. Of course, this is one of the features that has caused it to be prized above other Native American autobiographies.[17] It greatly complicates the book, however, making it ghostwritten in two profoundly different and competing senses. As a visionary narrative, it is ghostwritten in the sense that it originates with the ghosts of ancestors and the spirits of the earth, rather than with a living individual. (Black Elk's authorship is that of augmentation: he is essentially a custodian and transmitter of a tribal legacy.) But it is also ghostwritten in the sense that it is conveyed to the page by a surrogate, amanuensis, collaborator—call him what you will. The vision, therefore, if not the entire narrative, is twice mediated: first from his ancestors through Black Elk, and then from Black Elk through Neihardt. (Unlike the poet, the holy man admits that the vision is ineffable and that he is an imperfect vehicle.) In spite of Black Elk's efforts to locate the narrative's authority in a communal and transcendent source, the basis for that authority has slowly but inexorably shifted: from the supernatural to the secular, the tribal to the individual, the Lakota to the English, and the visionary and oral to the written and printed.

V

After Black Elk's death, Neihardt became a medium in a different sense—the living person who answered questions on behalf of the deceased. He increasingly emphasized his own role in the production of the book when interviewed. In his proprietary attitude toward the published book, as well as in his editing of the transcripts, he tended to assume the authority of origination rather than that of augmentation. Despite the increasing recognition of Neihardt's contribution, however, some critics have seen it as somehow enhancing the book's special status and authority. The following represents what we may call the canonical reading of *Black Elk Speaks*:

> The shape that Neihardt lent to Black Elk's narrative, particularly through his arrangement and partial writing of the first and final chapters, both unifies the narrative and lends it an authenticity unequalled by the life stories recorded for the purpose of scientific study.
>
> ....
>
> Neihardt's structure for *Black Elk Speaks* reflect[s] and define[s] Black Elk's identity. . . . For these reasons, *Black Elk Speaks* represents a genuine marriage between Native American consciousness and Western literary form, thus becoming what I take the liberty to call the first American Indian autobiography.[18]

Though it seems to me that these claims cannot be true, this view has had considerable currency among readers, both lay and academic. For example, Hilda Neihardt Petri, who witnessed the recording of the narrative, asserts, in her foreword to *The Sixth Grandfather*:

> *Black Elk Speaks* is authentic; it does convey with faithful sincerity Black Elk's message. But in presenting this message to the reader, Neihardt created a work of art, and true art in all its forms is an intensification and greatly clarified form of communication (xviii).

Even Demallie expresses a similar attitude toward the text. While he warns that many have underestimated the extent of Neihardt's editing, he adds that others have failed "to appreciate the sincerity of Neihardt's commitment to make the book speak for Black Elk faithfully, to represent what [he] would have said if he had understood the concept of literature and if he had been able to express himself in English" (xxii).

Of course, DeMallie's presumption is not equal to Neihardt's, and his full account of the collaborative transaction arms future readers against past suppositions by exposing the text's artifactuality. Yet, in a way, DeMallie compounds the problem. Basing his claim on thorough scholarship rather than on mystical communication, he professes in effect that *his* book does what Neihardt's failed to do: "The intention of this book is to allow readers direct access to Black Elk, the historical personage" (xxiii). Such access is not possible, for as we have seen, the transcripts' language is several removes from Black Elk's.

Though Black Elk's motives and intentions are irrecoverable, DeMallie's research permits us to reconstruct Neihardt's. Evidently, as early as the fall before the dictations, he had conceived of the book as covering the story of the tribe up to the Battle of Wounded Knee. (The implications of this preconceived ending will be discussed in Section VI.) He also intended to pay Black Elk for his time (29). Although there is no evidence that profit was an important motive for either party, it is wise, in view of the distaste expressed by many critics for the work of paid informants, to acknowledge that this privileged collaboration was not without an economic dimension.

DeMallie's publication of the transcripts also makes very clear one of Neihardt's editorial practices—the consistent suppression of Black Elk's awareness of white culture and technology (52). When this extends to the substitution of descriptive phrases for the names of certain cities, the result is sometimes ironic, if not comic: Omaha becomes "a very big town" and Chicago "a much bigger town" (220). Without knowing what Black Elk's locutions were, we should not make too much of this. But Neihardt's expunging of Biblical phrases such as "many were called but few were chosen" serves to conceal crucial facts about Black Elk (facts still not known to many readers of the book): he became a Roman Catholic early in this century and, more startling perhaps, served as a catechist and missionary to other Sioux for a period of decades thereafter.

Black Elk's conversion to Christianity was apparently less a matter of profound and total inner change than of accommodation to the repression of traditional religious practices. While Black Elk gave up conjuring and healing, his conversion and his subsequent career as a catechist evidently allowed him to continue to function in a traditional role and to participate in an ongoing communal life (DeMallie, 23, 26, 92). Of course, the local priests viewed his conversion differently: Black Elk was considered a model convert and a paragon of piety, and Church pamphlets prominently displayed pictures of him, dressed in tribal clothing, giving religious instruction to his daughter, who was dressed in Western clothes. Thus, the publication of *Black Elk Speaks* aroused considerable consternation among the reservation clergy. Indeed, their reaction was so strong that Black Elk was induced to "speak" again in 1934: in a document signed by him and witnessed by his daughter and his priest, he reaffirmed his faith in Christianity. Furthermore, in a letter to missionaries, he complained that he had realized none of the promised profits and that Neihardt had denied his request to append an account of his conversion to the narrative (DeMallie, 59–63).

This reavowal of his Christianity did not prevent him from participating in pageants in which he reenacted his practice as a healer, nor from passing on traditional teachings in further interviews with white collaborators. (The first, with Neihardt in 1944, resulted in

When the Tree Flowered, and the second, with Joseph Epes Brown in 1947, issued in *The Sacred Pipe.*) Such behavior may seem self-contradictory from a Western perspective, but taken as a whole, the evidence suggests that, rather than desiring to renounce *Black Elk Speaks,* he wished merely to appease the local authorities. Probably he saw little conflict between his roles as catechist and as repository of the suppressed—and thus endangered—religion of his ancestors. (This may help to explain his willingness, even eagerness, to share his ancestral vision with Neihardt some twenty-five years after his apparent renunciation of the old beliefs.)

In any case, some time after he granted his first set of interviews, Black Elk discovered that the authorities found his published "pagan" self inconsistent with their Christian image (indeed, icon) of him, and that they had a larger stake than he in the Western ideas of consistency, orthodoxy, and conversion. At this historical distance, it is not easy to know his motives for collaborating with Neihardt and Brown or the exact nature of his beliefs. What seems clear is that while *Black Elk Speaks* gratified his desire to give his power vision permanent form and wider currency—to smuggle it off the reservation—it also represented him in a way that made his life difficult. As a result of his collaboration with Neihardt, he found himself caught between two irreconcilable "selves." Both were produced in cooperation with white men, and both claimed to be historically authoritative. Unable to retain—or to regain—authority over his narrative, he created living space for himself by supplementing it with other texts. Haunted by a ghostwritten text, he found refuge in the camouflage of proliferating texts and selves.

VI

If biography is the literary equivalent of murder—character assassination in print—and autobiography is the literary equivalent of suicide—the taking of one's own life in words—as Henry Adams suggested,[19] then collaborative autobiography may be a kind of literary mercy-killing—the taking of one person's life, by mutual agreement and prearrangement, by another. With literary as with literal euthanasia, however, the quality of mercy is sometimes strained: it is not always clear whose interests the act serves. When the already equivocal act involves members of different—and historically hostile—races, then the arrangement becomes especially charged.

Thanks to the work of Holler, Demallie, and others, we are now in a better position to assess the editorial operation that produced *Black Elk Speaks*. Neihardt's role as editor was especially decisive at the borders of the narrative, beginning with the title page. Although the use of proper names in Native American narratives is somewhat complicated by the custom of using various names over a lifetime (Brumble, 7), one can question Neihardt's decision to refer to the holy man as "Black Elk," which is an unhappy medium between his Lakota name, Hehaka Sapa, and his Christian name, Nicholas Black Elk. Neihardt's choice perfectly exemplifies his contradictory desires to characterize Black Elk as an unreconstructed "longhair" and to render him accessible to a white audience. (In any case, if Neihardt is to have "Flaming Rainbow" after his name, in recognition of his initiation into the tribe, perhaps Black Elk ought to have his Lakota name after his English one to signify his existence outside of English. The use of two names for each collaborator would at least put them on numerically equal terms.) As problematic as its subject's name is the book's title. Hilda Neihardt Petri has cited it as evidence of her father's desire to make the book Black Elk's from the start (Demallie, xviii), but *"Black Elk Speaks"* is not Black Elk's speech. The editor's initial gesture, intended to identify Black Elk as the source of what follows, effectively displaces him from the first to the third person. Moreover, though hardly avoidable, the use of a title introduces to the narrative the assumptions of print culture, which labels stories and binds them to individual authors in a way foreign to oral culture. From the outset, then, there is some uncertainty as to who is entitled to the narrative that follows.

It is never easy to identify individual contributions to a collaboratively produced text, but given the politically sensitive nature of boundaries in the history of white–Indian relations, producers and consumers of bicultural texts need to demonstrate particular tact in this regard. In this case, the efforts of scholars to determine the respective contributions of John Neihardt and Black Elk have yielded especially interesting—and damaging—revelations. For example, in an interview with Sally McCluskey shortly before he died, Neihardt declared that the narrative's very first lines were his own creation: "My friend, I am going to tell you the story of my life, as you wish; and if it were only the story of my life, I think I would not tell it" (1).[20] Here "Black Elk" concedes more than he knows, since his story will be told not so much *in response to* the white man's request ("as you wish") as *in the way that* Neihardt desires (or, in effect, wills).

Thus, the opening uncannily betrays white encroachment on native grounds.

In effect, what we have here is not Black Elk speaking through the passive medium of John Neihardt; it is Neihardt, self-proclaimed author of the book, speaking through the mask of Black Elk (i.e., creating a literary character by means of invented speech). While the opening words appear to be Black Elk's explanation to his collaborator of the distinctively tribal nature of the story he is about to convey, they are in fact Neihardt's justification to his reader of a feature of the text—its tribal focus—that his own editing had already diminished. Moreover, the opening passage brings the text into conformity with mainstream models: Franklin, Thoreau, and Adams—to name a few canonical American autobiographers—all begin their narratives with gambits that deflect the charge of egotism. In the case of Black Elk, the gesture is made necessary only by the preconceptions of his editor about "autobiography."

Intended to correct the impression that he had merely recorded the narrative, Neihardt's interview with McCluskey made it evident that Black Elk's speech had not been translated, but transformed—and at times invented. (Ironically, as DeMallie points out, the text's most frequently quoted passages are ones for which Neihardt has claimed authority [55].) It also retroactively blurred the boundary Neihardt had originally drawn—by means of the shift from "frame" to "narrative" and by the deployment of first- and second-person pronouns—between his textual space and Black Elk's. Other problematic features of the narrative suggest that what is true in one sense of the opening paragraphs is true in another of the entire text: it is an act of bicultural ventriloquism.

If dialogue is a form of political struggle for representation on the territory of the utterance, as Bakhtin suggested,[21] then *Black Elk Speaks* is at best governed by a form of benevolent dictatorship. Consider the book's tone of voice: for lack of the original Lakota, we cannot definitively assess the translation (as we have seen), but comparison reveals that the book's dignified style has less in common with that of the transcripts than with that of earlier Neihardt works (DeMallie, 52) and even perhaps the King James Bible (McCluskey, 241). Another problematic feature is the book's focus on Black Elk rather than on Lakota religion. As McCluskey points out, the transcripts include more description of ritual than the book; indeed, she asserts that, as a result of the editing, "Black Elk appears here as a priest second, a man first" (233). But this is presumably not the way he perceived or presented himself. Moreover, she reports that Neihardt referred to the use of the first person as "a literary device" (232)—further evidence that Neihardt's editing, which he may have thought would make the narrative more autobiographical, was what made it "autobiography" in the first place.

The narrative's chronology also subtly imposes alien values on the narrative. Chronology is so conventional in Western autobiography that it seems a natural, even inevitable, ordering principle. It apparently seemed so to Neihardt. According to Walter J. Ong, however, "Oral narrative is not greatly concerned with exact sequential parallelism between the sequence in the narrative and the sequence in extranarrative referents. Such a parallelism becomes a major objective only when the mind interiorizes literacy" (147). Thus, Neihardt's statement, or boast, to McCluskey that "he had to fashion Black Elk's story from many days of talk, many reminiscences recalled not necessarily in order" (232) suggests that the "transcription" was shaped by assumptions foreign to Black Elk. Perhaps even more relevant here is the fact that central both to Black Elk's vision and to Ghost Dance religion is the belief in a world that transcends simple chronological progression. To commit this narrative to a firm timeline is to privilege historical time over mythic time and to violate the Lakota sense of time as cyclical rather than linear. The cumulative effect of such decisions is to shape the book according to expectations irrelevant to Lakota culture; the medium (Euramerican autobiography) becomes the message.

The ending also reveals Neihardt's designs and preconceptions. In claiming credit for the narrative's organization, in his interview with McCluskey, he asserted that he concluded it with the Battle of Wounded Knee because he considered that to be its most dramatic event. He also acknowledged that he shaped the whole for a white audience: "The translation—or rather the *transformation*—of what was given to me was expressed so that it could be understood by the white world" (238–39). It should be remembered here that when Neihardt first approached Black Elk, he was seeking material about the Ghost Dance religion for his poem cycle, which was to end with that battle as the climax of white conquest of the West. Though a different book resulted from his visit, the ending was the same; in this sense, at least, it was a foregone conclusion.

Indeed, the terminus is forecast in the third paragraph, where the story is described as that of a "mighty vision, given to a man too weak to use it . . . and of a people's dream that ended in bloody snow"

(2). Although much did end at Wounded Knee—one does not want to downplay its calamitousness—Black Elk's life did not, nor did his vision. Indeed, he maintained the dream long afterward, and it was the function, and the burden, of his vision to deny the finality of these events. His vision is oriented toward a redemptive future. By contrast, the narrative moves toward an apocalypse that seems the fulfillment of all that precedes it.[22] The narrative structure implies that traditional culture ended with the battle. The final paragraphs say so explicitly:

> I did not know how much died there. . . . And I, to whom so great a vision was given in my youth—you see me now a pitiful old man who has done nothing, for the nation's hoop is broken and scattered. There is no center any longer, and the sacred tree is dead (276).

These paragraphs, however, like the first three, are Neihardt's creation, as are the attitude of failure and the tone of despair they impart. (DeMallie suggests that Neihardt may have misread the conventional tone of humility in Lakota prayer as expressing an attitude of hopelessness toward history [56].) The effect of the premature ending is to dismiss Black Elk's reservation life as nonexistence—which parallels and reinforces the effect of Neihardt's suppression of his Christianity. (In the transcripts, it is evident that the remembering consciousness is informed by a Christian perspective.) Because of its erasure of assimilated traits of the reservation Indian, *Black Elk Speaks* characterizes its narrator as spiritually close to, though temporally remote from, the life of the Plains. There is considerable truth in this, of course, but the effect of such editing is to characterize Black Elk as a man who has aged but not changed in the intervening years.

The relationship among the theologies successively embraced by Black Elk—traditional Lakota religion, Ghost Dance religion, and Christianity—is difficult to assess. Clyde Holler argues that from Black Elk's perspective they were compatible and complementary rather than contradictory—different means to the same end, the survival and perpetuation of the tribe (31–37). At the same time, he argues that Neihardt subtly but significantly distorted Black Elk's theology. According to Holler, *Black Elk Speaks* reinforces the implication of Neihardt's *Cycle of The American West* that "the Indian future does not lie with the revitalization of the traditional religion and values, which were discredited at Wounded Knee, but with assimilation and conversion" (34). The crucial misrepresentation is the speaker's renunciation of the Ghost Dance religion: "Neihardt's Black Elk regrets joining the Ghost Dance; the real Black Elk regrets not using a more powerful vision against the whites" (35). The historical ironies here are terrible: like the reservation administrators of the 1890s, Neihardt unfairly and unilaterally put down the Ghost Dance movement.[23]

As we have seen, Neihardt suppressed all references to the holy man's conversion to Roman Catholicism. Neihardt thus misread or misrepresented the subtle syncretism of Black Elk's theology—whether of the 1890s or of the 1930s. On the one hand, he rehabilitated a "heathen" —by minimizing the militancy of his traditional power vision and by distancing him from the revitalization cult. On the other hand, he "cannibalized" a Christian—by concealing the fact of his conversion. (There is also an element of figurative cannibalization in Neihardt's consumption and digestion of Black Elk's dictations.) The effect of his dissociating Black Elk both from Ghost Dance religion and from Christianity is to portray the holy man as caught between two worlds, and to characterize the Lakota cause as hopeless. In the very act of receiving the power vision from Black Elk, Neihardt portrayed its source as powerless in the face of white encroachment.

The effect of Neihardt's editing is to stop the clock on Lakota life, in both its personal and communal dimensions, and thus to threaten its legacy. Indeed, ending the narrative so *conclusively* with the Battle of Wounded Knee is the literary equivalent of killing off the survivors—a kind of metaphorical genocide. The conclusion encourages white readers to indulge in uncomplicated pathos at the demise of a noble (savage) way of life rather than to compel them to contemplate its tenuous survival in assimilated forms. While Neihardt translates the vision in a compelling—because preternaturally clear—prose, he fails to devise a narrative form that can present it in any but a pathetic and nostalgic way. His book does not entirely transcend that romantic cliche—the song of the dying Indian.

VII

Neihardt's literary biographer, Blair Whitney, has claimed that "[t]hough Neihardt says Black Elk spoke though him, it is equally correct to say that Neihardt speaks through Black Elk, since the Sioux holy man asserts many of Neihardt's personal beliefs and dramatizes in his narrative some of Neihardt's own themes."[24] Whitney's casual reversal of the usual account of the collaboration unwittingly suggests the problematic nature of the book's provenance. (Indeed, in his Twayne volume, Whitney treats *Black Elk Speaks* like any other text in Neihardt's oeuvre, stressing the features it shares with his other work and its role in his development as a writer.) It also suggests that Neihardt's background emboldened him to take liberties another collaborator might have declined to take. In any case, his admission that he wrote the first and last paragraphs is devastating, for it literally changes the formal boundaries of the narrative, the point at which the Lakota and the white wor(l)ds meet. As Neihardt encroaches on Black Elk's verbal territory, the book unintentionally inscribes the process it explicitly and eloquently condemns: the historical expropriation of tribal country by whites—if not by violence, then by means of manipulative verbal contract.

It is especially ironic that Neihardt's own divulgences began to expose the flaws in an apparently innocent collaboration. But when we have grasped the implications of Neihardt's editing, we may see that his own testimony and the revelations of McCluskey and DeMallie were not necessary to disclose the book's defects: its own tropes deconstruct it. (Judging from the transcripts, they are almost all Neihardt's: the use of metaphor was one of his means of giving the book poetic distinction and power.) For example, the lament for the displacement of the tribe from round tipis based on sacred archetypes to frame houses based on Western models indicts the use of the framed narrative and the confinement of an oral narrative to blocks of print. Similarly, Black Elk's childhood fear of being "rubbed out" by Wasichus (whites) is tragically realized by Neihardt's editing, which erases some of his distinctive Lakota features, even as it exaggerates others. Finally, the condemnation of the white hunters who slaughtered buffalo for their tongues inculpates the process by which the white reader acquires and consumes Black Elk's preserved speech.

When Black Elk relinquished his precious vision to Neihardt in the hope that he could translate it intact out of the reservation, on which tribal religion had been literally outlawed, he surrendered it to a process whose outcome he could neither foresee nor control. Ultimately, Neihardt's narrative remains confined within the invisible reservations of its own unconscious ethnocentrism. What is surprising is not that the narrative is tainted with ethnocentrism, but that it passed for authentic for so long. The reason for this is perhaps not far to seek: the truth of Indian–white relations is so intolerable that we seek desperately to deny it. Lacking historical instances of harmonious relations between the races, we invent literary ones. Witness the well-documented tradition of idealized relations between white males and males of color in the novels of Cooper, Melville, Mark Twain, Faulkner, and others. While most critics of *Black Elk Speaks* have treated it as historic, and historical, model of communication and cooperation between the races, it may be just another fictive one.

Neihardt's narrative speaks with a forked tongue in several senses. (In the transcripts, though Black Elk complained about the Wasichus' lies, he never uses the phrase "forked tongue.") It speaks with a cloven tongue in the way that all collaborative autobiography does because it conflates two consciousnesses (and in this case languages and cultures) in one undifferentiated voice. It also misleads by not fully acknowledging the extent and the tendencies of its editing. The book also falsifies because of the contradictory senses in which it *contains* the tensions between Wasichus and Lakotas. First, it *includes* them as its subject, and, by explicitly indicting them, it purports to *check* them. By *confining* them to the distant past and erasing them from the present, however, it surreptitiously accommodates them. Thus, the book's greatest deception is its most subtle one—its pretense that its own production escaped the cultural imperialism that it condemns. The preface claims that the collaboration was mutual and egalitarian—in effect, that it took place outside of the historical conditions it describes. But the editing is clearly implicated in—and thus encodes—cultural imperialism.

Thus, finally, the text *undoes* what it says: it reenacts the process it condemns. Black Elk repeatedly refers to his present predicament, and his vision points to a distant future, but the narrative produced is largely retrospective. Black Elk's "failure" to narrate events in temporal sequence is "corrected" by Neihardt's editing, and the narrative's truncation severs the tragic past from the present. Black Elk remains marooned in time, and confined to rectangles of print surrounded by white space. His speech is preserved here as Lakota culture is preserved on the reservation: in conditions neither wholly of its making nor freely of its choosing. Neihardt is also caught in a trap of his own creation. In treating the narrative as autobiography (rather than as sacred history), he made it less tribal, but in trying to make it more traditional (editing out evidence of Black Elk's assimilation), he made it less autobiographical (a less accurate expression of Black Elk's life and being), until "Native American autobiography" is revealed to be a misnomer, if not an oxymoron.

The more closely one examines the text in its context, the more elusive its authority (and its author) becomes. To put it differently, the more one knows about *Black Elk Speaks*, the less difference one perceives between it and the white-produced "Indian shows" in which Black Elk participated. Its proper epigraph might be his remark about Buffalo Bill's Wild West Show: " 'I liked the part of the show we made, but not the part the Wasichus made' " (221). Indeed, its *actual* epigraph (attributed to Black Elk)—"What is good in this book is given back to the six grandfathers and to the great men of my people" —can be constructed in just this way. In speaking what proved to be the first words of his book, perhaps Black Elk also in some sense spoke the last words on it. In such oblique and ironic ways is the oppositional potential of Native American autobiography realized.

9

Biculturalism in Contemporary Autobiography: Richard Rodriguez and Maxine Hong Kingston

I

Two recent autobiographies—*Hunger of Memory: The Education of Richard Rodriguez, An Autobiography* (1982), and Maxine Hong Kingston's *The Woman Warrior: Memoir of A Girlhood Among Ghosts* (1976)—illuminate the predicament of the contemporary minority autobiographer. Neither Rodriguez nor Kingston wishes to be read simply as a minority writer, of course, and neither presumes to represent an entire group, yet both have spoken out on minority issues. Rodriguez's autobiography rose out of his early articles on bilingual education and affirmative action; in turn, it gave rise to more articles, speeches, and media appearances on these and related subjects. Similarly, Kingston has given lengthy interviews in which she avowed her feminism, championed other Chinese-American writers, and criticized Caucasian misreading of her writing.

Hunger of Memory and *The Woman Warrior* are bicultural autobiographies in the sense that they recount lives that originated in distinctive minority subcultures but did not end there. They were not produced in collaboration with members of the dominant culture. Thanks to their impressive academic credentials and impeccable English, Rodriguez and Kingston were able to function more or less autonomously as autobiographers: these minority writers did not have their narratives written for them or otherwise appropriated by Caucasians. Unlike the case in most Native American autobiography or slave narrative, there is no race ritual apparent in the production or presentation of these texts; and yet both have been involved in disputes over the reception of their stories: for reasons having to do with their ambiguous cultural status, the authority of both autobiographies has been questioned.

In his chapter on higher education, Rodriguez argues that, at least in his case, the term "minority student" was not only a misnomer but an oxymoron: "The reason I was no longer a minority was because I had become a student."[1] For Rodriguez, education is inherently assimilating because it confers public identity, which ethnicity denies. His book seems to imply that ethnic autobiography is also a contradiction in terms: to write and publish one's life is to achieve full citizenship as an unhyphenated American. For Rodriguez, then, autobiography is not merely the most democratic of genres, but a literary melting pot. In effect, *Hunger of Memory* seems to declare the end, or nonexistence, of minority autobiography—the impossibility of bicultural autobiography.

As Rodriguez is well aware, however, the issue is not up to him to decide; he understands that he cannot entirely control how his own autobiography will be presented to, and read by, the public:

> Let the bookstore clerk puzzle over where it should be placed. (Rodriguez? Rodriguez?) Probably he will shelve it alongside specimens of that exotic new genre, "ethnic literature." Mistaken, the gullible public will—in sympathy or in anger—take it that I intend to model my life as the typical Hispanic-American life (7).

Thus, although Rodriguez is in a position to resist editorial interference or appropriation of his text, he cannot completely control its marketing or its reception. The ill-considered decision of a harried bookstore clerk might fundamentally misrepresent his book, creating an expectation that the text could confound but never destroy.

Understandably, some readers have resented and resisted his denial of his ethnicity. Hispanic activists and critics in particular have attacked Rodriguez for preaching assimilationism, accusing him, as he notes in his prologue, of being "a brown Uncle Tom" (4), a traitor to his people. They not only impugn his assertion that he and others like him suffer no significant disadvantage; they also challenge his right to speak for (or against) them. For example, Raymund Paredes charges:

> In his attacks on affirmative action and bilingual programs and his support of traditional American education, institutionalized religion, and ethnic assimilation, Rodriguez quickly emerged as the designated "Hispanic" intellectual of the 1980s. In a political climate turning chilly towards minorities, Rodriguez eloquently justified, from the dominant point of view at least, a retreat from a national agenda to address their concerns.[2]

Thus, some Hispanic readers have publicly disputed the authority of his autobiography.

Ironically, it is members of Rodriguez's ethnic group who seek to appropriate his experience, to interpret his life, in the belief that the force of his opinions lies largely in the "authority" of his personal history. Indeed, they virtually deny him a private life separate from their collectivity. In the most sustained and sophisticated attack on Rodriguez, Ramon Saldivar has argued that

> it is the very private quality of his confessional mode that has made his book of political consequence to the Right. Who would read another editorial on affirmative action? But who can turn away from an anguished denunciation of it by one who has benefitted from affirmative action?[3]

(Rodriguez has admitted that his views on issues like bilingual education have been solicited precisely because his sponsors consider him to be, in some sense, what he denies he is—a Chicano.)

Kingston's book has been far less controversial, and she has been warmly embraced by minority readers and critics (especially feminists). Some reviewers, however, characterized her book in terms of the stereotypes she thought she had demolished; indeed, some referred to her as Chinese, rather than Chinese-American, thereby unconsciously denying her citizenship. By literally reviewing her reviewers, she reasserted her authority over her autobiography in an extraordinary way.[4]

The two complementary examples of Rodriguez and Kingston suggest that autobiography—presumably a genre equally accessible to all Americans today—is still an especially complicated undertaking for members of minority groups. Granted, for the most part these two writers have met with exceptional acclaim as autobiographers. Reviewers, critics, and anthologists have canonized their texts, and both writers were, for a time, minor(ity) celebrities in the American fashion. Rodriguez was featured in *People* magazine, and Kingston was named a Living Treasure of Hawaii, where she resided. Yet both have had to defend their texts after publication, and both have had assertions about their ethnic, racial, or cultural identities (their status as "hyphenated Americans") called into question. Their reception suggests that members of minority groups are still liable to have the rights to their literary lives publicly contested, especially if their narratives have controversial political agendas. Both books, then, illustrate the complex circumstances and dynamics of bicultural autobiography in contemporary America.

II

The feature of their bicultural backgrounds that causes Kingston and Rodriguez most concern and confusion is language. Both self-consciously confront the issue of the relationship of the self to language and culture—of the autonomy of the self in and out of autobiography. As children, both were painfully torn between assimilation into mainstream culture and allegiance to their respective subcultures, which were passed on by bilingual or non-English-speaking parents. Both characterize their familial discourses as distinctive but difficult environments for character-formation. Rodriguez associates mellifluous Spanish with an all-embracing intimacy and a profound public alienation; Kingston finds a rich repertoire of stories and a frustrating ambiguity—not to mention an embarrassingly un-American loudness—in her family's Chinese. While both experienced racial discrimination, they found linguistic barriers more difficult to surmount than color lines; thus, both focus on their audible rather than visual distinction from the norm.

In both cases, the ethnic language is experienced as an obstacle to full selfhood as an American: in making the transition from private (family) life to public life (in school), from Chinese or Spanish to English, both suffered temporary speech impediments. Both eventually broke through the language barrier to become exceptionally literate and well-educated in English, as is demonstrated by their success as writers; however, both recognized that in writing autobiography, they broke powerful cultural proscriptions. (Indeed, both books are dedicated to parents who either cannot read or cannot accept their autobiographical writing.) Thus, while both are "success stories," both associate pain, loss, and confusion with their assimilation.

Despite all of these similarities, there are crucial differences in the way Rodriguez and Kingston apprehend and express their ethnicity. Rodriguez was encouraged toward assimilation by parents who were apparently aware of, and willing to pay, its price. (They intentionally moved into an Anglo neighborhood to advance their children's acculturation, rather than their own.) Perhaps it should come as no surprise, then, that Rodriguez feels less bound to, and by, his ethnicity. While sensitive to the pain of assimilation, he explicitly—and provocatively—celebrates his accession to a public identity by means of his monolingual education. He also denies that he suffered significant disadvantage because of his language, his ethnic background, or his skin color, once that education took hold. While he is eloquently nostalgic for the Edenic world of his preschool years, he makes no attempt to recover or to voice his Hispanic heritage in his autobiography.

In contrast to Rodriguez's parents, Kingston's did not wish assimilation for themselves or their children—they never learned to speak or read English. Settling in a Chinese-American community in Stockton (indeed, in a neighborhood populated by people from their village in China), they apparently lived in the hope and expectation of one day returning from "Gold Mountain" to China—from which they were, in a sense, political refugees. Despite Kingston's deep reservations about her Chinese heritage—in particular, she harshly indicts its crippling sexism—it is perhaps understandable that she is less sanguine than Rodriguez about assimilation. In any case, her book essays a fusion of the cultural forms of China and America, East and West. These autobiographers differ, then, in how much they were shaped by ethnic culture; they differ, too, on the public viability and value of their respective subcultures.

Thus, while both are acutely aware of the power of language to shape the self, their autobiographies cast them in very different relations to their "mother tongues." As an autobiographer, Kingston circles back repeatedly to the rich linguistic and cultural resources of her childhood to fashion a genuinely bicultural memoir. Her narrative ultimately achieves a novel accommodation between minority and mainstream culture. In contrast, Rodriguez plots his narrative as a more or less steady march away from a private identity defined by Spanish toward a public identity defined by English. Moreover, despite a disclaimer—"I write of one life only. My own" (7)—he does not hesitate to generalize his experience:

> The bilingualists insist that a student should be reminded of his difference from others in mass society, his heritage. But they equate mere separateness with individuality. The fact is that only in private—with

> intimates—is separateness from the crowd a prerequisite for individuality. (An intimate draws me apart, tells me that I am unique, unlike all others.) In public, by contrast, full individuality is achieved, paradoxically, by those who are able to consider themselves members of the crowd. Thus it happened for me: Only when I was able to think of myself as an American, no longer an alien in *gringo* society, could I seek the rights and opportunities necessary for full public individuality. The social and political advantages I enjoy as a man result from the day that I came to believe that my name, indeed, is *Rich-heard Road-ree-guess*. . . . [D]espite the anonymity of the crowd and the fact that the individuality I achieve in public is often tenuous—because it depends on my being one in a crowd—I celebrate the day I acquired my new name (27).

But Rodriguez's text sometimes induces invalid conclusions from his experience. In particular, his views on bilingualism do not cohere or convince. His narrative is certainly better at describing the pain that attended his progressive alienation from the intimacy of his Hispanic family than it is at arguing the necessity and desirability of that process. His remarkable first chapter vividly conveys the subtle but devastating changes brought about by the family's compliance with his teachers' request that they practice English at home. Consider his dismay upon hearing his parents shift from Spanish to English when he entered a room. (They did so to facilitate his understanding of his second language, not of them.) The change instantaneously redefined him, and his relationship with his parents, in public terms. It reflected the conversion, at least temporarily, of the whole family into students, and of the home into a school. While he later achieved intimacy with family members, as well as with his Caucasian friends, in English, his text demonstrates the costs of the intrusion of English into family life: his relatives' confusion and resentment at his dis-ease with Spanish (his increasing fluency with English was accompanied by a block with spoken Spanish, as though his tongue could accommodate only one language at a time), and his father's increasing deference to his mother's more confident English, followed by his lapsing into silence.

Rodriguez credits his monolingual education for his empowering transformation from Ricardo into Richard Rodriguez, and the book focuses on the ways in which his identity is linguistically produced. Three of the narrative's six chapters ("Aria," "The Achievement of Desire," and "Mr. Secrets") deal directly with his production or consumption of discourse: his speaking, reading, and writing English, respectively. (A fourth, "Credo," also reflects on the transforming power of language when it criticizes the new English Mass.) In particular, his crucial first chapter conflates the achievement of a public identity with the acquisition of English. Its very first sentence portrays his entry into a monolingual school as his true genesis: "I remember to start with that day in Sacramento—a California now nearly thirty years past—when I first entered a classroom, able to understand some fifty stray English words" (11). The decisive point, the moment of conversion, comes in the fourth paragraph:

> The nun said, in a friendly but oddly impersonal voice, "Boys and girls, this is Richard Rodriguez." (I heard her sound out: *Rich-heard Road-ree-guess.*) It was the first time I had heard anyone name me in English. "Richard," the nun repeated more slowly, writing my name down in her black leather book. Quickly I turned to see my mother's face dissolve in a watery blur behind the pebbled glass door (11).

The first chapter recounts the narrator's baptism and confirmation as an American—in a Catholic school that was anything but "parochial." The imagery of this passage however, suggests its own, less affirmative meaning because Richard's literal inscription in the class roll of his monolingual school is accompanied by the dissolution of his mother's familiar face behind the classroom door's translucent panel—a visual barrier that stands for the sound barrier that was to come between them. The official pronouncement of his new name irrevocably alters his relation to his family. (Of course, from his mother's point of view, *Ricardo* was slipping inexorably away, but her viewpoint would be increasingly inaccessible to her son.) Moreover, his new name is truncated; the dropping of one syllable destroys the symmetry and the rhythm of his Spanish name. (Symptomatically, his transcription of it, rather than being simply phonetic, renders all but one of its syllables into English *words:* instead of a familiar integral, his name becomes a series of alien words whose reference and significance were yet to be determined.)

The chapter's last image—the mortician's arrangement of his grandmother's face for display in her coffin—also testifies to the distorting effect of shaping by others.[5] Her "expression" in death is recognizable but unsettling:

> Her face appeared calm—but distant and unyielding to love. It was not the face I remembered seeing most often. It was the face she made in public when the clerk at Safeway asked her some question and I would have to respond. It was her public face the mortician had designed with his dubious art (40).

Her public face, though functional in the larger world, is distressing to her relatives. It is especially distressing here because it is imposed on her by strangers on the occasion of her death. This instance of facial distortion implicitly contests the book's explicit celebration of assimilation—which is also, after all, the superimposition of a public mask on one's distinctive features. Moreover, insofar as autobiography is itself the making of a public face—a "dubious art" of public self-presentation (akin to embalming, as P. T. Barnum demonstrated when he arranged for his wife to write his autobiography's "Last Chapter")—this final image deconstructs the authenticity of the narrative that contains it. *The Education of Richard Rodriguez* functions surreptitiously as the epitaph of Ricardo Rodriguez: beneath the narrative's rational surface we occasionally glimpse his ghostly image—his remains.

To some extent, then, the narrative's images seem to deny what Rodriguez explicitly affirms—the desirability of monolingual education. Suspecting as much, he hastens to justify himself:

> My awkward childhood does not prove the necessity of bilingual education. My story discloses instead an essential myth of childhood—inevitable pain. If I rehearse here the changes in my private life after my Americanization, it is finally to emphasize the public gain. The loss implies the gain (27).

His crucial move here is to displace responsibility for his loss from any historically conditioned agency—his teachers, representing an educational system that denigrates or suppresses the first language of many of its most vulnerable students—onto an unquestioned, and by implication, unquestionable universal—the pain of growing up. (At the same time, by putting his Hispanic identity in opposition to his American one, he reinforces a system of cultural hegemony whose existence he refuses to acknowledge.) The point here is not to contradict Rodriguez's claim that, in his case, the gain outweighed the loss, but to point out that his own narrative sometimes suggests otherwise. In any case, the loss is not borne by him alone, and his satisfaction with the outcome does not necessarily legitimize the policy behind it.

While Rodriguez confesses that he "wrongly believed that English was intrinsically a public language and Spanish intrinsically a private one" (20), he does not acknowledge the extent to which his exceptional circumstances led him to false arguments against bilingual education. Had he been a barrio child, he would have already possessed a public Hispanic voice and identity when he entered school. At that point, he would still have had to cross a formidable linguistic frontier, but he would have needed only to supplement an existing public identity, not to forge one for the first time with an alien tongue. Nor would bilingual education have required the sacrifice of family intimacy or of his sense of private selfhood that Rodriguez's monolingual schooling did.[6] A bilingual classroom would have welcomed rather than silenced his first language and thus suggested that Spanish, while not the language of the ruling elite, is nevertheless capable of valid public utterance.

Rodriguez clearly, but mistakenly, believes that to accede to authority in public he needed to abandon Spanish, and to erase Ricardo from his consciousness. By refusing to acknowledge the political determination of this transformation, however, Rodriguez makes it seem more natural and necessary than it is. By first identifying Spanish with family intimacy, and then by exposing that equation as false, Rodriguez manages to sentimentalize, and then to minimize, the cost of the transition. The adoption of English only *seemed* to destroy the harmony of the home; in the end, the family recreated intimacy in English: *"Intimacy is not created by a particular language;* it is created by intimates" (32). What is "lost" here—what *Rodriguez* suppresses—is the intrinsic association of Spanish with a particular cultural heritage and with loyalty to it—with community solidarity: it is this that accounts for his relatives' hurt and angry reaction to his stumbling, stuttering Spanish. By refusing to understand the basis of their response, he inverts a conventional feature of minority autobiography: discrimination at the hands of the majority culture. The aspiring hero of this narrative is discouraged by members of his own ethnic group; instead of suffering rejection by *los gringos,* his attempts at assimilation are scorned by other Mexican-Americans who are threatened by, or jealous of, his incipient assimilation.

In any case, Rodriguez's whole attack on bilingual education can be read as classic case of the resolution of cognitive dissonance. Having undergone, by his own testimony, a painful process of immersion in a monolingual school, Rodriguez could either denounce the pain as unnecessary or he could justify it. The latter strategy was psychologically more economical. Indeed, one wonders in what sense *Richard* Rodriguez could have condemned the educational/linguistic transformation that, by his own account, *produced* him. The function of much of his book is to enumerate the reasons he is unable to go home again.

III

Rodriguez has written, presumably on purpose, a virtually monolingual, monocultural, and monologic text. Its subtitle, "The Education of Richard Rodriguez, An Autobiography," associates it unmistakably with *The Education of Henry Adams,* a canonical intellectual autobiography by a member of the elite. So does its structure: the chapters recount in chronological order his education by a series of cultural institutions—the English language ("Aria"), primary school ("The Achievement of Desire"), the Church ("Credo"), skin color ("Complexion"), higher education ("Profession"), and autobiography itself ("Mr. Secrets").

Like Adams, he subordinates character and narrative to analysis and argument. Indeed, in resisting his editor's preference for the former, he replays, from a position of power, the struggle of earlier minority autobiographers for authority over their texts:

> But the New York editor is on the phone and he can't understand: "Why do you spend so much time on abstract issues? Nobody's going to remember affirmative action in another twenty-five years. The strength of this manuscript is in the narrative. You should write your book in stories—not as a series of essays. Let's have more Grandma."
>
> But no. Here is my most real life. My book is necessarily political, in the conventional sense, for public issues . . . have bisected my life and changed its course (6–7).

Far from urging him to emphasize the book's political agenda, his editor requests more local color, more ethnic character(s)—precisely that which Rodriguez is least inclined to offer. To some extent, the narrator's predicament here recalls that of the abolitionist slave narrator, whose role was to supply vivid personal testimony, rather than to devise his own ideology. Yet this highly educated Chicano has sufficient clout to resist the guidance of his New York editor—even to flaunt that resistance. Thus, unlike slave narrators, whose editors generally validated their words by surrounding them with documentation, Rodriguez is in a position to exhibit his authority by quoting, and then overruling, his editor in his Prologue.

Familiarity with slave narrative may inform a related passage in the Prologue. Like many abolitionist narrators, Rodriguez rehearsed his autobiography on the lecture platform. In his opening, he wittily reenacts the ritual of being introduced to a live audience, interpolating his own ironic commentary:

> "Mr.? . . ."
>
> Rodriguez. The name on the door. . . . The name I carry from my parents—who are no longer my parents, in a cultural sense. This is how I pronounce it: *Rich-heard Road-ree-guess.* This is how I hear it most often.
>
> The voice through a microphone says, "Ladies and gentlemen, it is with pleasure that I introduce Mr. Richard Rodriguez."
>
> I am invited very often these days to speak about modern education in college auditoriums and in Holiday Inn ballrooms. . . .
>
> "Mr. Rodriguez has written extensively about contemporary education."
>
> Several essays. I have argued particularly against two government programs—affirmative action and bilingual education.
>
> "He is a provocative speaker."
>
> I have become notorious among certain leaders of America's Ethnic Left. I am considered a dupe, an ass, the fool. . . . (4).

Though his remarks are self-deprecating, here Rodriguez internalizes and inverts the apparatus of authentication, displaying the extent to which contemporary minority members may be free to control the production and presentation of their printed lives.

Evidently, Rodriguez can have his way with his text. His way with his autobiography, however, is to not to reach back to his Chicano origins for models or materials—"Caliban won't ferry a TV crew back to his island, there to recover his roots" (5)—but to rely on those made accessible by his academic training. Hence his idea of his book as a middle-class pastoral, elaborated in his Prologue (as well as his allusion to the Tempest). Hence, too, his reliance on Richard Hoggart's *The Uses of Literacy,* which he discovered while escaping from his dissertation in the British Museum. There, in self-imposed exile from his Chicano background, Rodriguez had sought a sense of relation in the community of scholars; instead, he found solace and self-understanding in Hoggart's discussion of a type of the "scholarship boy: good student, troubled son."

> The child is "moderately endowed," intellectually mediocre, Hoggart supposes—though it may be more pertinent to note the special qualities of temperament in the child. High-strung child. Brooding. Sensitive.

> Haunted by the knowledge that one *chooses* to become a student. (Education is not an inevitable or natural step in growing up.) Here is a child who cannot forget that his academic success distances him from a life he loved, even from his own memory of himself (48).

He invokes Hoggart to explain, in a kind of sociological shorthand, the impact of his own primary education, rather than to confirm his ideas on education. But Hoggart does more than supply Rodriguez with a template for his younger self, and a plot for the book. The graduate student, even the author of the book, is still very much a scholarship boy:

> I realized that I had not neatly sidestepped the impact of schooling. My desire to do so was precisely the measure of how much I remained an academic. . . . My need to think so much and so abstractly about my parents and our relationship was in itself an indication of my long education. . . . The ability to consider experience so abstractly allowed me to shape into desire, what would otherwise have remained indefinite, meaningless longing in the British Museum. If, because of my schooling, I had grown culturally separated from my parents, my education finally had given me ways of speaking and caring about that fact (72).

Thus, he understands, with Hoggart's help, the extent to which his longing for his remote ethnic past is a function of the education that obliterated it. He sees that instead of reducing his distance from that past, his articulation of his longing may increase it—by stimulating the hunger of memory.

The larger revelation here is the exposure of the extent to which Rodriguez *is* what he has *read*. The characteristic scene in this chapter is one in which Rodriguez endeavors to transcribe onto himself—through his reading—the attributes of his teachers, or to inscribe himself into the tradition out of which they emerged. Like Franklin, he fondly and proudly recollects his early reading, but Rodriguez seems less sure that his identity transcends its textual sources:

> The scholarship boy is a very bad student. He is the great mimic; a collector of thoughts, not a thinker; the very last person in class who ever feels obliged to have an opinion of his own. In large part, however, the reason he is such a bad student is because he realizes more often and more acutely than most other students—than Hoggart himself—that education requires radical self-reformation. . . . He becomes in every obvious way the worst student, a dummy mouthing the opinions of others. But he would not be so bad—nor would he become so

> successful, a *scholarship* boy—if he did not accurately perceive that the best synonym for primary "education" is "imitation" (67).

Rodriguez's insistence that the essence of education is imitative self-reformation leads him toward an unusual autobiographical tactic: rather than urging the uniqueness of its author's identity, his narrative seems at times content to portray it as a composite, a textual construct. Far from reflecting a taste for poststructuralism, however, this tendency affirms his assimilation into the dominant culture.

In his very eagerness to blend into that culture, however, there are indications that his book is somewhat of an American anomaly, an authoritarian's autobiography—one that values obedience to authority over individual judgment. His intolerance of ambiguity, both intellectual and otherwise, is implicit in this comment on the *Baltimore Catechism:*

> Beyond what the answer literally stated, two things were communicated. First, the existence of a question implies the existence of an answer. (There are no stray questions.) And second, that my questions about religion had answers. (The Church knows.) (88).

Similar sentiments are explicit in his assertion that he remains at least a "cultural" Catholic: "I am a man who trusts a society that is carefully ordered by figures of authority" (102). His authoritarianism also surfaces in his endorsement of rote learning:

> Stressing memorization, my teachers implied that education is largely a matter of acquiring knowledge already discovered. And they were right. For contrary to more progressive notions of learning, much that is learned in a classroom must be the already known; and much that is already known must be learned before a student can achieve truly independent thought.
>
> Stressing memorization, the nuns assumed an important Catholic bias. . . . [T]hey believed that learning is a social activity; learning is a rite of passage into the group. Remembrance is itself an activity that establishes a student's dependence upon and union with others (89).

In part, the appeal of rote learning may have been that it would somehow offset the tendency of the monolingual classroom, by weaning him abruptly from his mother tongue, to throw him unprotected into the public arena; rote learning offered a new resource, and a new impersonal affiliation. It gratified his desire for community at a vulnerable moment. *Hunger of Memory,* therefore, is a curious and somewhat contradictory text: an autobiography that celebrates the education that transformed its author, but whose dominant tone is one of yearning for a world as secure as the one from which English uprooted him. The real heresy of the book lies not in its controversial views on minority issues—which, after all, are shared by many—but in its expression of dissatisfaction with a society so tolerant of diversity that it not only accepts but celebrates ethnic distinctions and idiosyncrasy. Rodriguez sometimes seems to imply that diversity is impossible; at other times he seems to imply that it is unhealthy.

As we have seen, Rodriguez's models are academic (in the case of Hoggart), or canonical (in the case of Adams)—assimilationist rather than ethnic. His reference to St. Augustine is interesting in this regard, because rather than invoking this preeminent autobiographer as a Catholic precursor, Rodriguez converts him into a Protestant:

> There was a time in my life when it would never have occurred to me to make a confession like this one. There was a time when I would never have thought to discuss my spiritual life—even with other Catholics I knew intimately. It is true that in high school I read Augustine's *Confessions,* but that extraordinary autobiography did not prompt my imitation. Just the reverse: There seemed to me something non-Catholic about the *Confessions.* I intuited that such revelations made Augustine a Protestant church father more than a Catholic father (109).

Rodriguez deliberately forgoes an opportunity to locate his autobiography within a tradition congruent with his origins. While he does invoke Augustine as a forefather, he associates him with seventeenth-century Puritan autobiographers, who eschewed institutional ritual and sacramental confession for new written forms of confession and profession of faith. What the Catholic youth found alien, the graduate student in English finds congenial: the canonical status of the text is part of its eventual appeal as a model.

This purposeful misreading of Augustine is part of a larger strategy by which Rodriguez self-consciously reminds the reader that the very act in which he is engaged is proscribed by ethnic and family tradition. Indeed, he devotes his whole last chapter to illustrating and elaborating the point. This chapter is the most self-reflexive one because it is about the writing of the book that contains it: it is the autobiography's autobiography. In recapitulating his career as a student and writer here, Rodriguez notes his early resistance to, or incomprehension of, assignments calling for autobiographical writing. (In "Complexion," he notes his reluctance even to fill in his color in early self-portraits.) His coming around finally to autobiography is part of the process by which he passes over from the hermetic Hispanic world of his family to what he calls "the sliding-glass door informality of middle-class California family life" (179). Thus, the message of his medium itself is assimilationist—his book says implicitly what his speeches say explicitly: I am not a Chicano. (According to Rodriguez, Chicanos don't write autobiography, or at least not in this mode: they do not discuss private family matters in public.)

At first, like his parents, he sensed an essential incompatibility between the valued privacy of the home and the publicity of written discourse. Even his rationale for his autobiography betrays a trace of his parents' attitude:

> I do not make my parents' sharp distinction between public and private life. With my mother and father I scorn those who attempt to create an experience of intimacy in public. But unlike my parents, I have come to think that there is a place for the deeply personal in public life. This is what I have learned by trying to write this book: There are things so deeply personal that they can be revealed only to strangers (185).

What apparently licensed the writing of *Hunger of Memory* was Rodriguez's growing sense of the buffering impersonality of writing, acquired through access to mechanical modes of producing or reproducing it: the printing of his articles in the school newspaper, in which "Richard Rodriguez" became a by-line rather than a name, and the typing of his college papers, which enabled him to read his writing (now "prose") with an objective eye—the "I" and the voice of another:

> Each morning I make my way along a narrowing precipice of written words. I hear an echoing voice—my own resembling another's. Silent! The reader's voice silently trails every word I put down. I reread my words, and again it is the reader's voice I hear in my mind, sounding my prose (186–87).

The defamiliarization of his writing by mechanical reproduction is for Rodriguez, I think, a trope for the healthy process of achieving a valid public identity. Of paramount importance here is the evolution of his image of his reader—first, an intimate reading over his shoulder, then, teachers increasingly removed from his family situation, and finally people whom he did not know and who knew him only as a writer:

> Now I am struck by the opportunity. I write today for a reader who exists in my mind only phantasmagorically. Someone with a face

> erased; someone of no particular race or sex or age or weather. A gray presence. Unknown, unfamiliar. All that I know about him is that he has had a long education and that his society, like mine, is often public (*un gringo*) (182).

He can essay autobiography only when he can imagine his audience as anonymous strangers, Caucasians who will welcome his self-exposure, and who cannot be betrayed by it. In contrast, thinking of his audience as his parents blocks his writing: "Many mornings at my desk I have been paralyzed by the thought of their faces, their eyes. I imagine their eyes moving slowly across these pages. That image has weakened my resolve" (184–85). When his mother is dismayed by an article he had published, they discuss it in correspondence rather than in person or on the phone: "The impersonality of the written word made it the easiest means of exchange" (189). (In short, Rodriguez learns to treat his mother like an anonymous reader, rather than vice versa.) The publication of family matters becomes itself a family matter, but one that defies the normal channels of communication and resolution. Not only do autobiography's public disclosures violate his parents' sense of the family's integrity, but the act of publication itself resists integration into family discourse.

Seen in this light, the act of writing autobiography becomes psychologically fraught and morally ambiguous. His autobiography's assertion, in form as well as content, of his status as a fully assimilated, no longer hyphenated, American suggests that Rodriguez may be driven in part by self-doubt, i.e., that his sense of his own exclusion and inferiority, so candidly confessed in "Complexion," has not been entirely conquered. Thus, when Rodriguez says, "I do not give voice to my parents by writing about their lives. I distinguish myself from them by writing about the life we once shared" (186), his assertion is simultaneously an overt admission of the impossibility of giving genuine utterance to others and a covert confession of subconscious intention. What Rodriguez had said of Alex Haley's *Roots* (in putting down the idea of "minority literature") could serve as a gloss on his own book: "That book tells us more about his difference from his illiterate tribal ancestors that it does about his link to them. . . . The child who learns to read about his nonliterate ancestors necessarily separates himself from their way of life" (161). His autobiography is not merely essays *on,* but also an essay *in,* the making of an American:

> I think my mother sensed that afternoon that the person whose essay she saw in a national magazine was a person unfamiliar to her, some

> Other. The public person—the writer, Richard Rodriguez—would remain distant and untouchable. . . . And that afternoon she seemed to accept the idea, granted me the right, the freedom so crucial to adulthood, to become a person very different in public from the person I am at home (189–90).

His autobiography pledges his allegiance to the America his parents intended him for: it affirms and consolidates the public identity, the public acceptance, audibility, and intelligibility that were inaugurated in his enrollment in school as Richard Rodriguez. It also suggests, however, that beneath all of his intellectual self-assurance may be doubt about the provisionality of his identity—fear that "Richard Rodriguez" is an unacknowledged pseudonym, and guilt for having adopted it. Thus, while it is very much an academic autobiography (in more than one sense), intended primarily for the eyes of educated Caucasians, the text is also burdened by the author's sense of his debt to those, including his parents, who cannot or will not read it:

> You who read this act of contrition should know that by writing it I seek a kind of forgiveness—not yours. The forgiveness, rather, of those many persons whose absence from higher education permitted me to be classed a minority student. I wish that they would read this. I doubt that they ever will (153)

While this acknowledgment of the make-up of the book's audience functions to locate its author securely within the hegemonic culture, it also reminds him, and his audience, of the exclusiveness of that culture. At moments like this, the text may implicitly concede the desirability, if not the possibility, of a bicultural autobiography that would resist or reverse the effects of assimilation. For when autobiography enacts assimilation, as this one does, it threatens to function as a voice synthesizer that obliterates accents that need to be heard. *Hunger of Memory* is a bicultural autobiography only in the sense that it recounts Rodriguez's progress from one culture to another and powerfully renders that migration's emotional aftermath.

IV

The poignancy of *Hunger of Memory* is that Rodriguez seems genuinely attracted to two worlds that he cannot finally reconcile. While his book outwardly celebrates and formally reinforces his assimilation, there is a strong undercurrent of longing for the intimacy of his

Hispanic childhood. In contrast, there is little nostalgia in Kingston's account of her girlhood; indeed, at times she portrays both halves of her bicultural heritage as threatening: "Sometimes I hated the ghosts for not letting us talk; sometimes I hated the secrecy of the Chinese" (213). In addition to wariness of Caucasian ghosts, her book expresses her rage toward an ethnic heritage she found confusing, disabling, and oppressive. Moreover, Kingston's book is powerfully shaped by the fact that she is a member of a gender minority as well as an ethnic one: it both documents and indicts the strong constraints of Chinese-American culture on women. Perhaps the primary obstacle to the autobiography of a Chinese-American woman is the Confucian exaltation of family and community over the individual, and the privileging of men's lives over women's.[7] For example, Kingston notes, that "the Chinese word for the female *I* . . . is "slave."[8] While Kingston acknowledges the extent to which ethnicity, language, and gender determine identity, she also struggles to resist their domination and to turn their resources to her advantage. Though the book cannot *record* a happy marriage of the American and Chinese influences on her, it does finally manage to *achieve* one.

Like Rodriguez—like any self-conscious bilingual autobiographer—Kingston must face the quandary concerning the provenance of the self: In which language do "I" exist? For Kingston, the radical differences between competing linguistic systems created doubt as to the validity and viability of her viewpoint. Her girlhood troubles had much to do with her difficulty in translating her subjectivity into an alien tongue. The problem was perhaps exacerbated by her tendency to read the first-person pronoun in English as an ideograph, as though its visual features were significant, rather than arbitrary:

> I could not understand "I." The Chinese "I" has seven strokes, intricacies. How could the American " I," assuredly wearing a hat like the Chinese, have only three strokes, the middle so straight? Was it out of politeness that this writer left off strokes the way a Chinese has to write her own name small and crooked: No, it was not politeness; "I" is a capital and "you" is lower-case. I stared at that middle line and waited so long for its black center to resolve into tight strokes and dots that I forgot to pronounce it (193).

To Kingston's eye, accustomed to the intricate Chinese symbol, the English "I" was virtually a cryptogram—austere and minimal, yet assertive and integral. More important than the particulars of the contrast is its consequence: the refusal of the English pronoun to "resolve" itself into its Chinese equivalent made it virtually unutterable.

The problem of self-definition and self-translation had an aural dimension as well. Whereas Caucasian Americans, especially women, usually spoke in soft voices, Chinese-Americans seemed to shout (199):

> Normal Chinese women's voices are strong and bossy. We American-Chinese girls had to whisper to make ourselves American-feminine. Apparently we whispered even more softly than the Americans. Once a year the teachers referred my sister and me to speech therapy, but our voices would straighten out, unpredictably normal, for the therapists. Some of us gave up. . . . Most of us eventually found some voice, however faltering. We invented an American-feminine speaking personality, except for that one girl who could not speak up even in Chinese school (200).

Caught between two cultures with radically different signs and sorts of subjectivity, she found discourse easier at first in Chinese school, where the prevailing methods were collective chanting and private recitation before the teacher, rather than extemporaneous performance in an alien tongue. Even there, however, both her voice and her sister's voice sometimes sounded crippled. Her girlhood memories are full of relatives' unwelcome demands on her tongue—for example, to translate as they haggle with shopkeepers: "You can't entrust your voice to the Chinese, either; they want to capture your voice for their own use. They want to fix up your tongue to speak for them" (196). If the Chinese "I" is an intricate knot binding a female identity, the English alternative may also be a snare: either "I" can throttle her or tie her tongue. Like Rodriguez, Kingston experiences the problem of the relation between language and identity quite viscerally—not theoretically, but existentially. Like *Hunger of Memory, The Woman Warrior* is concerned with a crisis of self-translation from an ethnic first language into the language of the dominant culture.

The matter of narrative conventions for one's experience was also problematic. In addition to the double-bind of the female autobiography—whether to write a conventional story of female development, which would not count as autobiography, or to forge a culturally validated "masculine" story that would deny her gender[9]—Kingston encountered the dilemma of the bicultural autobiographer—how to express in one narrative, and in one language, the experience of two cultures. Kingston, the child of immigrants from a provincial village, did not have ready access to the most widely known Chinese mythology—the mythology of her parents' village was derived from "the small tradition," not the more prestigious "high tradition" of the Chinese classics.[10] Moreover, as Margaret Miller has noted, Chinese women were traditionally confined to oral and colloquial expression and excluded from the written classical literature (24).

Here, Kingston faced a more difficult predicament task than Rodriguez because she seems to have experienced her two heritages not merely as discontinuous but as virtually incapable of representation in the same narrative mode. She perceived America as substantial, practical, and real; China, as intangible, superstitious, and dreamlike: "To make my waking life American-normal, I turn on the lights before anything untoward makes an appearance. I push the deformed into my dreams, which are in Chinese, the language of impossible stories" (102). Moreover, her implicit frame of reference was opposed to that of her parents: "Whenever my parents said 'home,' they suspended America. They suspended enjoyment, but I did not want to go to China. In China my parents would sell my sisters and me . . . . I did not want to go where the ghosts took shapes nothing like our own" (116). Far from offering her a secure and intimate home, "China" threatened her with dispossession and gender bondage—as wife or slave. The story of her self needed to be bivocal and bicultural, if not literally bilingual.

As a result, *The Woman Warrior* is finally very different in tone and execution from *Hunger of Memory*. Whereas Rodriguez's appropriation of English and American academic models (Hoggart, Adams, the pastoral tradition) in effect advances as well as documents his assimilation, Kingston's fusion of genres—high and low, Eastern and Western—stages a lively, if unlikely, dialogue between two diverse and apparently divergent worlds. Indeed, according to her, the book *is* bilingual, in a limited sense:

> There are puns for Chinese speakers only, and I do not point them out for non-Chinese speakers. There are some visual puns best appreciated by those who write Chinese. I've written jokes in that book so private, only I can get them; I hope I sneaked them in unobtrusively so nobody feels left out.[11]

More generally, in its integration of elements of her Chinese background, it runs the risk of incorporating a quality stereotypically attributed to the Chinese: inscrutability. (Though most Caucasian readers will presumably miss the Chinese puns, other passages, such as Kingston's comments on the English "I," will remind them that inscrutability is a matter of cultural perspective.) In both texture and structure, *The Woman Warrior* is truly a bicultural text, one that achieves a tenuous rapprochement between the conflicting elements of Kingston's complex heritage.

Whereas Rodriguez's sources are literary or academic—and thus remote from, if not opposed to, his ethnic origins—Kingston's are often folk or popular, and thus proximate to, or directly derived from, her bicultural girlhood. In addition, whereas Rodriguez, enamored of the impersonality of type and print, documents his ascent from his origins by tracing his descent from canonical authors, Kingston finds her inspiration in improvisatory oral discourse that both perpetuates and revises traditional models. For example, she audaciously combines her mother's exotic talk-story and the American slang in which she and her siblings sought acculturation. Unlike Rodriguez, she evokes and develops the double repertoire of her bicultural childhood to fashion her memoir. What she experienced, as a girl, as irreconcilable, even unutterable differences, she exploits, as an autobiographer, as elements of a vibrant multivocal discourse. If growing up was for her profoundly dis-Orienting, her autobiographical project is an idiosyncratic attempt at self-reorientation: her identity as a Chinese-American emerges from the dialogue between her discrete voices.

Kingston also eschews a linear narrative from birth to the present. In Rodriguez's "[e]ssays impersonating an autobiography" (7), (personal) history *does* repeat itself: the force of his story accrues from the repetition, in chapter after chapter, of the essential action of assimilation. Like Rodriguez, Kingston might have sought refuge from the constraints of her ethnic subculture in assimilation, and constructed her story as a linear conversion narrative. As her name reveals, Maxine Hong Kingston is distanced somewhat from her Chinese-American origins by marriage to a Caucasian. As an autobiographer, however, she does not retrace the progress of her assimilation; rather, she immerses herself in her ethnic girlhood by recalling discrete narratives of Chinese-American women. Thus, her narrative treats time very differently from Rodriguez's—by leaping ahead, circling back, and shifting abruptly among disparate moments in her life. (Her birth is noted almost incidentally in the narrative as an event in her mother's life story.) According to Suzanne Juhasz, women's Lives may distinguish themselves from the male pattern of linear "careers" by just such plots: "[T]hey show less a pattern of linear development towards some clear goal than one of repetitive, cumulative, cyclical structure."[12] Thus, instead of conceiving her identity and her story in terms of conventions of the dominant culture, Kingston appropriates and revoices the tales and texts of her girlhood in a way that challenges or deauthorizes the discourse of the cultures—Caucasian, Chinese, and patriarchal—that threatened to condemn her to silence or marginality.

Vacillating between seemingly objective documentary and idiosyncratic fantasy, Kingston's text tries out a number of narrative methods and points of view. Perhaps, as Suzanne Juhasz suggests, "Kingston's [style] develops from the notion that fantasy, the life of the imagination, creates female identity" (222). Far from being fanciful, contrived, or self-indulgent, however, Kingston's idiosyncratic fusion of fact and fiction is rooted in the particular circumstances of her youth, when her mother's talk-story, already ambiguous, often merged with dreams. It is thus part of a deliberate strategy that favors resources that were accessible to her as a girl over those made available by her education and her reading as a woman. (The book is thus a memoir *of* girlhood in a special sense.) The integrity of Kingston's multifaceted book, then, derives in large part from the pervasiveness—and persuasiveness—of scenes of talking-story, and its power accrues from the development of a reciprocal relationship between her and her mother, Brave Orchid, who was her major source and influence.

V

Less explicitly self-reflexive than *Hunger of Memory, The Woman Warrior* nevertheless presents model after model of its own origins, theory, and practice. Perhaps the most striking of these, Kingston's complex response to her mother's ambiguous admonition, comes right at the opening of the first chapter, "No Name Woman": " 'You must not tell anyone,' my mother said, 'what I am about to tell you. In China your father had a sister who killed herself. She jumped into the family well. We say that your father has all brothers because it is as if she had never been born' " (3). The aunt is not completely expunged from family history: she is kept alive in mutilated form (bereft of a name) to impress on younger women their responsibility to the family.

The details of this story (the aunt's suicide followed an illegitimate pregnancy that shamed her family) as well as the timing of its telling (it coincided with Kingston's reaching puberty) make it an explicit warning against female self-assertion, whether sexual or verbal. Its apparent intent is to induct the daughter into a culture in which the authority to initiate intercourse or to shape family history is reserved to men. Genre is clearly gender-bound: women may be the subjects of stories but not their authors.

But her mother's passing on of the aunt's story in a way undermines her explicit message. Though the suppression of her aunt's name is intended to punish her—if not to deny her existence altogether—her invocation as a warning against female self-assertion not only perpetuates her memory, it permits, if it does not authorize, her rehabilitation or reclamation as a precursor by a Chinese-American descendant. Thus, the subtext of the tale is the ability of women to resist, if only through the whispered communication of secrets, the power of men to determine their fates even after death. There is also some doubt as to the story's veracity—it is a story whose authority is still to be determined: "Whenever she had to warn us about life, my mother told stories that ran like this one, a story to grow up on. She tested our strength to establish realities" (5). In this case, empirical "reality testing" is ruled out: the story's materials and manner of presentation make it impossible to verify. The aunt's existence, hitherto suppressed, would be categorically denied.

Instead, Kingston must test its authority by reconstructing it—first in her mother's words and voice, and then by means of an imaginative rehearsal that goes beyond its bare "facts" into motive and meaning. While sensitive to its original, historical context, she recognizes that its meaning for her cannot be purely Chinese (exclusively monocultural). Only by taking American liberties with the story can she establish a significant relationship with her proscribed relation: "Unless I see her life branching into mine, she gives me no ancestral help" (10). While publication of this story is a violation of her mother's warning, her inquiry into it is not; Kingston's speculative reconstruction of her aunt's circumstances is not as defiant of her mother as it may first appear. Indeed, it may be the desired response, for in a different context, her mother later remarks to her: "Chinese . . . like to say the opposite" (237). It is possible that the mother's reference to the no-name aunt is more a challenge than a warning. In any case, it provides the first instance in the narrative of its fundamental mode of production—the daughter's reworking of material supplied by her mother to produce an artifact that is both bicultural and woman-centered.

Kingston recognizes that she can not unilaterally restore her aunt to a position of respect in the family, but in giving her banished ancestor visibility in English and assigning her a role as a foremother, she begins to formulate her own ethics and esthetics, and to author her own self. It becomes evident that this is a model solution to the problem of cultural and gender conflict (in form as well as content) when, at the end of the chapter, Kingston likens her written reconstruction of her aunt's story to a kind of origami. She knows it is not a genuine folk artifact, the kind of paper gift traditionally proffered to honored ancestors (and deliberately denied the aunt)—it is not paper folded into replicas of shelter or clothing, but paper *un*folding to expose the inscription of an identity long hidden. The publication of her story will not restore the outlawed aunt to a place of honor in the family, but it diminishes the penalty of imposed anonymity, breaks the silence to which she had been condemned, and mitigates Kingston's complicity in her aunt's eternal punishment (18). It is also the beginning of a conspiratorial collaboration with her powerful mother: with the anonymous aunt as a kind of mute muse, they write the hitherto suppressed auto/biographies of the female side of the family. Thus, in *The Woman Warrior,* Kingston not only reconstructs her own heritage; she also inscribes an original form of what feminists call *herstory*.

In her second chapter, "White Tigers," she also elaborates on a story from her mother—this time that of a culture heroine rather than that of an outcast. Kingston's imaginative investment in the fantasy of being adopted, trained, and initiated as a woman warrior able to avenge family hurt is evident in her appropriation of the legend of Fa Mu Lan to the first person and in the yielding of the subjunctive mood to the indicative. Menstruation, which the story of No Name Woman associated with sexual shame, is treated here very differently: since its onset coincides with, but does not interrupt her training, the warrior simultaneously attains power to create and to destroy life. Even though it is fully elaborated, and dense with exotic and mythic details, the narrative is far from free-floating. On the one hand, it is derived from an ancient ballad sung to her by her mother, presumably in a more or less traditional manner, while on the other, it is adapted to Kingston's contemporary circumstances. The mythical emperor who drafts the heroine's brother has his American equivalent in the president who drafts Kingston's brother to fight in Vietnam, just as the offenses against Fa Mu Lan's family have their equivalent in the ravages of Red Guards against Kingston's relatives. Thus, like the story of her aunt, it is reconstructed so as to "anticipate" what has already happened in Kingston's life. Kingston acknowledges the sense in which her present shapes her (narrated) past, rather than vice versa.

Its fantastic tone, however, also suggests its incompatibility with her actual American girlhood. Only retrospectively, as an adult, is Kingston able to assimilate the story of Fa Mu Lan she listened to as a girl, and even then only as an adulteration of an ancient Chinese myth. (According to Kingston, it is deliberately and ironically syncretized—she intended it to read, in part, like a parody of a kung fu movie.[13]) In the latter half of the chapter, she admits its incongruity with the external realities of her past: "When urban renewal tore down my parents' laundry and paved over our slum for a parking lot, I only made up gun and knife fantasies and did nothing useful" (57). The woman warrior masquerading as a man can decapitate (symbolically emasculate) the emperor in response to his mistaken attempt at male-bonding, but when Kingston criticizes her boss's racism, she gets fired. The legacy of her mother's story, then, was ambiguous. It suggested the potential of feminine power without indicating how to realize it, and it identified the enemy, but not how to defeat them: "From the fairy tales, I've learned exactly who the enemy are. I easily recognize them—business-suited in their modern American executive guise, each boss two feet taller than I am and impossible to meet eye to eye" (57).

The traditional tale, then, remained a kind of paradoxical power vision—one that armed Kingston without truly empowering her. It exalted unquestioning filiality, authorizing aggressive behavior in women only in the service of patriarchy: Fa Mu Lan serves in the army in place of an aged and ailing father, and her gender is revealed only when her service ends, at which time she reverts happily to the lot of the conventional Chinese daughter.[14] Kingston's consciousness of Chinese sexism sets her decisively apart from Fa Mu Lan, for whom vengeance and filial duty are conveniently congruent. Both have family grievances, but some of Kingston's are *against* her family—against the very terms in which she is defined. The establishment of her autonomy as a Chinese-American woman involves revenge *on* as well as *for* her family. (Later in the narrative, she confesses: "I had vampire nightmares. . . . I hunted humans down in the long woods and shadowed them with my blackness. Tears dripped from my eyes, but blood dripped from my fangs, blood of the people I was supposed to love" [221].) Yet Kingston insists on her kinship with the fabulous swordswoman, as with her no-name aunt:

> What we have in common are the words at our backs. The idioms for *revenge* are "report a crime" and "report to five families." The reporting is the vengeance—not the beheading, not the gutting but the words. And I have so many words—"chink" words and "gook" words—that they do not fit on my skin (62–3).

Both have revenge carved on their backs; that is, both are indelibly scarred by hostile words, and as a writer, Kingston can at last enact a form of revenge. As a wordswoman, her tongue is freed at last; it will cut less dramatically and discriminately than that of Fa Mu Lan—and thus more dangerously.

Like the first two chapters, the third, "Shaman," is a critique of disabling Chinese-American sexism, and like them, it depends on mother–daughter collaboration. But it differs from both in tone and method. Neither a speculative reconstruction of an unknown ancestor's self-destruction nor a fanciful juxtaposition of a culture heroine's tale to her own childhood, this chapter retells the story of her mother's training and career as a doctor-midwife in China in her husband's absence. Though, like some of the other narratives, this one has its share of distancing implausibility, it arises not from Kingston's memory of an early maternal speech act but rather from still available evidence—documents and photos—which the mother has apparently explained in response to her daughter's questions.

The narrative (like her mother) cannily exploits a loophole in a tightly authoritarian culture. Thus, the book is centered, literally and symbolically, on an account of exceptional female self-determination.[15] This chapter also sets forth a distinctively Chinese-feminine and collective form of self-constitution. To set an example for the other, generally much younger, students, Brave Orchid slept in a haunted chamber and faced down a powerful ghost. In the morning, the others, unable to recall her spirit by chanting her proper "descent line," used a variant of the traditional practice:

> The students at the To Keung School of Midwifery were new women, scientists who changed the rituals. When she got scared as a child, one of my mother's three mothers had held her and chanted their descent line, reeling the frighted spirit back from the farthest deserts. A relative

> would know personal names and secrets about husbands, babies, renegades and decide which ones were lucky in a chant, but these outside women had to build a path from scraps. No blood bonded friend to friend. . . . The calling out of her real descent line would have led her to the wrong place, the village. . . . They pieced together new directions, and my mother's spirit followed them instead of the old footprints. Maybe that is why she lost her home village and did not reach her husband for fifteen years (88–89).

Performed in reciprocation for Brave Orchid's repelling of the Sitting Ghost, this ceremony is followed by a communal exorcism. The process does not simply restore Brave Orchid; rather, it relocates and redefines her in terms of gender rather than kinship. This collective act, undertaken by student midwives, is a kind of paradigmatic rebirth that changes Brave Orchid's identity, insofar as that identity is constituted by her relationships with others.

Kingston can no more chant her own descent line in traditional fashion than her mother's schoolmates could chant hers—her bicultural background has left too many gaps in her past. But she notes that even her mother adapted such customs to an American context:

> When my mother led us out of nightmares and horror movies, I felt loved. I felt safe hearing my name sung with hers and my father's, my brothers' and sisters.' . . . An old-fashioned woman would have called in the streets for her sick child. She'd hold its little empty coat unbuttoned, "Come put on your coat, you naughty child." When the coat puffed up, she'd quickly button up the spirit inside and hurry it home to the child's body in bed. But my mother, a modern woman, said our spells in private (89).

From one perspective, Kingston borrows from her mother's history a model she can use in her own, but from another, she *invents* one she can use to relate her mother's history more intelligibly—and liberally—to her own. What Kingston attempts in her text, therefore, is to recall her own spirit from the double-bondage of her girlhood by chanting her ascent/descent line in a deliberately improvisational and bicultural fashion.

Brave Orchid's achievement here—like Kingston's in the first chapter, and elsewhere in the narrative—is to demystify ghosts—in this case, the ghosts of traditional folklore. A relatively practical woman, Brave Orchid demonstrates a talent for naming the ghosts that haunt the medical school dormitory, and she hazards the paradoxically reassuring hypothesis that ghosts are not "the continuance of dead people [relatives] . . . but an entirely different species of creature" (77). Whatever their ontology, the chapter clearly implies that ghosts can be, and must be, controlled by the proper discourse. In any case, only by acknowledging and facing down her own ghosts, Asian as well as Caucasian, can Kingston give substance to her narrative. In addition, only by writing biography—her mother's story—can she write autobiography. It is appropriate, then, that the chapter ends with a tender scene in which the aged mother resigns herself to her married daughter's reluctance to spend long periods at "home." When Brave Orchid addresses her daughter as Little Dog, an intimate nickname not used in years, a weight lifts from Kingston; she has been released by, and reconciled with, her own (s)mothering ghost. Located at the very center of the narrative is the accommodation required for its genesis as a figuratively collaborative autobiography.

At first glance, the next chapter, "At the Western Palace," is remarkable for its formal "objectivity," i.e., its eschewal of a first-person point of view. Its confinement to a single episode and its strict chronology also set it apart from the other chapters. The internal consistency of this chapter makes it seem the least syncretic and the most monologic in form. Despite intermittent comedy, the tale it recounts is perhaps the book's most traumatic one—the story of Kingston's aunt, Moon Orchid, whose husband emigrated to California, established a successful medical practice, and then married a local Chinese-American woman as part of his new life-style. When Brave Orchid talks her sister into coming to America and then into confronting her husband, Moon Orchid cracks under the strain: she retreats into agoraphobia, paranoia, and madness, and finally dies.

Insofar as it has to do with the destruction of an aunt, this chapter recalls the first one, but it differs significantly from it. Unlike No Name Aunt, this woman is known to Kingston, and instead of happening in an inaccessible time and place, this tragedy plays itself out virtually in Kingston's own home. Moreover, its tragic outcome results from Brave Orchid's foolhardy attempt to script her sister's life according to a Chinese legend that proves sadly irrelevant in America. The proximity of this episode makes it, I think, a far more threatening instance of female vulnerability than the story of No Name Aunt. Indeed, the materials are fraught with personal implications: Moon Orchid is a kind of self-surrogate, suffering the fate Kingston sometimes feared—of being destroyed by Brave Orchid's unrealistic and willful demands, of being domineered into madness.

The challenge in telling the story of this aunt is not to reconstruct an obscure and fragmentary tale from the remote past, but to make sense of the too-well known facts of the present. Kingston adopts here the third-person omniscient point of view, a novelistic technique that simultaneously permits the penetration of other characters' consciousnesses and the disengagement of the self from the story. Indeed, though relatively "realistic," this chapter finally proves quite spooky in its own way, less because of the strangeness of the materials than because of the estrangement of the narrator, who refers to herself merely as one of Moon Orchid's several anonymous nieces and nephews—for example, as "[t]he child married to a husband who did not speak Chinese" (164), and as the "oldest girl who was absent-minded and messy. She has an American name that sounded like 'Ink' in Chinese" (152). The superficial "composure" of this chapter is, I think, the measure of Kingston's desperate need for distance from this episode, which involves not merely her aunt's failed assimilation, but also the annihilation of her sanity, and finally her subjectivity. The chapter admits, but holds at a safe distance, the specter of insanity that haunted Kingston's girlhood after her own breakdown, which followed her confrontation with an obvious alter ego in her grade school class (211).

Its invariable manner also dangerously resembles the inflexibility that dooms Moon Orchid, for the clinching symptom of Moon Orchid's insanity is not emotional imbalance or cognitive confusion, but discursive monotony:

> Brave Orchid saw that all variety had gone from her sister. She was indeed mad. "The difference between mad people and sane people," Brave Orchid explained to the children, "is that sane people have variety when they talk-story. Mad people have only one story that they talk over and over" (184).

In the next chapter, Kingston herself adopts a variant of this theory: "I thought talking and not talking made the difference between sanity and insanity. Insane people were the ones who couldn't explain themselves" (216). The cessation of discourse, particularly of improvisation, is a sign of mental illness. The issue was a vital one to Kingston: "I thought every house had to have its crazy woman or crazy girl, every village its idiot. Who would be It at our house? Probably me. . . . I had the mysterious illness. And there were adventurous people inside my head to whom I talked" (220).

The implicit esthetic, here, though it seems to indict this chapter's relative monologism, helps to explain and justify the technical variety of the memoir as a whole. Indeed, the esthetic is itself autobiographical; it confesses the narrator's fear of being judged insane because of the eccentricity of her discourse, and it self-protectively associates variety and volubility with mental health. The singular consistency of this chapter is part of a larger pattern of heteroglossia that confirms Kingston's avoidance of two complementary dangers: on the one hand, the monologism of complete assimilation—exemplified by Moon Orchid's husband, who rebuffs her and Brave Orchid as "people in a book I . . . read long ago" (179)—and, on the other hand, the monologism and silence of total alienation—exemplified by Moon Orchid. Unlike the fragile Moon Orchid, Kingston manages to enter and inhabit "the Western Palace" without sacrificing her subjectivity or suppressing her distinctively accented voice. Her aesthetic is thus self-justifying and self-authorizing.

In any case, the next chapter, "A Song for a Barbarian Reed Pipe," begins by exposing cracks in the apparently monolithic composure of its predecessor. First, Kingston identifies her brother as her source for the crucial confrontation between Moon Orchid and her husband, quoting the dialogue in which he divulged what he remembered of the encounter. Then, in a further twist, she identifies his interrogator as her sister, rather than herself:

> In fact, it wasn't me my brother told about going to Los Angeles; one of my sisters told me what he'd told her. His version of the story may be better than mine because of its bareness, not twisted into designs. The hearer can carry it tucked away without it taking up much room (189–90).

In this way Kingston reminds the reader that the previous chapter's "objective" manner and consistent point of view are every bit as artifactual, twisted into design, as some of her more exotic flights of fancy. She inaugurates the last chapter, therefore, by disclosing the complex subjectivity and inventiveness beneath the placid surface of the previous chapter. She also identifies the episode as a story passed from sibling to sibling, gaining in density and intricacy in the process. It is decidedly a story constructed by intra- rather than intergenerational collaboration. She continues:

> Long ago in China, knot-makers tied string into buttons and frogs, and rope into bell pulls. There was one knot so complicated that it blinded the knot-maker. Finally an emperor outlawed this cruel knot, and the nobles could not order it anymore. If I had lived in China, I would have been an outlaw knot-maker (190).

The knot analogy applies better to the book as a whole than to the chapter in question, but her trope reminds us of her defiance of the proscriptions of traditional Chinese patriarchy: it identifies autobiography as a risky and subversive activity.

With that, she turns to her girlhood struggle to free and control her tongue, in the chapter that is most autobiographical (in focus and narrative technique) by Western measures. The central episode here is her intimidation and exhortation of a girl who is even more silent than herself:

> "Don't you ever want to be a cheerleader? Or a pom-pom girl? What are you going to do for a living? . . . If you don't talk, you can't have a personality. . . . You think somebody's going to marry you, is that it? Well, you're not the type that gets dates, let alone gets married. Nobody's going to notice you" (210).

Afterward, she herself relapses into the condition of her victim, which is both "poetic justice" and psychological truth, since she unrealistically and unfairly demanded of the other girl exactly that which she could not manage herself.

This is also a period of great anxiety, verging on paranoia, about her parents' plans for her. Her fears focus on the possibility of a Chinese-style arranged marriage, and she tries to make herself sexually unattractive in order to frustrate the suspected marriage plot.[16] In this tumultuous period, the autobiographical impulse is born, or recognized: "Maybe because I was the one with the tongue cut loose, I had grown inside me a list of over two hundred things that I had to tell my mother so that she would know the true things about me and to stop the pain in my throat" (229). She envies the Catholic girls their weekly confession, but exaggerates the benefits of confidence: "If only I could let my mother know the list, she—and the world—would become more like me, and I would never be alone again" (230). Here she attributes to a proscribed confessional speech act the ability to make the world conform to her words.

When at last her "throat bursts," she indicts her mother's discourse as crippling in its ambiguity:

> "Even if I am stupid and talk funny and get sick, I won't let you turn me into a slave or a wife. I'm getting out of here. I can't stand living here anymore. It's your fault I talk weird. . . . I'm going to get scholarships and I'm going away. . . . And I don't want to listen to any more of your stories; they have no logic. They scramble me up. You lie with stories. You won't tell me a story and then say, 'This is a true story,'

> or, 'This is just a story.' I can't tell the difference. I don't even know what your real names are. I can't tell what's real and what you make up. Ha! You can't stop me from talking. You tried to cut off my tongue, but it didn't work" (234–35).

The effect is hardly conciliatory: her mother responds just as shrilly, denying any intention of pairing her off or of silencing her, and defending her ambiguity as potentially liberating:

> My mother, who is a champion talker, was, of course, shouting at the same time. "I cut it to make you talk more, not less, you dummy. You're still stupid. You can't listen right. I didn't say I was going to marry you off. Did I ever say that? Did I ever mention that? . . . Who would want you? Who said we could sell you? We can't sell people. Can't you take a joke? You can't even tell a joke from real life. You're not so smart. Can't even tell real from false" (235).

Far from easing tension, the shouting match temporarily exacerbates misunderstanding and increases alienation: confession merely creates further wounds and further words to avenge. But its reconstruction as the emotional climax of the narrative suggests that it made possible a later reconciliation.

In her words, Kingston needed to "leave home in order to see the world logically." She needed to master new discursive and intellectual conventions—to "[s]hine floodlights into dark corners: no ghosts" (237)—before she could attempt a conciliatory dialogue with her mother. However, her self-induced exile from her ethnicity, like Rodriguez's, drove her back on it, intellectually: "I've been looking up 'Ho Chi Kuei,' which is what the immigrants call us—Ho Chi Ghosts" (237). She had to look the term up because she had no one to ask what it meant; appropriately, the term's translation reminds her that assimilation makes *her* a ghost from her parents' perspective.

She ends her narrative with a story her mother told her, "not when I was young, but recently, when I told her I also talk-story. The beginning is hers, the ending, mine" (240). The first part tells of her grandmother's taking her family to see a play in spite of the threat of attack by bandits. Though the bandits attack the playgoers, the family comes through intact—"proof to my grandmother that our family was immune to harm as long as they went to plays" (241). The story suggests, if not the actual protective power of art, the therapeutic value of belief in it. The latter half has to do with Ts'ai Yen, a second-century woman poet who is captured by, and married to, a Tartar chief. Though her children do not speak or even understand the Chinese she tries to teach them, she overcomes the language barrier when she composes a song to the disturbing music of the barbarians' flutes:

> Then, out of Ts'ai Yen's tent, which was apart from the others, the barbarians heard a woman's voice singing, as if to her babies, a song so high and clear, it matched the flutes. Ts'ai sang about China and her family there. Her words seemed to be Chinese, but the barbarians understood their sadness and anger. Sometimes they thought they could catch barbarian phrases about forever wandering. Her children did not laugh, but eventually sang along when she left her tent to sit by the winter campfires, ringed by barbarians (243).

The appeal of this story, one guesses, lies in two features. First, its central role fits both mother and daughter in different ways; thus, the tale affirms, after much conflict, matrilineal continuity.[17] If Kingston told her own story in earlier chapters by elaborating on or revising her mother's, here she appends to her mother's contribution a Chinese legend that speaks for both of them. Second, although it acknowledges the pain of captivity and exile, it asserts the mutual intelligibility of alien cultures. Insofar as Kingston is analogous to the poet, the heroine's eventual return to her own tribe is mirrored in Kingston's new openness to Chinese culture. Indeed, the narrative hints that she has come to view China as a homeland worth investigating, if not as home. Near the end, she expresses a willingness to visit China, whose ghosts have become less threatening:

> I like to look up a troublesome, shameful thing and then say, "Oh, is that all?" The simple explanation makes it less scary to go home after yelling at your mother and father. It drives the fear away and makes it possible someday to visit China, where I know now they don't sell girls or kill each other for no reason (238).

By demystifying the homeland, she has halted her own private China syndrome, her fear of being melted down into the anonymous masses. Having "invented an American-feminine speaking personality" (200) in primary school, after much struggle, she succeeds, as an autobiographer, in inventing a Chinese-American feminist one.

VI

One of the common features of these autobiographies that seems linked to their biculturalism is that they are ghostridden, in various senses. Both authors acknowledge the insubstantiality of many of their characters and the obscurity of their own ethnic origins. *Hunger of Memory* contains characters made shadowy by their lying near or beyond the boundary defined by English: the limits of Rodriguez's recall seem as much a function of language as of memory or time. The narrative's chief ghost is the narrator's lost self, Ricardo, whose experience is virtually inaccessible to a consciousness constructed in, and by, English. Similarly, beginning with its subtitle, *The Woman Warrior* is densely populated by ghosts, including those of Chinese lore (sometimes threatening monsters, sometimes ancestors), those of Stockton (Americans made insubstantial by their sheer Westernism), and even, from their mother's perspective, the narrator and her siblings (as a result of their partial assimilation): "They would not tell us children [secrets] because we had been born among ghosts, were taught by ghosts, and were ourselves ghostlike. They called us a kind of ghost" (213–14). More than Rodriguez, however, Kingston engages her ghosts in discourse, exorcising some and honoring others.

Both books are also "ghostwritten" in ways related to their authors' ethnicity. As a result (in part) of their minority status, both writers turn (more openly than most autobiographers) to others for help in establishing an audible, credible voice. The crucial difference here is that one writer seeks models in the dominant culture, while the other employs the resources of ethnic culture. As we have seen, *The Uses of Literacy* is more than a source of ideas for Rodriguez's book: it is a powerful model in which a scholar examines his humble background in a way that combines academic and autobiographical impulses. *Hunger of Memory* is "ghost-written" insofar as Hoggart is the acknowledged "author" of the main character, and an important source of the narrator's sense of himself. *The Woman Warrior* is "ghostwritten " in the sense that Brave Orchid provides much of its material. While the narrative as a whole is told *by* Kingston, it depends fundamentally on stories told *to* her: the daughter's talk-story mimics, elaborates, and perpetuates her mother's. In different senses, each woman is the other's author. Kingston is Brave Orchid's in that she creates her on the page and Brave Orchid is Kingston's not only in bearing and nurturing her, but also in providing the formal example of vital talk-story. Perhaps the book's biculturalism, as well as its feminism, is best illustrated in Kingston's recognition and acceptance, if not her celebration, of her mother as her authorizer and virtual co-author.

Paul John Eakin has astutely noted that "[w]hat Kingston learns . . . is that the freedom and selfhood that speech enacts is not absolute and autonomous but bound and determined by culture. . . ."[18] Paradoxically, perhaps, the authority of her book is built on the forthrightness of that recognition and her concomitant refusal to surrender too much to it. She acknowledges the power of the seemingly insubstantial—whether ancestral ghosts or linguistic systems—to shape her psyche, her values, her identity, and her life-experience, yet her candid admission of that power enables her to challenge it, and to appropriate it to her own uses.

Indeed, the publication of her autobiography was contingent on the resolution of one bicultural dilemma. Kingston may exaggerate somewhat the nature of the Chinese prohibition of autobiography, yet, as she explains it, her background was hardly conducive to confession. The position of Chinese-Americans within the dominant culture has been analogous to that of women within Chinese-American culture, as illustrated in the story of Kingston's anonymous aunt: they have been vulnerable to expungement by means of the manipulation of their names and histories. Kingston summarizes parental advice:

> Lie to Americans. Tell them you were born during the San Francisco earthquake. Tell them your birth certificate and your parents were burned up in the fire. Don't report crimes; tell them we have no crimes and no poverty. Give a new name every time you get arrested; the ghosts won't recognize you (214–15).

Insofar as autobiography involves the forthright naming of names and the location of the self in a matrix of verifiable assertions, such discourse opposes its author to ethnic and familial custom. To put it differently, conformity to minority mores would seem to militate against authoritative autobiography.

In any case, Kingston's concern about the revelation of family secrets was strong enough to make her hesitate before publishing. As she explained to an interviewer, her "need for secrecy" drove her, like her mother, to an ambiguity that combined divulgence and concealment.[19] Commenting on her method in *The Woman Warrior* and *China Men* (1982), she explained:

> Actually, I'm as clear as I possibly can be, because I'm telling the story as these people give it, and some of the people have given their official version more often than they've given their secret version. They themselves can't afford to tell the truth. So they tell it the way I've told it. When I tell it with all these versions, I'm actually giving the culture

> of these people in a very accurate way. You can see where the people make up these fictions about themselves, and it's not just for fun. It's a terrible necessity (12).

Kingston makes an unconventional case here for the authority of her autobiography. Though literally untrustworthy at times, her autobiography is still, she insists, ethnographically valid, i.e., if some details are not factual, the tales are culturally authentic. Its authority is in a sense communal: instead of establishing the veracity of her narrative at the cost of her relatives' privacy (or protecting them by paranoically remaining silent), she passes along their own self-protective life stories. At the same time, she lays claim to a distinctively American authorization for her autobiography—some of the fictionalized stories she retells are licensed by the immigrants' desire to remain in the United States and to realize American freedoms. The truth of the autobiography resides paradoxically in its "fictional" methods: imaginative liberties were essential if a Chinese-American woman was to make public sense and significance of her conflicted girlhood. As a child, she had felt herself trapped between the demands of competing cultures, but here she explains how she carved out a textual space in which to maneuver without betraying either side of her heritage. In this and other ways, she has written an autobiography that bridges the two halves of her bicultural background. Insofar as it inscribes her story in relation to those of mute foremothers, her narrative also manages to elude the gender trap and to authorize a woman's Life.

10

Conclusion

> The word in language is half someone else's. It becomes "one's own" only when the speaker populates it with his own intention, his own accent, when he appropriates the word, adapting it to his own semantic and expressive intention. Prior to this moment of appropriation, the word does not exist in a neutral and impersonal language (it is not, after all, out of a dictionary that a speaker gets his words!), but rather it exists in other people's mouths, in other other people's contexts, serving other people's intentions: it is from there that one must take the word, and make it one's own.
>
> MIKHAIL BAKHTIN[1]

I

A valuable perspective on the authority of autobiography is provided by the contemporary awareness of the way in which the common sense of the term *author* was historically produced. As Arnold Krupat has pointed out in his discussion of Native American composition,

> In European and Euramerican culture, the rise of the author parallels the rise of the individual. Homologous with the bourgeois conceptualization of an opposition between the individual and society appears the corollary opposition between individual (private) and collective (public) production and composition. Individual composition means written composition, for only texts can have individual authors. From the eighteenth century forward, individual authors are protected by copyright laws. Authors are—the idea would seem to be obvious—the individual creators of the individual works which carry their names; accordingly, they are fully entitled to profit from the sale and circulation of their private property.

> With the development of the conception of individual authorship, half of the etymological sense of the word *author,* previously strong in ordinary understanding, dropped out of currency. "Author" is from the Latin *augere,* which means both to "originate" and "to augment." But from the eighteenth and, most particularly, from the nineteenth century on, authors were regarded strictly as originators.[2]

Like the phenomenon of autobiography, with which it is tightly linked, the common sense of "author" is culture-bound, confined in time and in space—itself limited in authority.

We have seen some of the implications of this already. Traditional or tribal cultures, which do not conceive of the individual as separable from, let alone opposed to, the community, generally do not understand authors as originators, nor do they produce autobiography. They do not, at least, produce autobiography without external stimulus: autobiography issues from such cultures only through contact or collaboration with individuals from literate cultures. In such situations, collaborative autobiography, which might seem oxymoronic within mainstream culture, may seem inevitable and valid; in these circumstances, autobiography would *necessarily* be collaborative. In addition, since traditional narrators have no idea of authority as "origination," it may seem that collaboration costs them nothing: incapable of producing their own autobiographies, the "native informants" can hardly claim to have had their life stories—their private property—stolen or appropriated. In a sense, the collaboration *endows* them with life-stories.

As we have seen, Black Elk sought to amplify his power, and extend his authority of augmentation, by sharing his vision with John Neihardt—a man who seemed ideally suited for the task. But, coming from another culture, one that conceived of authority as origination, Neihardt increasingly thought of himself as the book's "author" and sole proprietor. Certainly, as he aged, he increasingly emphasized his own role in the book's production. In any case, Black Elk had no way of controlling the book's form or of foreseeing the existential and political implications of producing a textual self-embodiment. Though the authority of such texts is difficult to determine (to apportion between the one who lived the life and the one who wrote it), we are beginning to recognize the troubling nature of bicultural collaborative production, particularly when the parties to collaboration understand authorship in fundamentally different ways.

Just as it is erroneous to treat collaborative texts such as *Black Elk Speaks* as wholly attributable to their subjects, it may also be fallacious to treat "single-author" texts as generated and controlled entirely by an isolated, autonomous individual. As we have seen, Benjamin Franklin did not live to complete his narrative, much less to oversee its publication; instead, his legacy to his immediate posterity was abused and corrupted, appearing in various unauthorized and unauthoritative versions. One of the book's ironies is that its printer-author did not live to correct its proofs. Even if he had, his authority over the text would not have been absolute because the manuscript itself admits—implicitly, at least—in the curious validation of Part Two, to a kind of corporate authorship. Moreover, Franklin's pervasive allusions to his wide reading acknowledge the extent to which his life story is a variant of other narratives, rather than an unmediated record of his life. Thus, even the Founding Father of American autobiography left some doubt about the paternity of his textual offspring; even the supposed progenitor of the American success story, which exalts individual autonomy, generated his Life by working from, with, and against a multiplicity of textual models.

II

Perhaps this book must end in paradox, by admitting, on the one hand, that the authority of autobiography is not susceptible to definitive determination, and asserting, on the other, that it is nevertheless necessary and desirable to monitor it carefully in each case. The reasons for this, if not already clear, can be demonstrated by reviewing three paradigms of language currently competing for dominion over the study of autobiography.[3] Each conceives of autobiography and its authority differently.

For a "correspondence theory" of language—with its sense of a "one-to-one correspondence between the objects in the world, the words in a language, and the concepts in our heads" (450)—autobiography is fundamentally a historical record of an antecedent set of phenomena. The expressivist variant of the correspondence theory—held by John Sturrock—holds that, as an index of the self, autobiography is automatically self-revealing and hence authoritative. This idea of the automatic correspondence between psyche and text has the immediate appeal—but also the limited force—of a tautology. Because it is true by definition, it provides little critical leverage;

because it endows all autobiography with authority, it fails to distinguish helpfully among particular examples.

For the empiricist version of the correspondence theory, the authority of autobiography is a matter of the verifiability of its "facts" and assertions. (The contractual corollary held by Lejeune and Bruss makes this a matter of ethical, and virtually legal, commitment.) In practice, of course, literal conformity to fact is not required of autobiographers. Few readers want to do the hard work of verification, even when it is possible, but they do want insurance against being fooled either by hoaxes, such as the Irving "autobiography" of Hughes, or by significant misrepresentations in authentically produced texts. Thus, they insist on the option of verification, and are reassured by the obligation that the "autobiographical pact" is thought to impose on the writer. Ironically, the theoretical "pact" is subscribed to not so much by skeptical readers as by credulous ones: in effect, the notion of verifiability serves to license the suspension of their disbelief in "nonfiction."

In any case, authority in the sense of verifiability is fraught with problems. If it is taken literally as correspondence of textual assertions to verifiable extratextual facts, it is of limited practical use. For one thing, as the Irving hoax reminds us, even when the "facts" check out, the "autobiography" that contains them may be wholly fraudulent. For another, such an approach ignores the issue of selection. Despite the use of the term "full-life narrative" by some critics, there is not, and there can never be, any such thing. At the very least, the fact that the author cannot include his own death denies autobiography the wholeness and the closure of biography. The most rigorously documented narrative would be inevitably riddled with gaps, and partiality (in the sense of incompletion) begets partiality (in the sense of bias). In any case, the most interesting autobiographical assertions are typically not verifiable. Self-aware autobiographers have long been aware of, and have sometimes drawn attention to, the aporias of the form. Mark Twain, P. T. Barnum, and Benjamin Franklin have all playfully demonstrated the limits of verifiability. This is not to say that "reality-testing" of autobiography is irrelevant or worthless; it is important to know when a text diverges from other accounts of the same events (and whether it is ghostwritten). But these determinations should begin rather than end investigations into the authority of autobiography. At best, verifiability is a negative, legalistic standard, which would ensure only the absence of outright lies, rather than the presence of truth. Though in some cases it may be ruled out, even factual authority is not something that can be definitively established. The "whole truth" is no more available to autobiography than it is to biography.

In any case, the notion of autobiography as issuing from, determined by, and referring to a pre-existent self has been shown to be problematic. In recent years, the critique of the subject has challenged the apparently distinctive features of the first-person singular—thus eroding, if not exploding, one basis of the genre's special privilege and validity. Thus, for structuralists, since language "always *precedes and exceeds* any individual subject," autobiography renders "not authors but authorial conventions, . . . not 'true selfhood' but only a metalepsis (i.e., an effect of language), a rhetorical figure that fills the empty places within discourse" (Morgan 452–53).

For those who conceive of the self as unique and integral—transcending the play of language—the idea that writing does not express a single prior self but somehow produces a provisional one may seem inconsistent with the idea of individual autonomy. But as Joseph Harris has argued, the structuralist and poststructuralist view of the self as a linguistic construct is not necessarily antiindividualistic.[4] The other side of the unsettling notion that the self depends necessarily and helplessly on language for its creation is that the vast repertoire of the language gives the self a high degree of freedom and flexibility:

> What is really happening is that one idea of the self is being exchanged for another. . . . [T]he self is seen not *merely* as a single simple essence, but as an incredibly rich and layered tapestry of languages we constantly weave and reweave. The task of writers is not to make language adhere to some mystic and wordless vision of their selves, but to use language in a way that begins to *constitute* a self . . . (162).

That subjectivity may not exist outside of or against discourse does not necessarily mean that one is a passive product of language: "Style is not simply an effusion of self, nor is it mere adherence to prevailing norms of usage and decorum. Rather it is to be found in the tension between the two, between the writer and his community of discourse, idiolect and dialect" (164).

Thus, while the recent critique of the subject is genuinely powerful and important, its implications have sometimes been too negatively construed. That the self is socially constructed and contextually variable is not inconsistent with individual freedom and power. That the self may be not only conditioned but in some sense produced by language may challenge our sense of our individual originality and uniqueness, but the resources of the language are vast, and our selves are perhaps more enabled than constrained by their linguistic dimensions. Just as the self may be artifactual without being artificial, autobiography may be fictive without becoming fiction.

Still, for a theory that views the self entirely as a linguistic construct, the authority of autobiography would be a nebulous matter of textual effects, i.e., a function of the play of signs, tropes, and conventions—which would perpetually defer definitive meaning and the presence of the self. Some texts might have perceptibly more authority than others, but the distinctions among them would be relatively insignificant—a matter of the pecking order among inmates in the prisonhouse of language. (Some texts might be arguably less determined by linguistic features than others, but none would have any significant claim to extratextual authority.) Thus, like the expressivist view, but for different reasons, the structuralist model fails to distinguish very helpfully among autobiographies on the basis of authority.

For a dialogical paradigm, linguistic elements may precede, but they do not entirely predetermine the self. Transpersonal conventions are amenable to personal appropriation:

> Meaning cannot be attributed exclusively to either the speaker or the linguistic structure, but is a shared project of both interlocuters. Meaning depends upon the differential positions (race, gender, class) of those who speak/write and upon the degree of freedom of those who transvalue such speech/writing . . . (Morgan, 454).

According to this model, autobiography neither refers transparently to the self, nor produces it; rather, like all discourse, it is a kind of playground—or battlefield—on which the self struggles to establish its presence and to consolidate its power.

A dialogical view of language would "shift our attention to the split and multivocal nature of any speech act. . . . It would also attend to the ideology of literary forms and the sociality they encode" (Morgan, 455). Thus, whereas the correspondence theory privileges the pre-existent self as the textual referent and the structuralist model assigns autonomy to the linguistic system, the dialogical model conceives of the autobiographer as engaged in a dynamic struggle for authority:

> A dialogic approach would . . . mainly raise questions: What is it possible/impossible to speak of in this discourse? What subject-positions and versions of sociality are inscribed in it? What meanings and contests for meaning does it display? Most importantly, what and whose interests does it serve? (Morgan 456).

Authority is located neither in correspondence to an extratextual reality, nor in the self-determining agency of language, but in the engagement of contending parties and voices in the world.

The implications of some of these different models can be illustrated by rehearsing the way they might engage a particular mode of autobiography. Even aside from the practical problems of verifying a text and the theoretical challenge to the assumptions underlying the correspondence theory, the legalistic notion of the factuality of autobiography presents another problem: like all laws, it may be inconsistently and unfairly enforced. The classic case of some autobiographies being held more strictly accountable than others is that of slave narratives, whose verifiability was a major issue from the start. Early black autobiographers were held to a stringent autobiographical pact; editors and readers expected a particular literal, historicist form of authority in slave narratives. Thus, the slave narrators were caught in a vise that threatened to squeeze the vitality out of their lifewriting.

The fact that slave narrative tended toward strict conventionality—conformity to a "master plot"—suggests that factuality was not the (only) point, and that authority was not finally, or wholly, a matter of literal factuality and verifiability. The emergence of a rigid formula exposes the irrelevance of documentation—the authority of the narratives apparently lay as much in their manipulation of the formula as in their presentation of the facts. Ultimately, one suspects, authority was as much a matter of internal coherence and rhetorical effectiveness as it was of verifiability.

The narrative straitjacket was presumably made necessary by the genre's function as antislavery propaganda; however, the ironic result was that the *form* threatened to enslave the narrators. Efforts to endow the narratives with authority in either of two senses—correspondence to otherwise verifiable facts or conformity to conventions—threatened to deprive the narrators of authority in a more important sense—control over their own narratives. The elaborate apparatus of authentication associated with abolitionist narratives reveals that authority was also a function of extraliterary authorization. This is also true for the cross-referencing of *Uncle Tom's Cabin* and Josiah Henson's narrative—Stowe's novel might need the factual ballast supplied by slave narratives, but those presumably factual narratives could also borrow stature from her novel.

What is demanded of autobiography, really, is not some unimpeachable empirical authority—the facts and nothing but the facts—but a convincing *show* of authority. Autobiography may be, as Howells said, the most democratic province of letters, but it no utopia; not everyone is admitted to citizenship, at least not on equal terms. No one is admitted without a pass, so to speak, and passes are granted at different rates to different groups. In the case of slave narrative, authority is granted by the apparatus of authentication, but that apparatus reinforces as well as reflects the disadvantaged status of the narrator. Thus, the apparatus of authentication exposes the uneven way in which autobiographical authority is measured and distributed.

The demonstration of authority is very different in Franklin's case. In Part One, he indulged in gestures of playful self-authorization that would hardly be tolerated in a minority autobiographer of his time. Under close examination, the two letters prefacing Part Two, the very letters that give his continuation quasi-official sanction, seem to compromise his authority over his text. Still, in contrast to the case of slave narrative, the informal apparatus of authentication devised to sanction his autobiography tends to reflect his extraordinarily privileged position. Franklin and his friends can take liberties with his textual authority precisely because his extratextual authority is so secure—precisely because his life can be assumed to be exemplary.

The authority of autobiography never resides exclusively in the text or the self, or even in the correspondence between them; rather, it is something negotiated, and renegotiated, between the autobiographer and others—collaborators, editors, critics, biographers, historians, and lay readers. One of the uses of slave narrative today is to demonstrate the ways in which the rules vary from subgenre to subgenre and from text to text. At their best, these narratives demonstrate how the prevailing rules could be evaded, bent, or rewritten to the benefit of a disadvantaged writer. For example, Amy Post's letter appended to Harriet Jacobs' narrative helps to redefine authority in terms of the cost of the act of confidence rather than extensiveness of documentation; it thus negotiates a credence for her narrative that most pseudonymous autobiography would automatically forfeit.

Similarly, narrators' metadiscourse may arrogate authority by demonstrating the unfair way in which it is conventionally dispensed.

Indeed, one premise of a dialogical approach to lifewriting might be that the authority of an autobiography is proportional to the narrator's recognition and articulation of threats to it. Though the limits on slave narrators were in some cases stifling, the narrators' acute awareness of those limits stimulated forceful and empowering dialogical narratives in others. Metadiscourse could moderate, by exposure, the race ritual of authentication. Slave narrators might not always be able to evade the strict conventions of the master plot, but they could comment on them in a way that enhanced the text's authority without affecting its historicity.

This is in part why we may tolerate novelization. Thus, Harriet Jacobs' narrative gains authority not merely from the positive outcome of her verbal war with her master, which her freedom helped to consolidate, but from its very sophisticated rhetorical construction. To adduce a case from outside this subgenre, while Chesnut's novelization of her journal sacrifices the authenticity of immediacy and of correspondence to "fact," it is part of a strategy that negotiates independent authority for a woman's point of view in a patriarchal world. Similarly, Kingston's forthright acknowledgment of the ways in which her bicultural girlhood threatened to tongue-tie her helps to secure tolerance of her flights of fantasy; we see that these are necessary stratagems for finding her own Chinese-American voice.

A remark Jerome Bruner made in a different connection may be relevant here:

> [I]t is far more important . . . to understand the ways human beings construct their worlds . . . than it is to establish the ontological status of the products of these processes. For my central ontological conviction is that there is no "aboriginal" reality against which one can compare a possible world in order to establish some form of correspondence between it and the real world.[5]

Far from being an anomaly, then, *Black Elk Speaks* may represent the general condition of autobiography, which always seeks—but always fails—to recapture "aboriginal" experience, and whose ontological status is perhaps less important than the question of how it was produced or constructed.

Without being programmatic, this book has attempted to explore the various ways in which the authority of particular autobiographies has come into question. It has tried to emphasize the processes by which authority—in and over autobiography—has been discursively negotiated: the explicit exchange between Franklin and his son in

Part One, and between him and his epistolary authorizers in Part Two; the interplay between Barnum's various autobiographical texts; the curious deformation of the historical Samuel Clemens into the pseudonymous Mark Twain, and the clash between Mark Twain and his authorized biographer; the barbed dialogue between slaves and their owners, and the more subtle interchange between slave narrators and their sponsors; the externalization of private monologue in Mary Chesnut's text, in part through the use of literary dialogism; the collaboration between Black Elk and John Neihardt, which ironically reenacted and exposed the historical betrayal of Native Americans by English words; and finally, the dialogue between Richard Rodriguez and Maxine Hong Kingston, on the one hand, and their respective families and subcultures, on the other.

Admittedly, there are constraints on all self-lifewriting. Indeed, one currently fashionable view is that one can no more write one's life autonomously than one can live it completely independently—that autobiography is impossible. (However current it seems, this view is not new; it haunted Mark Twain's final years.) Yet autobiography continues to be produced and consumed at an astounding rate: oblivious to its own impossibility, the genre has taken on a life and a momentum of its own. Far from lacking authority altogether, it engages in a constant struggle to negotiate its authority in novel ways.

Notes

CHAPTER 1

1. The source for the information in this chapter about the Hughes "autobiography" is Stephen Fay, Lewis Chester, and Magnus Linklater, *Hoax: The Inside Story of the Howard Hughes-Clifford Irving Affair* (New York: Viking Press, 1972). Hereafter, page numbers will be included in parentheses in the text.

2. *The Education of Henry Adams* (1918, rpt; ed. Ernest Samuels, Boston: Houghton Mifflin, 1973), 512.

CHAPTER 2

1. For the use of "democracy," see Raymond Williams, *Culture and Society* (1958), xiv; for the origins of "autobiography" see the Oxford English Dictionary.

2. "Autobiography and America," *Virginia Quarterly Review*, 47 (1971): 253, 256.

3. "Autobiography and the Making of America," in James Olney, ed., *Autobiography: Essays Theoretical and Critical* (Princeton: Princeton University Press, 1980), 147. Similarly, in my first book, *American Autobiography: The Prophetic Mode* (Amherst: University of Massachusetts Press, 1979), I argued that "prophetic autobiography" constituted an important, perhaps distinctive, tradition in American letters from the Puritans to the present.

4. "American Autobiography and Ideology," in *The American Autobiography: A Collection of Critical Essays*, ed. Albert E. Stone (Englewood Cliffs, N.J.: Prentice-Hall, 1981), 95.

5. *Autobiographical Acts: The Changing Situation of a Literary Genre* (Baltimore: Johns Hopkins University Press, 1976), 8.

6. Robert Lyons, *Autobiography: A Reader For Writers* (New York: Oxford University Press, 1977), vi.

7. Kenneth J. Gergen, "Theory of the Self: Impasse and Evolution," in *Advances in Experimental Social Psychology*, V. 17, ed. Leonard Berkowitz (New York: Academic Press, 1984): 100.

8. John F. Kihlstrom and Nancy Kantor, "Mental Representations of the Self," in Berkowitz, 13.

9. Morton Hunt, *The Universe Within* (New York: Simon and Schuster, 1982), 90.

10. *Fictions of the Self: Studies in the Art of Self-Invention* (Princeton: Princeton University Press, 1985), 195. See all of Chapter Four, "Self-Invention in Autobiography: The Moment of Language" (especially pages 191–209) for a lucid discussion of the relation between self and language.

11. *Literary Theory: An Introduction* (Minneapolis: University of Minnesota Press, 1983), 107.

12. In Olney, 28–48.

13. Avrom Fleishman, *Figures of Autobiography: The Language of Self-Writing in Victorian and Modern England* (Berkeley: University of California Press, 1983), 7.

14. "The Impact of Critical Theory on the Study of Autobiography: Marginality, Gender, and Autobiographical Practice," *Auto/Biography Studies* III, No. 3 (Fall 1987): 2.

15. "The New Model Autobiographer," *NLH* 9, No. 1 (Autumn 1977): 52.

16. Paris: Seuil,1975.

17. Michael Ryan,"Self-Evidence," *Diacritics* 9, No. 1 (June 1980): 2–16.

18. *A Critique of Modern Textual Criticism* (Chicago: University of Chicago Press, 1983), 42–43.

CHAPTER 3

1. *When Words Lose Their Meaning: Constitutions and Reconstitutions of Language, Character, and Community* (Chicago: University of Chicago Press, 1984), 231.

2. "An Exploration of the Nature of Authority and Some of its Sources," *Authority,* ed. Carl Friedrich (Cambridge: Harvard University Press, 1958), 27.

3. *Sons of the Fathers: The Civil Religion of the American Revolution* (Philadelphia: Temple University Press, 1976), 184.

4. "Jefferson's 'Slave Narrative': The Declaration of Independence as a Literary Text," *Early American Literature,* 8 (1974): 239–256.

5. Of course, the official encouragement of authorship was somewhat offset by the American failure to honor international copyright law in the early nineteenth century, which did much to perpetuate the domination of the American literary marketplace by English writers. In any case, as the wording of Section 8 suggests, the Anglo-American notion of copyright granted authors narrowly defined rights in order to benefit the community. By contrast, in the French tradition copyright was considered a natural right of authors. James Lardner, "Annals of Law: The Betamax Case, Part I," *New Yorker,* April 6, 1987: 66.

6. Of course, the requirement extends only to the legislative branch, but recent presidents, and their advisers, have often proceeded as though retired members of the executive branch were compelled to write memoirs.

7. *The Examined Self: Benjamin Franklin, Henry Adams, Henry James* (Princeton: Princeton University Press, 1964), 41.

8. *The Devil's Dictionary* (1911; rpt. New York: Dover, 1958), 59.

9. *Problems in General Linguistics,* trans. Mary Elizabeth Meek (Coral Gables: University of Miami Press, 1971), 202.

10. *A Grammar of Motives* (New York: Prentice-Hall, 1945), 360–61.

11. *The Creation of the American Republic, 1776–1787* (Chapel Hill: The University of North Carolina Press, 1969), 524–26.

12. "Government by Fiction: The Idea of Representation," *Yale Review* 72, No. 3 (Spring 1983): 338–39.

13. *The Autobiography of Benjamin Franklin,* ed. Leonard Labaree et al. (New Haven: Yale University Press, 1964), 261. This is the edition used for quotations; hereafter citations will be parenthetical.

14. James M. Cox, "Autobiography and America," *Virginia Quarterly Review* 47, No. 2 (Spring 1971): 261.

15. J. A. Leo Lemay and P. M. Zall, eds., *The Autobiography of Benjamin Franklin: A Genetic Text* (Knoxville: University of Tennessee Press, 1981), xx.

16. Christopher Looby has argued against this view: " 'The Affairs of the Revolution Occasion'd the Interruption': Writing, Revolution, Deferral, and Conciliation in Franklin's *Autobiography,*" *American Quarterly* 38, No. 1 (Spring 1986): 72–96. Indeed, he suggests that just as Franklin's diplomacy tended to delay or defer the political rupture, "A chief motive guiding Franklin's composition of the *Autobiography* was a desire to repress the Revolution" (73). Though we are occasionally in disagreement, his article, which came to my notice after this manuscript was complete, nicely complements this chapter.

17. "The Printer as a Man of Letters: Franklin and the Symbolism of the Third Realm," in *The Oldest Revolutionary: Essays on Benjamin Franklin,* ed. J. A. Leo Lemay (Philadelphia: University of Pennsylvania, 1976), 3–4.

18. *The History of Sexuality,* Volume I, *An Introduction,* trans. Robert Hurley (New York: Pantheon, 1978), 61–62.

19. For example, see J. A. Leo Lemay, "Benjamin Franklin," in *Major Writers of Early American Literature,* ed. Everett Emerson (Madison: University of Wisconsin, 1972), 238.

20. William Sterne Randall, *A Little Revenge: Benjamin Franklin and His Son* (Boston: Little Brown, 1984), 6, 249, and Hugh J. Dawson, "Fathers and Sons: Franklin's 'Memoirs' as Myth and Metaphor," *Early American Literature* 14 (1979–1980): 286n.

21. Jay Fliegelman, *Prodigals and Pilgrims: The American Revolution against Patriarchal Authority* (Cambridge: Cambridge University Press, 1982), 97–100.

22. Quoted in Dawson, 275. In addition, in his will, which disinherited William, he said: "The part he acted against me in the late war, which is of public notoriety, will account for my leaving him no more of an estate he endeavored to deprive me of" (Randall, 492).

23. "Knowledge, Tradition, and Authority: A Note on the American Experience," in Carl Friedrich, ed., *Authority* (Cambridge: Harvard University Press, 1958), 120. See also Gordon Wood: "[the colonists] sincerely believed that they were not creating new rights or new principles prescribed only by what ought to be, but . . . claiming . . . the traditional rights and principles of all English men, sanctioned by what they thought had always been" (13).

24. Vaughan's idea that autobiography can preempt bad biography curiously anticipated (or perhaps inspired) Henry Adams's similar suggestion in a letter to Henry James, May 6, 1908: "The volume is a mere shield of protection in the grave. I advise you to take your own life in the same way, in order to prevent biographers from taking it in theirs." *The Education of Henry Adams* (1918; rpt. ed. Ernest Samuels, Boston: Houghton Mifflin, 1973), 512.

25. *The Forms of Autobiography: Episodes in the History of a Literary Genre* (New Haven: Yale University Press, 1980), 57.

26. "Unspeakable Practices, Writable Acts: Franklin's *Autobiography*," *Hudson Review* 32, No. 2 (Summer 1979): 235.

27. In this connection, it is worth noting Jay Fliegelman's assertion that "The multiple editions of Franklin's *Autobiography* published in the 1790s and the calls at the end of the decade to imitate the great Washington were attempts to ensure that the national character would be formed before the course of violent events . . . 'demoralised' it forever" (235).

28. Hubert L. Dreyfus and Paul Rabinow, *Michel Foucault: Beyond Structuralism and Hermeneutics* (Chicago: University of Chicago, 1982), 159.

29. "Afterword: The Subject and Power," in Dreyfus, *Foucault,* 212.

30. *Studies in Classic American Literature* (1923; rpt. New York: Viking Press, 1964), 9.

31. See the Introduction to the Labaree introduction, 1–3, for a brief account of some possible sources and influences.

32. Jay Fliegelman has described as Lockean "Franklin's faith that one can form one's own character as easily as the printer can 'impress' his own 'characters' " (112).

33. The information in the preceding two paragraphs is derived from the introduction to *The Autobiography of Benjamin Franklin: A Genetic Text,* ed. Lemay and Zall, xxxvii–lvii.

CHAPTER 4

1. The current bestseller is *Iacocca,* whose one-word title proclaims the openness of the form to the assimilated ethnic, and whose collaborative authorship attests to the popular acceptance of ghostwritten autobiography. At the same time, the failure of the ghostwriter, William Novak, to share in the book's unexpectedly huge royalties reveals the imbalance between the celebrity subject and the virtually anonymous scribe. See Peter Wyden, "The Blockbustering of Lee Iacocca," *New York Times Book Review,* September 13, 1987: 1, 54–55.

2. P. T. Barnum, *Struggles and Triumphs, or Forty Years Recollections of P. T. Barnum, Written by Himself* (1869; rpt. New York: Arno, 1970), 396. Hereafter cited parenthetically.

3. Benjamin Franklin, *The Autobiography of Benjamin Franklin,* ed. Leonard Labaree et al. (New Haven: Yale University Press, 1964), 126.

4. Johnnes Dietrich Bergmann, "The Original Confidence Man," *American Quarterly* 21 (Fall 1969): 560–77.

5. (New York: Redfield, 1855). Hereafter to be cited parenthetically.

6. Barnum's consciousness of his role as an exhibit in his Museum is evident in his story of a customer who, upon spotting the proprietor, promptly left the premises, asserting that he had got his money's worth (*Struggles and Triumphs,* 161).

7. Constance Rourke was the first to observe that "the whole museum constituted a practical joke," *Trumpets of Jubilee* (New York: Harcourt Brace, 1927), 392. Neil Harris has usefully extended this observation in his analysis of Barnum's aesthetic, *Humbug: The Art of P. T. Barnum* (Boston: Little, Brown, 1973).

8. Introduction to *Struggles and Triumphs,* edited and abridged by Carl Bode (1869; rpt. New York: Penguin, 1970), 20.

9. Quoted in Harris, *Humbug,* 227.

10. Introduction to *Struggles and Triumphs,* 23–24.

11. "The Style of Autobiography," in *Autobiography: Essays Theoretical and Critical,* ed. James Olney (Princeton: Princeton University Press, 1980), 78–79.

12. M. R. Werner, *Barnum* (New York: Harcourt Brace, 1927), 372.

13. "The New Model Autobiographer," *NLH* 9, No. 1 (Autumn 1977): 55–56.

14. Irving Wallace, *The Fabulous Showman: The Life and Times of P. T. Barnum* (New York: Knopf, 1959), 176.

15. *The Confidence Man in American Literature* (New York: Oxford University Press, 1982), 7.

16. "Autobiography as Presentation of Self for Social Immortality," *NLH* 9, No. 1 (Autumn 1977): 176.

CHAPTER 5

1. Hamlin Hill has commented briefly but cogently on the Barnum–Twain relationship, which involved mutually admiring correspondence. See "Barnum, Bridgeport, and *The Connecticut Yankee,*" *American Quarterly* 16 (Winter 1964): 615–16. He notes that Albert Bigelow Paine counted Twain's autographed copy of Barnum's *Struggles and Triumphs* as one of his favorite books that "showed usage." (*Mark Twain: A Biography, The Personal and Literary Life of Samuel Langhorne Clemens* [New York: Harper and Brothers, 1912], III, 1540.)

2. "Mark Twain's Experiments in Autobiography," *American Literature* 53, No. 2 (May 1981): 202.

3. *Mark Twain's Autobiography,* ed. Albert Bigelow Paine (New York: Harper and Brothers, 1924), I,96. Hereafter to be cited parenthetically.

4. *Of Huck and Alice* (Minneapolis: University of Minnesota Press, 1983), 11.

5. *Mark Twain: The Fate of Humor* (Princeton: Princeton University Press, 1966), 20–21.

6. Leonard Labaree, "Introduction," *The Autobiography of Benjamin Franklin,* ed. Labaree et al. (New Haven: Yale University Press, 1964), 15.

7. *Mark Twain's Burlesque Autobiography and First Romance* (New York: Sheldon and Company, 1871), 3. Hereafter to be cited parenthetically.

8. John Sturrock, "The New Model Autobiographer," *NLH* 9, No. 1 (Autumn 1977): 52.

9. *Mr. Clemens and Mark Twain* (New York: Simon and Schuster, 1966), 124, 196.

10. "Introduction," *Mark Twain of the Enterprise: Newspaper Articles & Other Documents, 1862–1864* (Berkeley: University of California Press, 1957), 9.

11. Quoted in Alan Gribben, "Autobiography as Property: Mark Twain and his Legend," in *The Mythologizing of Mark Twain,* ed. Sara de Saussure Davis and Philip D. Beidler (University: University of Alabama: 1984), 51.

12. Quoted in Guy Cardwell, "Samuel Clemens' Magical Pseudonym," *New England Quarterly* 48, No. 2 (June 1975): 180.

13. "Mark Twain: The Writer as Pilot." *PMLA* 93, No. 5 (October 1978): 888.

14. *Life on the Mississippi,* in *Mississippi Writings* (New York: Library of America, 1982), 516. Hereafter to be cited parenthetically. For convenience, citations from

"Old Times on the Mississippi" are from the earlier chapters (IV to XVII) of this same text.

15. Jacques Derrida, *The Ear of the Other: Otobiography, Transference, Translation,* ed. Christie V. McDonald and trans. Peggy Kamuf (New York: Schocken, 1985), 77–78.

16. P. T. Barnum, *Struggles and Triumphs, or Forty Years' Recollections* (1869; rpt. New York: Arno, 1970). Hereafter to be cited parenthetically.

17. Quoted in Burde, 882.

18. For an important discussion of the meaning of the pseudonym in another context, see Cox, 123–24.

19. "Mark Twain's South: Tom and Huck," *The American South: Portrait of a Culture,* ed. Louis D. Rubin, Jr. (Baton Rouge: Louisiana State University Press, 1980), 203.

20. *Mark Twain: God's Fool* (New York: Harper and Row, 1973), xii–xiii.

21. New York: C. L. Webster, 1885–1886.

22. *Mark Twain: A Biography, The Personal and Literary Life of Samuel Langhorne Clemens* (New York: Harper and Brothers, 1912), III, 1368–69.

23. *Mark Twain–Howells Letters: The Correspondence of Samuel L. Clemens and William D. Howells,1872–1910,* 2 Vols., ed. Henry Nash Smith and William M. Gibson (Cambridge: Harvard University Press, 1960), II, 778–82. Hereafter to be cited as MTH.

24. Letter to Howells, January 16, 1904, MTH, II, 778.

25. Bernard DeVoto, ed., *Mark Twain in Eruption: Hitherto Unpublished Pages about Men and Events* (New York: Harper and Brothers, 1940), 125–31. Hereafter cited parenthetically.

26. "The Turning Point of My Life," in *The Works of Mark Twain,* 19, *What Is Man? and Other Philosophical Writings,* ed. Paul Baender (Berkeley: University of California Press, 1973), 455.

27. Hill, 157, 183.

28. Quoted in Hill, 268.

29. Hill, 208, 212, 242, 260.

CHAPTER 6

1. Quoted in John Blassingame, "Introduction," *Slave Testimony* (Baton Rouge: Louisiana State University Press, 1977), xxx.

2. "Historical Discourse," in *Introduction to Structuralism,* ed. Michael Lane (New York: Basic Books, 1970), 145.

3. *Expression and Meaning: Studies in the Theory of Speech Acts* (Cambridge: Cambridge University Press, 1979), 12–13.

4. See Philippe Lejeune, *Le Pacte Autobiographique* (Paris: Editions du Seuil, 1975).

5. Robin Winks, "Introduction," *An Autobiography of The Reverend Josiah Henson ("Uncle Tom") From 1789 to 1881,* ed. John Lobb (1881; rpt. Reading, Mass.: Addison-Wesley, 1969), xxii, xxvi.

6. "Introduction: The Language of Slavery," *The Slave's Narrative,* ed. Charles

T. Davis and Henry Louis Gates, Jr. (New York: Oxford University Press, 1985), xvii.

7. William Andrews, *To Tell a Free Story: The First Century of Afro-American Autobiography, 1760–1865* (Urbana: University of Illinois Press, 1986), 16.

8. "The Slave Narratives as History," *The Slave's Narrative,* 36.

9. In "The Blockbustering of Lee Iacocca," Peter Wyden chronicles the unhappy fate of Iacocca's ghostwriter, William Novak. Little known before this collaboration, Novak signed a contract that tendered him only a flat fee and expenses. To everyone's surprise, however, the book sold well and made millions—for Iacocca and the publisher. When Novak's request for a percentage of the paperback royalties was denied, he felt that collaboration had proven to be exploitation. *New York Times Book Review,* September 13, 1987: 1, 54–55.

10. (Westport: Greenwood, 1978), 10–11. Smith does discuss the complex behavior of "masking," but locates it in slave behavior rather than in slave narrative strategies (15–16).

11. *From Behind the Veil: A Study of Afro-American Narrative* (Urbana: University of Illinois, 1979), 6–8.

12. "Introduction," *Narrative of the Life and Adventures of Henry Bibb, An American Slave, Written by Himself* (1849; rpt. *Puttin' On Ole Massa,* ed. Gilbert Osofsky [New York: Harper and Row, 1969]), 53.

13. " 'I Was born': Slave Narratives, Their Status as Autobiography and as Literature," *The Slave's Narrative,* 152–53.

14. Indeed, Frances Smith Foster has suggested that the needs of the abolitionist program and the limitations of its audience may have encouraged narrators to describe slave life in ways that unwittingly reinforced pernicious stereotypes—for example, that slaves of mixed ancestry were more intelligent, aggressive, and rebellious; or that the black family and black culture were weak. *Witnessing Slavery: The Development of Ante-bellum Slave Narrative* (Westport: Greenwood, 1979), 128–41.

15. "The Problematic of Self in Autobiography: The Example of Slave Narrative," in *The Art of Slave Narrative,* ed. John Sekora and Darwin Turner (Macomb: Western Illinois University Press, 1982), 101.

16. The conundrum of the slave narrative—how a literate narrator could emerge from the conditions whose horror his literacy made so vivid—was exposed but not addressed by Sidonie Smith's dichotomy between the oppression of slavery and the freedom of the slave narrative, *Where I'm Bound,* ch. 1.

17. Significant steps in this direction were taken in some of the essays in *The Art of Slave Narrative* (1982). Raymond Hedin argued that slave narratives did not submit unconsciously to the conventions of genteel literature they sometimes used. For example, he suggests that the slave narrative often creates a black variant of the picaresque in which the fugitive resists rather than accepts the amoral possibilities of his liminal status ("Strategies of Form in the American Slave Narrative," 26–28). Similarly, Lucinda MacKethan isolated rhetorical and narrative devices that create metaphors of mastery over their situations ("Metaphors of Mastery in the Slave Narratives," 55–70), and Keith Byerman stressed the use of black folk materials that might be "translated" without black dialect. He made the provocative suggestion that the very adoption of genteel conventions might be a form of masking behavior, puttin' on old massa—with massa now as white audience, if not as sponsoring abolitionists ("We Wear the Mask: Deceit as Theme and Style in Slave Narratives," 70–83). Such assertions

move toward the recovery of authentic black selfhood even from forms that seem to deny it.

18. (Buffalo: Miller, Orton, and Mulligan, 1854), 26. Hereafter to be cited parenthetically.

19. Indeed, Robert Stepto has cited this narrative as an example of "integrated narrative" —in which the narrator achieves a significant role in the authentication of his narrative. As evidence Stepto cites the relatively short preface, Northup's effort to establish his own links with, and credibility in, the Northern white community, and the use of Henry Northup's intervention as a model for reforming his readers (12–16). Stepto acknowledges that the appending of a series of affidavits is a feature of the eclectic narrative (15), but claims that in this case the assemblage of documents amounts to an instructional booklet on how to free blacks sold into slavery.

20. *Narrative of the Life of Frederick Douglass, An American Slave, Written by Himself,* ed. Houston Baker, Jr. (1845; rpt. New York: Viking Penguin, 1982), 62.

21. *Narrative of William Wells Brown, A Fugitive Slave, written by himself* (1847; rpt. *Puttin' On Ole Massa,* ed. Gilbert Osofsky [New York: Harper and Row, 1969]), 203.

22. Harriet Jacobs, *Incidents in the Life of a Slave Girl, Written by Herself,* ed. L. Maria Child (1861; rpt. ed. Jean Fagan Yellin, Cambridge: Harvard University Press, 1987), 3. Hereafter to be cited parenthetically.

23. See Jean Fagan Yellin's introduction, xxiii, and Jacobs' letter to Post, 242.

24. Andrews, 247. The confessions Jacobs recounts within the story—to her grandmother and to Reverend Durham—reinforce the image of the implied reader (Andrews 249–50). For an insightful discussion of how the narrative obstructs certain kinds of readings and encourages others, how it avoids becoming "pious pornography," and how it characterizes Jacobs' liaison with Mr. Sands as subversion rather than surrender, see Andrews, 250–53.

25. Yellin's sleuthing has been documented in increasing detail in *"Written by Herself:* Harriet Jacobs' Slave Narrative," *American Literature* 53 (Nov. 1981): 478–86; "Texts and Contexts of Harriet Jacobs' *Incidents in the Life of a Slave Girl: Written by Herself,"* in *The Slave's Narrative,* 262–82; and in her recent scholarly edition of the text, which includes relevant letters.

26. This account is based on Yellin's research as documented in her scholarly edition of the narrative, especially pp. xv–xxiv.

27. See Yellin's introduction for a discussion of Jacobs' ambiguous sense of the ethics of this decision, xxix–xxxi.

28. 17–20. For his account of Douglass' response to these texts, see page 20–26.

29. Stepto has noted that Douglass turns the tables by seizing the apparatus of authentication but does not seem to view this as a satire on the procedure itself, 26.

30. "Apostrophe," in *The Pursuit of Signs: Semiotics, Literature, Deconstruction* (Ithaca: Cornell University Press, 1981), 139, 142.

CHAPTER 7

1. Sidonie Smith, *A Poetics of Women's Autobiography: Marginality and the Fictions of Self-Representation* (Bloomington: Indiana University Press, 1987), 18. Hereafter to be cited parenthetically.

2. *Patriotic Gore: Studies in the Literature of the American Civil War* (New York: Oxford University Press, 1962), 279.

3. *Mary Chesnut's Civil War,* ed. C. Vann Woodward (New Haven: Yale University Press, 1981). Hereafter to be cited parenthetically as MCCW.

4. Full accounts of the complex, intermittent process of composition can be found in the publications by C. Vann Woodward and/or Elisabeth Muhlenfeld cited below.

5. "The Masterpiece That Became a Hoax," April 26, 1981, p. 9; reprinted in *The Air-Line to Seattle: Studies in Literary and Historical Writing about America* (Chicago: University of Chicago Press, 1983), 51. Hereafter to be cited parenthetically.

6. C. Vann Woodward, "Mary Chesnut in Search of Her Genre," *Yale Review* 73, No. 2 (Winter 1984): 203–4.

7. "What Is the Chesnut Diary?" *South Carolina Women Writers,* ed. James Meriwether (Spartanburg, SC: Reprint Co., 1979), 196–97. This volume contains the Proceedings of the Reynolds Conference at the University of South Carolina, October 24–25, 1975.

8. "Mary Chesnut in Search of her Genre," 205.

9. *Private Chronicles: A Study of English Diaries* (London: Oxford University Press, 1974), 40. Hereafter to be cited parenthetically.

10. Chapter 7. As Sidonie Smith has noted, approaches like Fothergill's may result in gender bias because the dichotomy between "self-conscious artistry" and "spontaneity" is often aligned with that between "masculine" and "feminine" (16).

11. "What Is the Chesnut Diary?" 198–200.

12. "The Confederate Elite in Crisis: A Woman's View," *Yale Review* 71, No. 1 (Autumn 1981): 123.

13. *The Private Mary Chesnut: The Unpublished Civil War Diaries,* ed. C. Vann Woodward and Elisabeth Muhlenfeld (New York: Oxford University Press, 1984), 42. Hereafter to be cited parenthetically as PMC.

14. "Mary Boykin Chesnut's Autobiography and Biography: A Review Essay," *Journal of Southern History* 47, No. 4 (November 1981): 589.

15. "Literary Elements in Mary Chesnut's Journal," *South Carolina Women Writers,* 246–47.

16. Sandra Caruso Mortola Gilbert and Susan Dreyfus David Gubar, "Ceremonies of the Alphabet: Female Grandmatologies and the Female Authorgraph," *The Female Autograph,* ed. Domna C. Stanton and Jeanine Parisier Plottel (New York: New York Literary Forum, 1984), 26. The authors' names—more extensive, complex, and matrilinear here than those they have used elsewhere—reinforce their explicit message. Their co-authorship is perhaps also an exemplary response to the predicament they describe.

17. Mary Boykin Chesnut's name clearly locates her within a patriarchal society. While her "maiden" name, Mary Boykin Miller, was the same as her mother's married name, it identifies her not so much *with* her mother as *in relation to* her father and her mother's father (from whom her mother's "maiden" name of course derived). The fact that her married name suppresses "Miller" rather than "Boykin" probably owes less to affection for her mother than to the greater prominence of her mother's family. Like her mother's name, then, her married name erases much of her premarital and matrilineal identity. I shall refer to her as "Mary Chesnut," "Mary Boykin Chesnut" or, when the context allows it to be unambiguous, "Chesnut." While these names are undeniably patriarchal, they seem preferable to the alternatives. "Mrs. Chesnut" iden-

tifies her solely as her husband's wife; "Mary Boykin" conceals or denies her married status; "Mary" alone is patronizingly familiar.

18. See Mary G. Mason, "The Other Voice: Autobiographies of Women Writers," *Autobiography: Essays Theoretical and Critical,* ed. James Olney (Princeton: Princeton University Press, 1980), 207; Elizabeth Winston, "The Autobiographer and Her Readers: From Apology to Affirmation," *Women's Autobiography: Essays in Criticism,* ed. Estelle C. Jelinek (Bloomington, Ind.: Indiana University Press, 1980), 95; and Patricia Meyer Spacks, "Selves in Hiding," *Women's Autobiography,* 111–12.

19. Estelle C. Jelinek, "Introduction: Women's Autobiography and the Male Tradition," *Women's Autobiography,* 7–8.

20. Quoted in Elisabeth Muhlenfeld, *Mary Boykin Chesnut: A Biography* (Baton Rouge: Louisiana State University Press, 1981), 197. Hereafter to be cited parenthetically as MBC.

21. Quoted here from *Mary Chesnut's Civil War,* for which Woodward appropriated it, 3–4.

22. Both entries are quoted in Muhlenfeld, "Literary Elements," 247–48.

23. Muhlenfeld, "Literary Elements," 246.

24. PMC 41. Words appearing in double side-angle brackets—<< >>—had been erased.

25. On Dickinson, see Sandra Gilbert and Susan Gubar, *The Madwoman in the Attic: The Woman Writer and the Nineteenth-Century Imagination* (New Haven: Yale Univ. Press, 1979), 633–35.

26. William L. Andrews, *To Tell A Free Story* (Urbana: University of Illinois Press, 1986), 256.

27. For a brief but helpful discussion of Chesnut's "diary" in context, see Estelle C. Jelinek, *The Tradition of Women's Autobiography: From Antiquity to the Present* (Boston: Twayne, 1986), 85–86.

28. "On Diaries," *Diacritics* 16, No. 3 (Fall 1986), 64.

29. "Autobiography in a Different Voice: Maxine Hong Kingston's *The Woman Warrior,*" *Auto/Biography Studies* III, No. 3 (Fall 1987): 30.

30. MCCW 172. Words in double side-angle brackets—<< >>—indicate excerpts from other versions (in this case the 1860s journal) inserted in the text.

31. "What Is the Chesnut Diary?" 267.

CHAPTER 8

1. Georges Gusdorf, "Conditions and Limits of Autobiography," *Autobiography: Essays Critical and Theoretical,* ed. James Olney (Princeton: Princeton University Press, 1980), 29.

2. New York: Morrow,1932. Hereafter to be cited parenthetically.

3. Vine Deloria, Jr., "Introduction," John G. Neihardt, *Black Elk Speaks* (Lincoln: University of Nebraska Press, 1979), xiv.

4. In a discussion of Lucullus Virgil McWhorter, *Yellow Wolf: His Own Story* (Caldwell, Idaho: Caxton Printers, 1940)—which he considers a more successful collaboration—Arnold Krupat points out that this device is adapted from the telling of coup stories. *For Those Who Come After: A Study of Native American Autobiography* (Berkeley: University of California Press, 1985), 121.

5. H. David Brumble, III, *An Annotated Bibliography of American Indian and Eskimo Autobiography* (Lincoln: University of Nebraska Press, 1981), 2.

6. "Toward an Oral Poetics," *NLH* 8, No. 3 (Spring 1977): 513–17.

7. *"In Vain I Tried to Tell You": Essays in Native American Ethnopoetics* (Philadelphia: University of Pennsylvania Press, 1981), passim.

8. Raymond J. DeMallie, ed. *The Sixth Grandfather: Black Elk's Teachings Given to John G. Neihardt* (Lincoln: University of Nebraska Press, 1984). Hereafter to be cited parenthetically.

9. Krupat, 10. The entire discussion of this issue in his introductory chapter is noteworthy. I will allude to it again in Chapter 10.

10. *The Gutenberg Galaxy* (London: Routledge and Kegan Paul, 1962), 131–32.

11. *The Domestication of the Savage Mind* (Cambridge: Cambridge University Press, 1977), 11–14.

12. Kathleen Mullen Sands, "American Indian Autobiography," in *Studies in American Indian Literature,* ed. Paula Gunn Allen (New York: MLA, 1983), 56.

13. Walter J. Ong, *Orality and Literacy: The Technologizing of the Word* (New York: Methuen, 1982), 69, 178.

14. "Vision and Experience in *Black Elk Speaks,*" *College English* 32 (1971): 512.

15. Brumble, 1, 3–4.

16. "Lakota Religion and Tragedy: The Theology of *Black Elk Speaks,*" *Journal of the American Academy of Religion* 52, No. 1 (1984): 21–23. Hereafter cited parenthetically.

17. Indeed, because of it, *Black Elk Speaks* quite nicely fits my own definition of "prophetic autobiography." (See *American Autobiography: The Prophetic Mode* [Amherst: University of Massachusetts Press, 1979], 2–3.) Its participation in that mode of autobiography, however, cannot be wholly ascribed to Lakota elements; it is partly because of Christian elements assimilated by Black Elk or infused by Neihardt. That is, its sharing of a prophetic impulse with works like *Walden* and *The Education of Henry Adams* is partly a function of its unacknowledged syncretism.

18. Carol Holly, "*Black Elk Speaks* and the Making of Native American Autobiography," *Genre* 12 (Spring 1979): 120, 121.

19. Letter to Henry James, May 6, 1908, quoted in *The Education of Henry Adams,* ed. Ernest Samuels (Boston: Houghton Mifflin, 1973), 512–13.

20. Sally McCluskey, "*Black Elk Speaks:* and So Does John Neihardt," *Western American Literature* 6 (Winter 1972): 237. Hereafter to be cited parenthetically.

21. Katerina Clark and Michael Holquist, *Mikhail Bakhtin* (Cambridge: Harvard University Press, 1984), 15.

22. According to Ong, lengthy climactic plots are themselves inconsistent with oral performance; they originate with written composition (145–46). Print further encourages complete closure (132–33).

23. Despite his incisive exposure of Neihardt's theological bias, Holler asserts in his conclusion that "*Black Elk Speaks* is a great work of American literature and a classic interpretation of the plight of the American Indian. . . . As a work of art, the book is a valuable portrait of an eminent Lakota *wicasa wakan* [holy man] and a record of the effect his teaching had on an eminent American poet. . . . [I]t provides us with a unique and personal perspective on Black Elk and native American religion that supplements the information from more scholarly reports" (41). Unfortunately, such

a conclusion seems to deny the very connections between "literature" and "art," on the one hand, and politics and religion, on the other, that his essay so nicely illuminates.

24. *John G. Neihardt* (Boston: Twayne, 1976), 93.

CHAPTER 9

1. Richard Rodriguez, *Hunger Of Memory: The Education of Richard Rodriguez, An Autobiography* (New York: Bantam, 1982), 147. Hereafter to be cited parenthetically.

2. "Autobiography and Ethnic Politics: Richard Rodriguez's *Hunger of Memory,*" *Auto/Biography Studies* 3, No. 2 (Summer 1987): 18.

3. "Ideologies of the Self: Chicano Autobiography," *Diacritics* 15, No. 3 (Fall 1985): 28. For other reviews critical of Rodriguez, see George Blanco, *Modern Language Journal* 67, No. 3 (Autumn 1983): 282–83; Carlos R. Hortas, *Harvard Educational Review* 53, No. 3 (August 1983): 355–59; Michael A. Olivas, *Journal of Higher Education* 54, No. 4 (July/August 1983): 472–75; and Horace A. Porter, "Ethnic Secrets," *American Scholar* 52 (Spring 1983): 278–85.

4. She makes the argument that the proper term for her is "Chinese American," rather than "Chinese-American." In the latter term, hyphenation implies terms of equal weight, whereas in the former, "Chinese" functions as an adjective modifying the substantive "American." "Cultural Mis-reading by American Reviewers," *Asian and Western Writers in Dialogue: New Cultural Identities,* ed. Guy Amirthanayagam (London: Macmillan, 1982), 60.

5. Carlos Hortas has suggested a link between this disturbing image and Rodriguez's block with spoken Spanish, Review of *Hunger of Memory: The Education of Richard Rodriguez, Harvard Educational Review* 53, No. 3 (August 1983): 357.

6. Hortas points out that one purpose of bilingual education is to preclude precisely the kind of guilt and shame Rodriguez feels toward his parents, 356.

7. Margaret Miller, "Threads of Identity in Maxine Hong Kingston's *The Woman Warrior,*" *Biography* 6, No. 1 (Winter 1983): 15.

8. Maxine Hong Kingston, *The Woman Warrior: Memoirs of a Girlhood Among Ghosts* (New York: Random House, 1976), 56. Hereafter to be cited parenthetically.

9. See Sidonie Smith, "The Impact of Critical Theory on the Study of Autobiography: Marginality, Gender, and Autobiographical Practice," *Auto/Biography Studies* III, No. 3 (Fall 1987): 3.

10. Arturo Islas, "Maxine Hong Kingston: Interview," *Women Writers of the West Coast,* ed. Marilyn Yalom (Santa Barbara: Capra Press, 1983), 13–14.

11. "Cultural Mis-reading," 65.

12. "Towards a Theory of Form in Feminist Autobiography: Kate Millett's *Flying* and *Sita;* Maxine Hong Kingston's *The Woman Warrior,*" *Women's Autobiography: Essays in Criticism,* ed. Estelle C. Jelinek (Bloomington: Indiana University Press, 1980), 223.

13. "Cultural Mis-reading by American Reviewers," 57.

14. Sidonie Smith, *A Poetics of Women's Autobiography: Marginality, and the Fictions of Self-Representation* (Bloomington: Indiana University Press, 1987), 158.

15. Sidonie Smith has noted that in its overall outline—separation from family, education, empowerment, and ultimate return to the family fold—it parallels the story of Fa Mu Lan. Thus, it too is double-edged, 161.

16. Patricia Lin Blinde has noted the centrality of the impulse here to Kingston's book: "If there is a consistent theme that can be detected in *The Woman Warrior,* it is the constant attempt on the part of the author to evade social, philosophical, and racial limitations that meet her at every level of life. . . . [I]ndividual life is always somehow governed by the accounts or 'fiction' devised by and implemented by someone else." She goes on to note that for Kingston the "inability to formulate a totalized sense of self . . . is not cause for despair—the irresolution amounts to a certain freedom to 'rewrite' her mother's fictions, social, racial and sexual definitions and ultimately her own life." "The Icicle in the Desert: Perspective and Form in the Works of Two Chinese-American Women Writers," *MELUS* 6, No. 3 (Fall 1979): 64–65, 66.

17. For further discussion of this theme, see Stephanie Demetrakopoulos, "The Metaphysics of Matrilinearism in Women's Autobiography: Studies of Mead's *Blackberry Winter,* Hellman's *Pentimento,* Angelou's *I Know Why the Caged Bird Sings,* and Kingston's *The Woman Warrior," Women's Autobiography: Essays in Criticism,* ed. Estelle C. Jelinek (Bloomington: Indiana University Press, 1980): 180–205.

18. *Fictions in Autobiography: Studies in the Art of Self-Invention* (Princeton: Princeton University Press, 1985), 269.

19. Phyllis Thompson Hoge, "This is the Story I Heard: A Conversation with Maxine Hong Kingston and Earll Kingston," *Biography* 6, No. 1 (Winter 1983): 10.

CHAPTER 10

1. *The Dialogic Imagination,* trans. Caryl Emerson and Michael Holquist (Austin: University of Texas Press, 1981), pp. 293–94.

2. Arnold Krupat, *For Those Who Come After* (Berkeley: University of California Press, 1985), 10–11.

3. The overview of language theories here follows Bob Morgan, "Three Dreams of Language: Or, No Longer Immured in the Bastille of the Humanist Word," *College English* 49, No. 4 (April 1987), 449–58.

4. "The Plural Text/The Plural Self: Roland Barthes and William Cole," *College English,* 49, No. 2 (February 1987): 158–170. Hereafter to be cited parenthetically.

5. *Actual Minds, Possible Worlds* (Cambridge: Harvard University Press, 1986), 46.

Selected Bibliography

Albanese, Catherine L. *Sons of the Fathers: The Civil Religion of the American Revolution.* Philadelphia: Temple University Press, 1976.

Andrews, William L. *To Tell a Free Story: The First Century of Afro-American Autobiography, 1760–1865.* Urbana: University of Illinois Press, 1986.

Bakhtin, Mikhail. *The Dialogic Imagination.* Trans. Caryl Emerson and Michael Holquist. Austin: University of Texas Press, 1981.

Barnum, P. T. *The Life of P. T. Barnum, Written by Himself.* New York: Redfield, 1855.

———. *Struggles and Triumphs, or Forty Years Recollections of P. T. Barnum, Written by Himself.* 1869. Rpt. New York: Arno, 1970.

Bibb, Henry. *Narrative of the Life and Adventures of Henry Bibb, An American Slave, Written by Himself.* 1849. Rpt. *Puttin' On Ole Massa.* Ed. Gilbert Osofsky. New York: Harper and Row, 1969, pp. 51–171.

Blassingame, John. Ed. *Slave Testimony.* Baton Rouge: Louisiana State University Press, 1977.

Brown, William Wells. *Narrative of William Wells Brown, A Fugitive Slave, Written by Himself.* 1847. Rpt. *Puttin' On Ole Massa.* Ed. Gilbert Osofsky. New York: Harper and Row, 1969, pp. 173–223.

Brumble, H. David, III. *An Annotated Bibliography of American Indian and Eskimo Autobiography.* Lincoln: University of Nebraska Press, 1981.

Bruss, Elizabeth. *Autobiographical Acts: The Changing Situation of a Literary Genre.* Baltimore: Johns Hopkins University Press, 1976.

Cardwell, Guy. "Samuel Clemens' Magical Pseudonym." *New England Quarterly* 48, No. 2 (June 1975): 175–93.

Clark, Katerina, and Michael Holquist. *Michael Bakhtin.* Cambridge: Harvard University Press, 1984.

Cox, James. "Autobiography and America." *Virginia Quarterly Review,* 47 (1971): 252–77.

———. *Mark Twain: The Fate of Humor.* Princeton: Princeton University Press, 1966.

Dawson, Hugh. J. "Fathers and Sons: Franklin's 'Memoirs' as Myth and Metaphor." *Early American Literature* 14 (1979–1980): 269–92.

Davis, Charles T., and Henry Louis Gates, Jr., eds. *The Slave's Narrative.* New York: Oxford University Press, 1985.

DeMallie, Raymond J., ed. *The Sixth Grandfather: Black Elk's Teachings Given to John G. Neihardt.* Lincoln: University of Nebraska Press, 1984.

Devoto, Bernard, ed. *Mark Twain in Eruption: Hitherto Unpublished Pages about Men and Events.* New York: Harper and Brothers, 1940.

Douglass, Frederick. *Narrative of the Life of Frederick Douglass, an American Slave, Written by Himself.* 1845. Rpt. Ed. Houston Baker. New York: Viking Penguin, 1982.

Dreyfus, Hubert L., and Paul Rabinow. *Michel Foucault: Beyond Structuralism and Hermeneutics.* Chicago: University of Chicago, 1982.

Eagleton, Terry. *Literary Theory: An Introduction.* Minneapolis: University of Minnesota Press, 1983.

Eakin, Paul John. *Fictions of the Self: Studies in the Art of Self-Invention.* Princeton: Princeton University Press, 1985.

Fay, Stephen, Lewis Chester, and Magnus Linklater. *Hoax: The Inside Story of the Howard Hughes-Clifford Irving Affair.* New York: Viking Press, 1972.

Fleishman, Avrom. *Figures of Autobiography: The Language of Self-Writing in Victorian and Modern England.* Berkeley: University of California, 1983.

Fliegelman, Jay. *Prodigals and Pilgrims: The American Revolution against Patriarchal Authority.* Cambridge: Cambridge University Press, 1982.

Fothergill, Robert A. *Private Chronicles: A Study of English Diaries.* London: Oxford University Press, 1974.

Foucault, Michel. "Afterword: The Subject and Power." Hubert L. Dreyfus and Paul Rabinow. *Michel Foucault: Beyond Structuralism and Hermeneutics.* Chicago: University of Chicago Press, 1982, pp. 208–226.

Franklin, Benjamin. *The Autobiography of Benjamin Franklin.* Ed. Leonard Labaree et al. New Haven: Yale University Press, 1964.

———. *The Autobiography of Benjamin Franklin: A Genetic Text.* Ed. J. A. Leo Lemay and P. M. Zall. Knoxville: University of Tennessee Press, 1981.

Gittleman, Edwin. "Jefferson's 'Slave Narrative': The Declaration of Independence as a Literary Text." *Early American Literature* 8 (1974): 239–256.

Gribben, Alan. "Autobiography as Property: Mark Twain and his Legend." *The Mythologizing of Mark Twain.* Ed. Sara de Saussure Davis and Philip D. Beidler. University: University of Alabama: 1984; pp. 39–55.

Harris, Neil. *Humbug: The Art of P. T. Barnum.* Boston: Little, Brown, 1973.

Henson, Josiah. *An Autobiography of The Reverend Josiah Henson ("Uncle Tom") From 1789 to 1881.* Ed. John Lobb. 1881. Rpt. Ed. Robin W. Winks. Reading, Mass.: Addison-Wesley, 1969.

Hill, Hamlin. *Mark Twain: God's Fool.* New York: Harper and Row, 1973.

Holler, Clyde C. "Lakota Religion and Tragedy: The Theology of *Black Elk Speaks.*" *Journal of the American Academy of Religion.* 52, No. 1 (1984): 19–45.

Holly, Carol. "*Black Elk Speaks* and the Making of Indian Autobiography." *Genre* 12 (Spring 1979): 117–36.

Jacobs, Harriet. *Incidents in the Life of a Slave Girl, Written by Herself.* Ed. L. Maria Child. 1861. Rpt. Ed. Jean Fagan Yellin. Cambridge: Harvard University Press, 1987.

Jelinek, Estelle C. *The Tradition of Women's Autobiography: From Antiquity to the Present.* Boston: Twayne, 1986.

———, ed. *Women's Autobiography: Essays in Criticism.* Bloomington: Indiana University Press, 1980.

Kingston, Maxine Hong. "Cultural Mis-reading by American Reviewers." *Asian and Western Writers in Dialogue: New Cultural Identities.* Ed. Guy Amirthanayagam. London: Macmillan,1982, pp. 55–65.

———. *The Woman Warrior: Memoirs of a Girlhood Among Ghosts.* New York: Vintage, 1977.

Krupat, Arnold. *For Those Who Come After: A Study of Native American Autobiography.* Berkeley: University of California Press, 1985.

Lejeune, Philippe. *Le Pacte Autobiographique.* Paris: Editions du Seuil, 1975.

Looby, Christopher. "The Affairs of the Revolution Occasion'd the Interruption': Writing, Revolution, Deferral, and Conciliation in Franklin's *Autobiography.*" *American Quarterly* 38, No. 1 (Spring 1986): 72–96.

McCluskey, Sally. "*Black Elk Speaks*—And So Does John Neihardt." *Western American Literature* 6 (Winter 1972): 231–242.

McGann, Jerome. *A Critique of Modern Textual Criticism.* Chicago: University of Chicago Press, 1983.

Meriwether, James, ed. *South Carolina Women Writers.* Spartanburg: Reprint Co, 1979, pp. 245–261.

Morgan, Bob. "Three Dreams of Language: Or, No Longer Immured in the Bastille of the Humanist Word." *College English* 49, No. 4 (April 1987): 449–458.

Morgan, Edmund S. "Government by Fiction: The Idea of Representation." *Yale Review* 72, No. 3 (Spring 1983): 321–339.

Muhlenfeld, Elisabeth. *Mary Boykin Chesnut: A Biography.* Baton Rouge: Louisiana State University Press, 1981.

Neihardt, John. *Black Elk Speaks, Being the Life Story of a Holy Man of the Oglala Sioux.* New York: Morrow, 1932.

Northup, Solomon. *Twelve Years a Slave: Narrative of Solomon Northup, a Citizen of New York, Kidnapped in Washington City in 1841, and*

Rescued in 1853, From a Cotton Plantation Near the Red River, in Louisiana. Buffalo: Miller, Orton, and Mulligan, 1854.

Olney, James, ed. *Autobiography: Essays Theoretical and Critical.* Princeton: Princeton University Press, 1980.

Paine, Albert Bigelow. *Mark Twain: A Biography, The Personal and Literary Life of Samuel Langhorne Clemens.* III. New York: Harper and Brothers, 1912.

Randall, William Sterne. *A Little Revenge: Benjamin Franklin and His Son.* Boston: Little Brown, 1984.

Rodriguez, Richard. *Hunger Of Memory: The Education of Richard Rodriguez, An Autobiography.* New York: Bantam, 1982.

Ryan, Michael. "Self-Evidence." *Diacritics* 9, No. 1 (June 1980): 2–16.

Saldivar, Ramon. "Ideologies of the Self: Chicano Autobiography." *Diacritics* 15, No. 3 (Fall 1985): 25–33.

Sayre, Robert. "Vision and Experience in *Black Elk Speaks.*" *College English* 32 (1971): 509–35.

Sekora, John, and Darwin Turner, eds. *The Art of Slave Narrative: Original Essays in Criticism and Theory.* Macomb: Western Illinois University Press, 1982.

Smith, Henry Nash, ed. *Mark Twain of the Enterprise: Newspaper Articles & Other Documents, 1862–1864.* Berkeley: University of California Press, 1957.

———, and William M Gibson, eds. *Mark Twain–Howells Letters: The Correspondence of Samuel L. Clemens and William D. Howells, 1872–1910.* 2 Vols. Cambridge: Harvard University Press, 1960.

Smith, Sidonie. "The Impact of Critical Theory on the Study of Autobiography: Marginality, Gender, and Autobiographical Practice. *Auto/Biography Studies* III, No. 3 (Fall 1987): 1–12.

———. *A Poetics of Women's Autobiography: Marginality and the Fictions of Self-Representation.* Bloomington: Indiana University Press, 1987.

———. *Where I'm Bound: Patterns of Slavery and Freedom in Black American Autobiography.* Westport: Greenwood, 1978.

Stanton, Domna C., and Jean Parisier Plottel, eds. *The Female Autograph.* New York: New York Literary Forum, 1984, pp. 5–22.

Starobinski, Jean. "The Style of Autobiography." *Autobiography: Essays Theoretical and Critical.* Ed. James Olney. Princeton: Princeton University Press, 1980.

Stepto, Robert. *From behind the Veil: A Study of Afro-American Narrative.* Urbana: University of Illinois, 1979.

Sturrock, John. "The New Model Autobiographer." *NLH* 9, No. 1 (Autumn 1977): 51–63.

Twain, Mark. *The Autobiography of Mark Twain, Including Chapters Now Published For the First Time.* Ed. Charles Neider. New York: Harper and Brothers, 1959.

———. *Life on the Mississippi. Mississippi Writings.* New York: Library of America, 1982.

———. *Mark Twain's Autobiography.* Two Volumes. Ed. Albert Bigelow Paine. New York: Harper and Brothers, 1924.

———. *Mark Twain's Burlesque Autobiography and First Romance.* New York: Sheldon and Company, 1871.

———. "The Turning Point of My Life." In *What Is Man? and Other Philosophical Writings.* Ed. Paul Baender. *The Works of Mark Twain.* Vol. 19. Berkeley: University of California Press, 1973, pp. 455–464.

White, James Boyd. *When Words Lose Their Meaning: Constitutions and Reconstitutions of Language, Character, and Community.* Chicago: University of Chicago Press, 1984.

Wood, Gordon S. *The Creation of the American Republic, 1776–1787.* Chapel Hill: The University of North Carolina Press, 1969.

Woodward, C. Vann. "Mary Chesnut in Search of Her Genre." *Yale Review* 73, No. 2 (Winter 1984): 199–209.

———, ed. *Mary Chesnut's Civil War.* New Haven: Yale University Press, 1981.

——— and Elisabeth Muhlenfeld, eds. *The Private Mary Chesnut: The Unpublished Civil War Diaries.* New York: Oxford University Press, 1984.

Index